The *Missouri* *Review*

Volume XIX Number 2   1996

University of Missouri – Columbia

EDITOR
Speer Morgan

MANAGING EDITOR
Greg Michalson

ASSOCIATE EDITORS
William Peden, Jo Sapp, Evelyn Somers

OFFICE MANAGER
Dedra Earl

SENIOR ADVISORS
Mary Creger, Reeves Hamilton, Kristen Harmon,
Hoa Ngo, Kirstin Rogers, Kris Somerville, Jeff Thomson

ADVISORS
Tracy Benbrook, Seth Bro, Ed Fogarty,
Joel Huggins, Stephanie Komen, Julie Laune,
Sarah Oster, David Schlansker, Melissa Wright

INTERNS
Brian Baker, Rebecca Fuhrman, Brad Hauck,
Tuan Heidenreich, Amy Kennebec, Abel Klainbaum,
Elizabeth Knapp, Nick Mullendore

The Missouri Review is published by the College of Arts & Science of the University of Missouri–Columbia, with private contributions and assistance from the Missouri Arts Council and the National Endowment for the Arts.

Web Page Site at http://www.missouri.edu/~moreview

Cartoons in this issue by Andrew Toos

The editors invite submissions of poetry, fiction, and essays of a general literary interest with a distinctly contemporary orientation. Manuscripts will not be returned unless accompanied by a stamped, self-addressed envelope. Please address all correspondence to The Editors, *The Missouri Review*, 1507 Hillcrest Hall, University of Missouri, Columbia, Missouri, 65211.

SUBSCRIPTIONS
1 year (3 issues), $19.00
2 Years (6 issues), $35.00
3 years (9 issues), $45.00

Copyright © 1996 by The Curators of the University of Missouri
ISSN 0191 1961   **ISBN** 1–879758–17–2
Typesetting by Stacia Schaefer   Printed by Thompson-Shore
Distributed by: Ingram Periodicals and B. DeBoer

The
Missouri
CONTENTS ***Review*** 1996

"I *liked your manuscript. Unfortunately, Mr. Handley here chose not to* accept it."

Foreword

The masthead of this magazine has stated for many years that we invite submissions "with a distinctly contemporary orientation." Someone recently asked me what that meant, and I responded with the less than impressive answer that I wasn't completely sure. Since in this issue David Wojahn writes about some of the influences and problems in today's poetry, it seems like an opportune time for me to come up with an assessment of what makes a short story "distinctly contemporary." First, a thing or two about the beginnings of the short story.

Storytelling has of course been around for longer than we will ever know, and the sacred books of the major religions are replete with narrative. But in the history of secular publishing, both short stories and novels are relative latecomers. The essay, the philosophical tract, epic and lyric poetry—most of the now classic genres of writing are bluebloods with ancient ancestry compared with these arrivistes. It wasn't until the growth of the periodic magazine in the 18th and 19th centuries that fiction was really launched.

It is probably something of an exaggeration to claim that Washington Irving, an American expatriate writer living in England, "invented" the short story. But his two best-remembered picturesque sketches, "The Legend of Sleepy Hollow" and "Rip Van Winkle," published in 1819, are key early examples of sketches that crossed over the line to what later was called the short story. One of their most important features is that they are presented as stories and nothing else, in which certain characters go through a complete narrative trajectory. They are not journalism or essays with fictional elements but fictional narratives, which speak for themselves.

The "lateness" of both novels and short stories in mass publishing was partly due to the fact that reading fiction was considered suspect, as movies and TV are suspect today. Many felt that the very medium itself was corrupting. As parents today (including me) tell kids that they will learn nothing but how to sit with their mouths open and brains turned off by watching television, moral authorities during the early years of fiction commonly suspected that there was something fundamentally corrupting about printed stories: being by definition "not true," fiction was false and dangerous and might instill the wrong habits (sloth, lewdness, etc.), particularly in female readers. To counter this, early writers and publishers often made extravagant declarations on title pages, and in prefaces and advertising, regarding the moral or educational value of a work.

Although Washington Irving got the idea for "Sleepy Hollow"—a tale of rivalry for the favors of "the buxom Katrina"—from German folklore, he set the story in lower New York among Dutch farmers. The use of exotic, mostly rural locales, characters, and speech was a common aspect of American fiction in the last half of the century. In the years 1875, '85, and '95, a little over half of the stories and serialized novels in *The Atlantic Monthly* (one of the best-edited American magazines) were local-color or dialect pieces, with the number declining by the last decade. Most of these stories are tiresome to readers today, due to their authors' exaggerated attempts to denote every oddity of speech. While revealing something about the variety of American idioms, such stories were so intent on describing "locals" that they failed to create true characters.

Since the days when local color was hot in America, there have been no small number of important writers whose characters lived in places like Yoknapatawpha County, Winesburg, Ohio, and rural Georgia. However, by 1920, coincidental with the shift of the American population toward a majority of city dwellers over country dwellers, American writers had become genuinely tired of rural and heartland life. Whereas early local colorists often lampooned artificial clowns of country life, their inheritors wrote about hypocrisy, ignorance, cruelty, and small-mindedness among real people. Colorful character types retreated to genre fiction and pure entertainment, such as the Western stories of writers like Zane Grey and Max Brand.

Which brings us to the "distinctly contemporary" story.

Fiction writers still use exotic locales, but often in a different way. The dramatic effect of such a setting is to present to characters an environment that operates according to its own insular, often strange rules. Such a world challenges the character's ability to maneuver, strips him of illusions, or teaches him something about what matters. Putting characters in "different worlds" is natural to storytelling in all forms. Good short fiction today typically uses a subtler kind of exoticism of place or avoids it altogether.

In an age saturated by visual media capable of picturing every nook and cranny of the world, story writers are less likely to search high and low for curious settings than to discover them at home, where one might not expect them to exist. This is hardly an innovation; Jane Austen left her young female protagonists physically in their original families, but launched them into the quite different milieu of the

marriage marketplace—a world of peril, disorder, and colorful characters—where their idealism and self-centeredness were invariably
challenged.

Ray Carver was a major influence on the contemporary American
short story. His slice-of-life stories in some ways were a throwback to
the hyper-realistic stories of Chekhov, in which sadly believable characters stumble along in disappointed, uncertain lives. Carver's realism
has added piquancy—or is boring, depending on one's point of
view—because he wrote about people who are rudderless, orally-fix-
ated, confused by alcohol, dope, and television. To these alienated
characters, even their own turf—the mundane world of televisions, re-
frigerators, and little houses—is an exotic environment. Given their
level of dysfunction, they might as well be walking around on Planet
X, bumping into hidden force fields.

There are any number of ways by which today's wily short story writers depict the "other" place. Gerald Shapiro's artist protagonist in this
issue's "The Twelve Plagues" stumbles into such a world when he goes
off to an eastern suburb to receive his artistic award: the Cajun swamps
it ain't, but suburban New Jersey can get pretty strange to the West
Coaster. This issue's story "Swimming in the Dark," by Nancy Zafris, is
about a Japanese stewardess enamored of American culture. From her
perspective, very little about her own life is interesting; not her highfly-
ing, globe-hopping work or the many places she visits, and certainly not
her own culture. She yearns for what to her is the exotic freedom of
Americans. The "other" place—the place of challenge, adventure, and
desire—is to the typical reader of this story an ordinary world.

Another feature of short stories today is that they don't usually try
to be openly "well made." Sometimes they flirt with confusion. Instead
of tight constructions that lead to inevitable fates, short-story writers
today may opt for inconclusiveness. This is one of the advantages the
story has over the visual mediums. Television entertainment and the
great majority of movies use the old, tired formula of rising action, climax, denoument. The results are almost always congruent with what
might be called vulgar poetic justice, with the bad guys getting exactly
what they deserve. To add a little realistic spice, the good guys may
suffer headaches and divorces, or have trouble arranging child care,
but still they march, week to week, from one dramatic triumph to
another.

Few people actually "believe" that such plots are realistic portrayals
of law firms, police work, etc. They watch such stories for diversion
and possibly a little back-door reassurance that poetic justic does exist
somewhere, if only in the dubious cunning of Hollywood producers.

The Missouri Review frequently receives in the mail stories written by people stuck in television consciousness, sometimes competent fairy tales about drug dealers and cops. We also get stories written by script writers with impressive lists of credits, who haven't yet mastered the short story and who don't understand how *real* fiction can be, how unruled by concepts fictional voice can be, and how "unstructured" the contemporary short story can seem by comparison with storytelling in the visual media.

In fact, almost from the beginning, short story writers have fiddled with different ways to organize stories and different sorts of outcomes. Most of the stories in James Joyce's collection *The Dubliners* (1914) are brief, spare X-rays of disappointment and futility among the people of Dublin. The concluding story "The Dead," however, is a fully narrated and explicated story, with a lot of action but a different sort of outcome: Its protagonist Gabriel Conroy is led not to a narrative climax, but to a climax of insight.

Spurred by the realization that in her youth his wife Greta had a more gallant lover than he can ever be, and by an almost delectably described mood of melancholy and mortality, he learns that he is not, after all, the center of his wife's universe. Indeed he has never really loved his wife or anyone in the way that her young lover did. This realization proves to be like a bowling pin that knocks over other assumptions that are already wobbling around in his and the reader's mind—that he is the Continental sophisticate among the locals, or the generous male figure over his extended family. As the story concludes in a lyrically written fadeout, Gabriel Conroy stands at a window, watching the snow falling all across Ireland, and all across the living and the dead, and we experience with him a sense of the infinite darkness. Conroy's revelation is scary in its intensity, conveying a feeling that reaches beyond his character into the condition of all Dubliners and all humankind.

"The Green Suit," Dwight Allen's wonderful comic story in this issue, shows how the moment of insight in contemporary fiction has become more subtle, more ambivalent, woven into the texture of a story rather than occuring in a lyrical burst. Allen's young male publishing assistant, swimming naked in the pond with another man's girlfriend, brings upon himself a very embarrassing moment indeed—which plainly suggests to him something that he should have figured out a while ago. Yet in this and many stories today the "epiphany" may not always be fully understood by the protagonist.

Another, somewhat surprising aspect of short stories in the nineties is how little good experimental short fiction is being written. From the sixties through the early eighties, influenced by the metafictional stories of John Barth, the paranoid, lyrical satire of Thomas Pynchon, the various experimental approaches of the Fiction Collective, and the magical realism of several South American authors, a creditable amount of such short fiction was written and published. At this time a healthy number of experimental novels are being written by authors like Milan Kundera, Kazuo Ishiguro (whose new novel is reviewed in this issue), and Salman Rushdie. However the stream seems to be sluggish in short fiction.

I frankly do not understand the reason for it, since the short story by its very briefness has always been a natural lab for experiment. The only guess I can make is that good short story writers sense how dated and mannered such stories can quickly become. When I note that John Barth has published his latest collection of metafictional short stories—fiction about fiction—I wonder if he is going for the all-time trophy for rehashing an old idea, twenty-five years and running.

In this issue, Pulitzer Prize winning writer Robert Olen Butler shows how natural experiment can be to the short story. Starting with the whimsical concept of writing a story based on a tabloid headline, Butler creates literary substance behind a ridiculous title: "Titanic Victim Speaks Through Waterbed" is told by a very real and oddly appealing man who sank on the Titanic and has since been finding his disembodied self in various vessels of water, from teacups and pisspots to the grand ocean itself. Mostly, though, the story is about the chance of a lifetime, in which a seemingly oblique and brief encounter with another person can change one's life—or at least one's understanding—quite literally forever.

Enjoy, Butler says, and we agree!

SM

Congratulations to two poets whose work we first introduced—E. C. Hinsey and Talvikki Ansel—for winning the 1995 and 1996 Yale Younger Poets awards. Congratulations also to Deborah Galyan, whose *Missouri Review* Editors' Prize story "The Incredible Appearing Man" was selected to be reprinted in the upcoming *Best American Short Stories*.

"I like stream-of-dream novels that take place over twenty years of inactivity, but the public can be fickle, Mr. Van Winkle."

"TITANIC VICTIM SPEAKS THROUGH WATERBED" / *Robert Olen Butler*

THIS IS A BIT of a puzzle, really. A certain thrashing about overhead. Swimmers with nowhere to go, I fear, though I don't recognize this body of water. I've grown quite used to this existence I now have. I'm fully conscious that I'm dead. And yet not so, somehow. I drift and drift, and I am that in which I drift, though what that is now, precisely, is unclear to me. There was darkness at first, and I failed to understand. But then I rose as some faint current from the depths of the North Atlantic and there were others around me, the corporeal creatures of the sea whom I had hitherto known strictly on fine china and dressed lightly in butter and lemon. I found that I was the very medium for the movement of their piscine limbs, and they seemed oblivious to my consciousness. In their ignorance, I could not even haunt them. But I understood, by then, of what my fundamental state consisted, something that had eluded the wisdom of Canterbury. Something for which I was unprepared.

And after many years—I don't know how many, but it is clear to me that it is not an inconsiderable sum—there are still surprises awaiting me. This impulse now to shape words, for instance. And the thrashing above me, the agitation it brings upon me. I returned to the first-class smoking lounge soon after I realized what had happened with the ship. I sat in an overstuffed leather chair and then looked about for a dry match to light my cigar. But I was well aware of what was going on out in the darkness beyond the window.

Perhaps that accounts for the slight betrayal of fear, something only I could notice, since on the surface I seemed to be in control: I sat down and reached for a match. But I sat down already fearing that the matches would be wet. I should have searched for the match and then sat down. But I sat. And then I looked about. And, of course, the room was quite dry. Just at arm's length was a silver-plate ashtray on the table with a silver matchbox engraved with the flag of the White Star Line rising on a pedestal from its center. It was full of matches. I took one and struck it against the side of the box and it flared into life and I held it to my cigar and I thought, What a shame that this quite charming ashtray will be soon lost. My hand was steady. To anyone watching, it would seem I had never doubted that the matches in this room were dry. Of course they were. At that hour the ship was beginning to settle into the water, but only like a stout fellow standing in this very room after a long night of cards and feeling heavy in his lower limbs. It was, of course, impossible for water to be in this room as of yet. That would come only very near the end. But still I feared that the matches would already be spoilt.

All through that night, the fear was never physical. I didn't mind so much, in point of fact, giving up a life in my body. The body was never a terribly interesting thing to me. Except perhaps to draw in the heavy curl of the smoke of my cigar, like a Hindu's rope in the market rising as if it were a thing alive. One needs a body to smoke a good cigar. I took the first draw there in that room just below the fourth funnel of the largest ship in the world as it sat dead still, filling with the North Atlantic Ocean in the middle of the night, and the smoke was a splendid thing.

And as I did, I felt an issue of perspiration on my forehead. This was not unpleasant, however. I sat with many a fine cigar on the verandah of my bungalow in Madras, and though one of the boys was always there to fan the punkah, I would perspire on my forehead and it was just part of smoking a good cigar out in India. With a whiskey and soda beside me. I thought, sitting on the sinking ship, to pour myself a drink. But I didn't. I wanted a clear head. I had gone to my cabin when things seemed serious and I'd gotten into evening dress. It was a public event, it seemed to me. It was a solemn occasion. With, I assumed, a King to meet somewhat higher even than our good King George. I didn't feel comfortable in tweeds.

What *is* that thrashing about above me now? The creatures of the sea are absent here, though I'm not risen into the air as I have done for some years, over and over, lifted and dispersed into cloud. I'm coalesced in a place that has no living creatures but is large enough that I don't quite sense its boundaries. Perhaps not too large, since I am not moving except for a faint eddying from the activity above. But at least I am in a place larger than a teacup. I once dwelt in a cup of tea, and on that occasion, I sensed the constraints of the space.

I yearn to be clothed now in the tuxedo I wore on that Sunday night in April in the year of 1912. I must say that a body is useful for formal occasions, as well. All this floating about seems much too casual to me. I expected something more rigorous in the afterlife. A propitiatory formality. A sensible accounting. Order. But there has been no sign, as yet, of that King of Kings. Just this long and elemental passage to a place I cannot recognize. And an odd sense of alertness now. And these words I feel compelled to speak.

Robert Olen Butler

There. I think I heard the sound of a human voice above me in this strange place. Very briefly. I cannot make out the words, if words this voice indeed uttered. It's been a rare thing for me, in all this time, to sense that a living human being might be close by. On that dark night in the North Atlantic, at the very moment we struck our fate out somewhere beneath the water line on our bow, I was in the midst of voices that did not resolve themselves into clear words, and none of us heard anything of that fateful event. I was sitting and smoking, and there was a voluble conversation over a card game near to me. It was late. Nearly midnight. I was reluctant to leave the company of these men, though I had not said more than two dozen words to any of them on this night, beyond "Good evening." I am an indifferent card player. I sat and smoked all evening and I missed having the latest newspaper. I don't remember what I might have thought about, with all that smoke. India perhaps. Perhaps my sister and her husband in Toronto, toward whom we had just ceased to steam.

What did become clear to me quite quickly was that we had stopped. I looked at the others and they were continuing to play their game unaware of anything unusual. So I rose and stepped out under the wrought iron and glass dome of the aft staircase. I had no apprehensions. The staircase was quite elegant with polished oak wall paneling and gilt on the balustrades and it was lit bright with electric lights. My feeling was that in the absence of the threat of native rebellion, things such as this could not possibly be in peril.

That seems a bit naive now, of course, but at the time, I was straight from the leather chair of the first-class smoking lounge. And I was tutored in my views by the Civil Service in India. And I was a keen reader of the newspapers and all that they had to say about this new age of technology, an age for which this unsinkable ship stood as eloquent testament. And I was an old bachelor whose only sister lived in the safest dominion of the empire.

Owing to the lateness of the hour, there was no one about on the staircase except for a steward who rushed past me and down the steps. "What's the trouble?" I asked him.

He waved a hot water bottle he was carrying and said, "Cold feet, I presume," and he disappeared on the lower landing.

I almost stepped back into the smoking lounge. But there was no doubt that we had come to a full stop, and that was unquestionably out of the ordinary. Two or three of the card players were now standing in the doorway just behind me, murmuring about this very thing.

"I'll see what's the matter," I said without looking at them, and I descended the steps and went out onto the open promenade.

The night was very still. There were people moving about, somewhat distractedly, but I gave them no notice. I stepped to the railing and the sea was vast and smooth in the moonlight. There were shapes out there, like water buffalo sleeping in the fields in the dark nights outside Madras. I would drive back to my bungalow in a trap, my head still cluttered with the talk and the music from the little dance band and the whirling around of the dancers, and I would think how the social rites of my own class sometimes felt as foreign to me as those of the people we were governing here. These pretenses the men and women made in order to touch, often someone else's spouse. I am not unobservant. But I would go to these events, nevertheless. Even if I kept to myself.

I looked out at these sleeping shapes in the water. A woman's voice was suddenly nearby.

"We're doomed now," she said in the flat inflection of an American.

It took a moment to realize that she was addressing me. She said no more. But I think I heard her breathing. I turned and she was less than an arm's length from me along the railing. In the brightness of the moon I could see her face quite clearly. She seemed rather young, though less than two hours later I would revise that somewhat. The first impression, however, was that she was young, and that was all. Perhaps rather pretty, too, but I don't think I noticed that at the time. There were certain things that I suppose were beyond my powers of observation.

When I realized to whom she was speaking, her words finally registered on me. "Not at all." I spoke from whatever ignorance I had learned all my life. "Nothing that can't be handled. This is a fine ship."

"I'm not in a panic," she said. "You can hear that in my voice, can't you?"

"Of course."

"I just know this terrible thing to be true."

I leaned on the rail and looked at these sleeping cattle. I knew what they were. I understood what this woman had concluded.

"It's the ice you fear," I said.

"The deed is done, don't you think?" she said.

Her breath puffed out, white in the moonlight, and I felt suddenly responsible for her. There was nothing personal in it. But this was a lady in some peril, I realized. At least in peril from her own fears. I felt a familiar stiffening in me, and I was glad for it. Dissipated now were the effects of the cigar smoke and the comfort of a chair in a place where men gathered in their complacent ease. But I still felt I only needed to dispel some groundless fears of a woman too much given to her intuition.

"What deed might that be?" I asked her, trying to gentle my voice.

"We've struck an iceberg."

I was surprised to find that this seemed entirely plausible. "And suppose we have," I said. "This ship is the very most modern afloat. The watertight compartments make it quite unsinkable. We would, perhaps, at worst, be delayed."

She turned her face to me, though she did not respond.

"Are you traveling alone?" I asked.

"Yes."

"Perhaps that accounts for your anxiety."

"No. It was the deep and distant sound of the collision. And the vibration I felt in my feet. And the speed with which we were hurtling among these things." She nodded to the shapes in the dark. I looked and felt a chill from the night air. "And the dead stop we instantly made," she said. "And it's a thing in the air. I can smell it. A thing that I smelled once before, when I was a little girl. A coal mine collapsed in my hometown. Many men were trapped and would die within a few hours. I smell that again . . . These are the things that account for my anxiety."

"You shouldn't be traveling alone," I said. "If I might say so."

"No, you might not say so," she said, and she turned her face sharply to the sea.

"I'm sorry," I said. Though I felt I was right. A woman alone could be subject to torments of the sensibility such as this and have no one to comfort her. I wanted to comfort this woman beside me.

Is this an eddy through what once was my mind? A stirring of the water in which I'm held? I ripple and suddenly I see this clearly: my wish to comfort her came from an impulse stronger than duty would strictly require. I see this now, dissolved as I have been for countless years in the thing that frightened her that night. But standing with her at the rail, I simply wished for a companion to comfort her on a troubling night, a father or a brother perhaps.

"You no doubt mean well," she said.

"Yes. Of course."

"I believe a woman should vote, too," she said.

"Quite," I said. This was a notion I'd heard before and normally it seemed, in the voice of a woman, a hard and angry thing. But now this woman's voice was very small. She was arguing her right to travel alone and vote when, in fact, she feared she would soon die in the North Atlantic Ocean. I understood this much and her words did not seem provocative to me. Only sad.

"I'm certain you'll have a chance to express that view for many decades to come," I said.

"The change is nearer than you think," she said with some vigor now in her voice, even irritation. I was glad to hear it.

"I didn't mean to take up the political point," I said. "I simply meant you will survive this night and live a long time."

She lowered her face.

"That's your immediate concern, isn't it?" I asked, trying to speak very gently.

Before she could answer, a man I knew from the smoking lounge approached along the promenade, coming from the direction of the bow of the ship. He had gone out of the lounge some time earlier.

"Look here," he said, and he showed me his drink. It was full of chipped ice. "It's from the forward well deck," he said. "It's all over the place."

I felt the woman ease around my shoulder and look into the glass. The man was clearly drunk and shouldn't have been running about causing alarm.

"From the iceberg," he said.

I heard her exhale sharply.

"I never take ice in my scotch and soda," I said.

The man drew himself up. "I do," he said. And he moved away unsteadily, confirming my criticism of him.

She stood very still for a long moment.

All I could think to say was something along the lines of "Here, here. There's nothing to worry about." But she was not the type of woman to take comfort from that. I knew that much about her already. I felt no resentment at the fact. Indeed, I felt sorry for her. If she wanted to be the sort to travel alone and vote and not be consoled by the platitudes of a stiff old bachelor from the Civil Service in India, then it was sad for her to have these intense and daunting intuitions of disaster and death, as well.

So I kept quiet, and she eventually turned her face to me. The moon fell upon her. At the time, I did not clearly see her beauty. I can see it now, however. I have always been able to see in this incorporeal state. Quite vividly. Though not at the moment. There's only darkness. The activity above me has no shape. But in the sea, as I drifted inexorably to the surface, I began to see the fish and eventually the ceiling of light above me. And then there was the first time I rose—quite remarkable—lifting from the vastness of an ocean delicately wrinkled and athrash with the sunlight. I went up into a sky I knew I was a part of, spinning myself into the gossamer of a rain cloud, hiding from the sea, traced as a tiny wisp into a great gray mountain of vapor. And I wondered if there were others like me there. I listened for them. I tried to call to them, though I had no voice. Not even words. Not like these that now shape in me. If I'd had these words then, perhaps I could have called out to the others who had gone down with the Titanic, and they would have heard me. If, in fact, they were there. But as far as I knew—as far as I know now—I am a solitary traveler.

And then I was rain, and the cycle began. And I moved in the clouds and in the tides and eventually I became rivers and streams and lakes and dew and a cup of tea. Darjeeling. In a place not unlike the one where I spent so many years. I had recently come out of the sea, but I don't think the place was Madras or near it, for the sea must have been the Arabian, not the Bay of Bengal. I was in a reservoir and then in a well and then in a boiling kettle and eventually in a porcelain cup, very thin: I could see the shadow of a woman's hand pick me up. I sensed it was Darjeeling tea, but I don't know how. Perhaps I can smell, too, in this state, but without the usual body, perhaps there is only the knowledge of the scent. I'm not sure. But I slipped inside a woman and then later I was—how shall I say this?—free again. I must emphasize that I kept my spirit's eyes tightly shut.

That was many years ago. I subsequently crossed the subcontinent and then Indochina and then I spent a very long time in another vast sea, the Pacific Ocean, I'm sure. And then, in recent times, I rolled in a storm front across a rough coast and rained hard in a new land. I think, in fact, I have arrived in the very country for which I'd set sail in that fateful spring of 1912.

Her country. I'm digressing now. I see that. I look at her face in this memory that drifts with me—I presume forever—and I am ready to understand that she was beautiful, from the first, and I look away, just as I did then. I talk of everything but her face. She turned to me and the moon fell upon her and I could not bring myself to be the pompous ass I am capable of being. I said nothing to reassure her. And that was an act of respect. I see that now. I wonder if she saw it. But neither did I say anything else. I looked away. I looked out to the sea that was even then trying to claim us both, and I finally realized she was gone.

She had said nothing more, either. Not good-bye. Nothing. Not that I blame her. I'd let her down somehow. And she knew that we were all in mortal peril. When I turned back around and found her gone, I had a feeling about her absence. A feeling that I quickly set aside. It had something to do with my body. I felt a chill. But, of course, we were in the North Atlantic with ice floating all about us. I wished I were in my bungalow near the Bay of Bengal, wrapped in mosquito netting and drifting into unconsciousness. I wished for that, at the time. I did not wish for her to return. I wanted only to be lying in a bed alone in a place I knew very well, a place where I could spend my days being as stiff as I needed to be to keep going. I wanted to lie wrapped tight, with the taste of cigars and whiskey still faint in my mouth, and sleep.

And now I feel something quite strong, really. Though I have no body, whatever I am feels suddenly quite profoundly empty. Ah empty. Ah quite quite empty.

I have cried out. Just now. And the thrashing above me stops and turns into a low murmur of voices. The water moves, a sharp undulation, and then suddenly there's a faint light above me. I had rushed through dark tunnels into this place and had no idea what it was, and now I can see it is structured and tight. The light is a square ceiling above me. I see it through the water, but there is something else, as well, blurring the light. Mosquito netting. A shroud. Something. It is quite odd, really.

I want to think on this place I'm in, but I cannot. There's only the empty space on the promenade where she'd stood. I turned and she was gone and I looked both ways and there were people moving about, but I did not see her. It was then that I knew for certain that she was right. I knew the ship would go down, and I would die.

So I went to my cabin and closed the door and laid out my evening clothes on the bed. There were footfalls in the hallway, racing. Others knew. I imagined her moving about the ship like some Hindu spirit taken human form, visiting this truth upon whomever would listen. I once again stood still for a moment with a feeling. I wanted her to have spoken only to me. That we should keep that understanding strictly between the two of us. I straightened now and put that thought from my head. That thought, not the sinking of the ship, made me quake slightly inside. I straightened and stiffened with as much reserve and dignity as possible for a man in late middle age standing in his underwear, and I carefully dressed for this terrible event.

When I came out again on the promenade deck, I hesitated. But only briefly. Something very old and very strong in me brought me to the door of the smoking lounge. This was the only place that seemed familiar to me, that was filled with people whose salient qualities I could recognize easily. I stepped in and the card game was still on. Several faces turned to me.

"It's all in for us," I said, matter-of-factly.

"Yes," one of them said.

"You can bet rather more freely," I said to him.

"Don't encourage him," said another at the table.

"Right," I said. Then I stood there for a moment. I knew that I'd come to join them. My chair sat empty near the card table. And I began to worry about finding a dry match. Force of habit—no, not habit; the indomitable instinct of my life—moved me into the room and to the chair, and I sat and I worried about the matches and then I found that they were dry and I lit my cigar and I took a puff and I thought about getting a drink and I thought about meeting a King more powerful than King George and then I suddenly turned away from all that. I laid my cigar in the silver-plate ashtray and I rose and went out of the lounge.

It took me the better part of an hour to find her. At first, things were civilized. They were beginning to put women and children into the boats and people were keeping their heads about them. These were first class passengers and I moved through them and we all of us exchanged careful apologies for being in each other's way or asking each other to move. With each exchanged request for pardon, I grew more concerned. From this very sharing of the grace of daily human affairs, I responded more and more to the contrast of the situation. I could tell there weren't enough lifeboats for this enterprise. Any fool could tell that. I searched these faces to whom I gently offered my apologies and who gently returned them, but I was not gentle inside. I wanted to find her. I prayed that if I did not, it was because she was already in a sound boat out on the sea, well away from what would soon happen.

Then I came up on the boat deck below the wheelhouse and I could see forward. The lights were still quite bright all over the ship and the orchestra was playing a waltz nearby and before me, at the bow, the forecastle deck already was awash. It was disappearing before my eyes. And now the people from steerage in rough blankets and flannel nightshirts and kersey caps were crowding up, and I felt bad for them. They'd been let down, too, trying to find a new life somewhere, and the gentlemen of the White Star Line were not prepared to save all these people.

A woman smelling of garlic pressed past me with a child swaddled against her chest and I looked forward again. The anchor crane was all that I could see of the forecastle. The blackness of the sea had smoothed away the bow of our ship, and I wanted to cry out the name of the woman I sought, and I realized that I did not even know it. We had never been introduced, of course. This woman and I had spoken together of life and death, and we had not even exchanged our names. That realization should have released me from my search, but in fact I grew quite intense now to find her.

There was a gunshot nearby and a voice cried out, "Women and children only. Be orderly." There was jostling behind me and voices rising, falling together in foreign words, full of panic now. I had already searched the first class crowd in the midst of all that, and I slipped through a passage near the bridge and out onto the port side of the boat deck.

And there she was. There was order here, for the moment, women being helped into a boat by their husbands and by the ship's officers, though the movements were not refined now, there was a quick fumbling to them. But she was apart from all that. She was at the railing and looking forward. I came to her.

"Hello," I said.

She turned her face to me and at last I could see her beauty. She was caught full in the bridge lights now. I wished it were the moon again, but in the glare of the incandescent bulbs I could see the delicate thinness of her face, the great darkness of her eyes, made more beautiful, it seemed to me, by the faint traces of her age around them. She was younger than I, but she was no young girl; she was a woman with a life lived in ways that perhaps would have been very interesting to share, in some other place. Though I know now that in some other place I never would have had occasion or even the impulse—even the impulse, I say—to speak to her of anything, much less the events of her life or the events of my own life, pitiful as it was, though I think she would have liked India. As I float here in this strange place beneath this muffled light I think she would have liked to go out to India and turn that remarkable intuition of hers, the subtle responsiveness of her ear and her sight and even the bottoms of her feet, which told her the truth of our doom, she would have liked to turn all that sensitivity to the days and nights of India, the animal cries in the dark and the smell of the Bay of Bengal and the comfort of a bed shrouded in mosquito netting and the drifting to sleep.

Can this possibly be me speaking? What is this feeling? This speaking of a bed in the same breath with this woman? The shroud above me is moving in this place where I float. It strips away and there are the shadows of two figures there. But it's the figure beside me on the night I died that compels me. She stood there and she turned her face to me and I know now that she must have understood what it is to live in a body. She looked at me and I said, "You must go into a boat now."

"I was about to go below and wait," she said.

"Nonsense. You've known all along what's happening. You must go into the lifeboat."

"I don't know why."

"Because I ask you to." How inadequate that answer should have been, I realize now. But she looked into my face and those dark eyes searched me.

"You've dressed up," she said.

"To see you off," I said.

She smiled faintly and lifted her hand. I braced for her touch, breathless, but her hand stopped at my tie, adjusted it, and then fell once more.

"Please hurry." I tried to be firm but no more than whispered.

Nevertheless, she turned and I fell in beside her and we took a step together and another and another and we were before the lifeboat and a great flash of light lit us from above, a crackling fall of orange light, a distress flare, and she was beside me and she looked again into my eyes. My hands and arms were already dead, it seemed, they had already sunk deep beneath the sea, for they did not move. I turned and there was a man in uniform and I said, "Officer, please board this lady now."

He offered his hand to her and she took it and she moved into the end of the queue of women, and in a few moments she stepped into the boat. I shrank back into the darkness, terribly cold, feeling some terrible thing. One might expect it to be a fear of what was about to befall me, but one would be wrong. It was some other terrible thing that I did not try to think out. The winch began to turn and I stepped forward for one last look at her face, but the boat was gone. And my hands came up. They flailed before me and I didn't understand. I could not understand this at all.

So I went back to the smoking lounge, and the place was empty. I was very glad for that. I sat in the leather chair and I struck a match and I held it before my cigar and then I put it down. I could not smoke, and I didn't understand that either.

But above me there are two faces, pressed close, trying to see into this place where I float. I move. I shape these words. I know that they heard me when I cried out. When I felt the emptiness, even of this spiritual body. They were the ones who thrashed above me. Not swimming in the sea. Not drowning with me in the night the Titanic sank. I stood before her and my arms were dead, my hands could not move, but I know now what it is that brought me to a quiet grief all my corporeal life long. And I know now what it is that I've interrupted with my cry. These two above me were floating on the face of this sea and they were touching. They had known to raise their hands and touch each other.

At the end of the night I met her, I put my cigar down, and I waited, and soon the floor rose up and I fell against the wall and the chair was on top of me, and I don't remember the moment of the water, but it made no difference whatsoever. I was already dead. I'd long been dead.

Robert Olen Butler won the Pulitzer Prize for fiction in 1993. This story is from his forthcoming collection, *Tabloid Dreams*, due out this fall and scheduled to premier as an HBO series this winter. His work has appeared several times in *MR*.

"I'd like to write a book about your view of the disaster. You have three minutes."

THE TWELVE PLAGUES / *Gerald Shapiro*

WHEN THE PHONE RANG, Rosenthal was kicking a canvas to shreds in the middle of his studio. He'd already thrown a can of wet brushes against the far wall and had kicked a tray of paint across the room, leaving an attractive boat-shaped smear of burnt sienna sailing along the whitewashed floorboards. The place should have been condemned, and so should Rosenthal: trapped inside another night of failure in a season of failure, locked in a listless, drifting orbit around a failing sun.

"Kenneth Rosenthal?" the woman's voice asked him.

"That's me," he panted into the receiver, still frenzied from his exertions. He wiped a damp hand across his brow.

"Kenneth Rosenthal, the painter?"

"The one and only," he muttered. "Who's this?"

"Naomi Glick is my name. I hope this isn't an awkward moment. I'm calling on behalf of the Rivka Hirschorn Kissner Foundation in New York City. Perhaps you've heard of us? We're devoted to supporting the work of unknown visual artists who are of interest and significance to the American Jew," the woman said. Her voice was portentous, as if she were reciting something etched on tablets of stone. "I am very pleased to inform you, Mr. Rosenthal, that you are this year's winner of the Rivka Hirschorn Kissner Prize. My heartfelt congratulations."

The Who? The What? But she'd said the word "prize." He stood with the phone pressed to his head, chilling his ear like an ice pack.

"I'm one of several judges," Naomi Glick continued. "We comb the length and breadth of this country, Mr. Rosenthal—the Judaic highways and byways, artistically speaking. We receive slides from scores of exhibitions at reputable galleries around the United States. We're tireless in our pursuit of new Jewish visual artists. We take this work seriously. Some years no one is deemed worthy, and in those years we decline to award the Kissner Prize to anyone. Our standards are high. Your series of paintings, *The Twelve Plagues*, recently came to my attention, and it took my breath away."

"*The Twelve Plagues!* How'd you hear about them?"

"The slides arrived in the mail last month. We received them from—let's see, I have it right here—the Umpqua Valley Arts and Crafts Festival, Roseburg, Oregon. Roseburg—is that by any chance a Jewish name?"

"I don't think so, Mrs. Glick."

"Call me Naomi, Kenneth—please. Such insufferable paintings, these *Twelve Plagues* of yours," she purred. "Obnoxious in the very deepest sense of the word, like a set of precocious eight-year-old boys yammering away. I should know. My son Max is eight years old, and someday soon I may kill him."

"Oh. Well." He hesitated. "Does that mean you liked them?"

"Positively haunted. All that slashing, the paint knifed onto the canvas as though it were trying to burrow through to the other side! All those reds and oranges and blacks saying to themselves, what in the name of God are we *doing* in these paintings? How can we get out of here? All that energy flaming up toward heaven, like it couldn't wait to get out of the frame! I adored them, Kenneth. They're what Jewish art is all about."

Rosenthal remembered the exhilarating, frightening experience of painting them, how they'd come to him like a bundle of gifts—no, like a string of anonymous letter-bombs in the mail—all twelve of them done in a week and a half of hysteria, a series of seizures a year ago, his last sustained and successful creative burst before something vital inside him dried up and blew away. Since then he'd wandered around his studio in a daze, an orphan in the wilderness.

"You don't know—you can't *possibly* know—what this means to me," he said into the receiver, and then he paused. He had no idea of what to say next; he'd never won anything before, in twenty years of labor at the easel. He'd entered one competition after another, submitted slides to foundations, shown his work in art festivals and fairs; he'd come close to recognition, so close he could feel it on his fingertips, but it had eluded him year after year. "To be recognized by such a prestigious foundation—to be honored by my own people," he heard himself say in a choked voice, and then he stopped. Who was he kidding? His people? When had he last stepped foot into a synagogue?

"You'll be interested to know that you're the very first winner of the Rivka Hirschorn Kissner Prize to live west of the Hudson River," Naomi Glick continued. "Oregon, of all places! Fur trappers, Lewis and Clark, Sacajawea—salmon fishing and lumber mills! One wouldn't have thought a Jew could survive in such a place! Are there Jews in Oregon?"

"There are Jews everywhere, Mrs. Glick. There are Jews in Yokohama."

"Our previous winners have all been New Yorkers," Naomi Glick continued, "which is natural, I suppose, given the fact that most serious American visual artists do seem to live in the New York area. Not that you're not serious, of course—I wasn't implying that at all. Believe me, we wouldn't have awarded you the Kissner Prize if you weren't absolutely first rate—and unknown, of course. But then you don't need me to tell you that, do you?"

Rosenthal surveyed the wreckage of his studio, the canvasses strewn here and there, the paints exploded, the brushes in splinters. "No," he said.

"Your paintings will be displayed at the Apawamis Jewish Community Center, the jewel of Westchester County, a monument to what money can buy, you'll love it, you really will," Naomi Glick went on. Her voice began to speed up, as though she were at a pay phone, running low on small change. "We'll arrange for shipment of the paintings. You'll be flown to New York for the awards presentation, there'll be a big dinner hosted by the donors, Sheldon Sperling and his wife Bernice, we'll invite the cream of New York's art critics and gallery owners to the awards ceremony, you'll be the toast of Apawamis, everyone will praise you to the skies, you'll have a lovely time. Believe me, Mr. Rosenthal, are you excited, of course you are, it's time to *shep* some *nakhes*, you lucky man."

A letter on Kissner Foundation stationery arrived three days later setting out the details of Rosenthal's upcoming trip to New York. He would have to give a short speech at the awards ceremony and then answer questions from the audience. The prize money and the airline tickets were on their way. He'd be met at La Guardia. Did he have any food allergies or preferences? All food would be prepared in a kosher kitchen during his visit, and no travel would be scheduled on the Sabbath, out of respect for his religious beliefs.

His religious beliefs! Rosenthal had a mirthless chuckle over that one. Once upon a time he'd believed. As a boy, he'd even toyed with the thought of becoming a rabbi. What had happened to his childlike devotion, his dutiful affection for God? Hebrew school from four to six in the afternoon, two or three days a week; training for his Bar Mitzvah, learning the entire portion of the Torah by heart; Sunday school; services on Friday nights and again on Saturday mornings, fasting, praying, chanting, beating his breast—at the age of thirteen he was a little Yeshiva *bucher, davening* with the best of them, rocking back and forth on his heels, locked in a dialogue with the Almighty. But once he'd finished with his Bar Mitzvah, stuffed all the gifts he'd received, the neckties, the wallets, the pen-and-pencil sets into a drawer, Rosenthal found himself without much left to say to God.

The trouble had been brewing for a while. In his teens he'd become increasingly aware that there was something despicable about his parents' version of Judaism, a kind of self-righteous, self-pitying one-upmanship. No one else had suffered like the Jews, his parents told him—no one else knew what deprivation was. Oh, sure, here and there in the history of the world, from time to time some other group had had their knuckles rapped with a ruler—but not like the Jews, *nothing* like the Jews. Competitive Suffering! It was an arcane athletic event his parents had invented, governed by one very simple rule: the Jews win. No arguing. Blow the whistle, the game's over, Jews win again. No matter what sorrow, what agony you might think had befallen you or your family or your people, you lose, because nothing that ever happened to anybody could compete with What Happened To The Jews.

Rosenthal remembered his Uncle Irwin coming to the house for dinner, a bleak little man so pale and nondescript that he tended to blend into the wallpaper. "When I was a child, we were so poor we ate grass," Uncle Irwin said during momentary conversational lulls at the family's dining room table. "I never tasted sugar until I was thirty-one years old. That's because we were Jewish. Nobody wanted us to have anything. That's why we had to eat grass. Pass the sugar, will you?"

The first time Uncle Irwin had said this—Rosenthal would have been perhaps nine—the pronouncement carried real drama with it (it beat the crap out of his mother's stories about hand-me-down shoes, for instance); but as the years went by and Irwin told the same story again and again, it lost its tragic bulk in Rosenthal's imagination, and floated up airily into the realm of comedy. Occasionally when Uncle Irwin wasn't there, Rosenthal would impersonate him: "We ate dirt. Sometimes when we had water, we made dirt soup. But we didn't have water very often. Once in a while they took away our dirt, and then we had to eat clothing. Shirts tasted pretty good—a little salt, a little pepper. But then they took away our salt and pepper, because we were Jews and they didn't want us to have any."

"You should be ashamed of yourself," Rosenthal's mother told him. "Such a comedian. Your Uncle went through a lot of deprivation. I'm talking about real deprivation, young man—not a joke."

By the time he was in college, Rosenthal's attitude had soured even further. His first semester, his philosophy professor spent the first ten weeks debunking various arguments supporting the existence of God. One after another, St. Anselm, Bishop Berkeley, Aquinas and the rest of them collapsed like so many mobile homes in a hail storm. At the holiday break, Rosenthal went home and called Rabbi Kravitz, the man who'd blessed him the day of his Bar Mitzvah. "I'm having a spiritual crisis," Rosenthal said. "I think I might be turning into an atheist. Can I come in to see you? It's kind of an emergency."

"This is a terrible week for me," Rabbi Kravitz said. He coughed into the phone.

"Look, I appreciate that, but I really need to talk to somebody."

"Listen to me, Kenny," Rabbi Kravitz said in his deep, tomb-like voice. "God exists. Trust me on this. He hears what you're saying and he's appalled. He's saying to himself, what's got into Kenny Rosenthal?"

"If there's a God, Rabbi Kravitz, just tell me this: why is there so much evil in the world? Why is there so much suffering?"

"You think you're the only one in the world who wonders about God's purpose? You think nobody's ever asked why there's suffering in the world?"

"No, I didn't think that."

"Well, you're not, my young friend," Rabbi Kravitz said in an aggrieved voice. "Listen—you're a Jew. You were born a Jew, you were raised a Jew, you're going to die a Jew. When the Nazis come to town, you think they're going to ask you if you're an atheist or not? You're a Jew! Into the ovens! It doesn't matter what kind of nonsense a professor tries to cram into your head, you're a Jew. Does that answer your question?"

Before Rosenthal could answer, the rabbi had hung up.

A month after the phone call from the Kissner Foundation, early on a Sunday afternoon that promised showers, a small, fragile-looking man in a seersucker sports coat met Rosenthal at La Guardia airport. The old man doffed his Yankees cap, revealing an ancient skull the color of aged parchment. "So you're the lucky artist," he muttered, and snatched Rosenthal's overnight bag with gnarled fingers. "I'm Sheldon Sperling," he said as they walked toward the parking lot. "Call me Chub, why don't you—everybody does. My wife and I, we're the donors of the prize you won. Don't worry, we can afford it. I'm in corporate law. Was, I should say—I just retired about two months ago, seventy-nine years old. Corporate law was my life—I still dream about it every few nights. Merger dreams, mostly—they're like flying dreams, tremendous sense of power there."

The car was a Mercedes station wagon, a big yellow tank of a car. Mr. Sperling threw Rosenthal's bag in the back. Slowly they drove through a skyless wasteland of urban blight, then gradually the scenery turned greener and the world opened up again as they left the city behind and entered lush, heavily wooded suburbs. "I'm taking you to your hotel—you can freshen up there for a while, then we'll send somebody to pick you up and bring you to dinner at our house. Our daughter Rachel came home just for this event. Isn't that something? Flew in from Chicago just for the occasion. She's some daughter. Married to a hotshot in marketing out there, the guy makes nothing but money. Heckuva guy. They've got one girl, beautiful, named Elena. Is that some name? Find that one in the Bible. I love that name. Our only grandchild."

"Gee," Rosenthal said. "That's some name."

"Our other daughter, Stephanie—married to a urologist. He has his own clinic, he's written up in medical journals all the time. They're in the south of France now, driving around drinking wine. Then there's our youngest, Randy, lives in the city. He won't be coming up this year. He says he can't get away. You'd like him—he's a designer. Very artistic guy."

"Sorry I won't get to meet him," Rosenthal said in a sadly philosophical tone, as if he'd really been hoping to meet the whole clan. They lapsed into silence. The streets had turned into avenues lined by arching maple trees, their leaves forming a continual canopy over the road, the afternoon light dappling the foliage.

"Before we get to the hotel, I have to ask you something," Sperling said. "Can I call you Dan?"

"Ken—it's Ken," Rosenthal said.

"It's not really my question, it's my wife's question. You ready?"

"Go right ahead."

"What the heck were you doing with those *Twelve Plagues*, anyway? Those paintings—what were you thinking about? What is that, is that your idea of Jewish art?" They stopped for a red light.

"Excuse me?" Rosenthal asked.

"Relax, don't get your hackles up. I mean, personally I don't care. I'm a lawyer, give me a contract I'll tell you what I think of it. Art is not my cup of tea. My wife, on the other hand—well, it's a different story. That's all I'm saying."

Rosenthal sat silently for a moment, mulling this over. You wait twenty years to win a prize, and now that you win one, you have to listen to this? Some aging shyster critiques your oeuvre for you? What had they brought him here for, anyway? "So, you're saying your wife didn't like my work?" he asked at last. "Is that it?"

"It isn't a question of liking or not liking. I'm just saying, you might want to think about what the heck you were doing, because *some* people might ask, that's all." The light changed and they pulled out into traffic again. "It doesn't bother me, understand. But *some* people," Sperling said, and then his voice trailed off. They drove on to the hotel, a nondescript brick building distinguished only by the extravagance of its landscaping. Sperling sat grimly at the wheel while Rosenthal got out of the car. "Just think about it, that's all," he called out. The Mercedes drove off, leaving Rosenthal standing at the curb with his bag.

At the check-in desk, the reservations clerk said, "Oh, so you're the Kissner winner this year." She flashed a lifeless smile at Rosenthal. "Congratulations on your prize. The room is taken care of—courtesy of the Kissner Foundation. Please don't make any long-distance phone calls—the phone is not taken care of. Neither is room service. And don't ask for anything special from Housekeeping. Last year's winner ran up a bill like you wouldn't believe. And whatever you do, don't watch HBO. It's not covered."

The bed was small but firm, and Rosenthal surprised himself by slipping into a light sleep. He awoke at a quarter to six, feeling refreshed and terror-stricken. He showered slowly, rehearsing the acceptance speech that he'd written for the occasion and had been practicing on and off for weeks. He wasn't very experienced at public speaking, but the tone of this speech seemed okay to him—a few jokes to establish the fact that he was an ordinary fellow, then the meat of the thing, short without being abrupt, humble but not groveling.

The shower itself felt wonderful; it was dark in there, and safe; the hot water hit him in the nape of his neck and cascaded down his back like a light massage. There was nobody in there but him, nobody saying, "So what the hell were you doing with those *Twelve Plagues,* anyway?" He got out reluctantly and towelled off, avoiding his gaze in the brightly lit mirror.

Rosenthal slowly got into his good clothes. Then he sat on the bed and looked at the blank television screen. Why had he come here? How could he have thought this prize would change the basic realities of his life, when nothing ever had changed them before? Flying three thousand miles to accept an award and shake hands with strangers— it was just the kind of thing that Lenore, his ex-wife, had warned him against in *The Price of Arrogance,* one of the series of cautionary treatises she'd written for him after their divorce, in an effort to "set him straight on life." Oh, he'd been set straight, all right.

By the time the phone rang, Rosenthal had retreated so far into himself that he thought the ringing sound was coming from the next room. After a few rings he summoned the presence of mind to pick it up.

"This is Chub Sperling. Did you get a nap in?"

"Yes—yes, I did."

"Good. I'm sending my daughter, Rachel, to pick you up. She's the one with the daughter. Her husband's the marketing hotshot. Nothing but money."

The yellow Mercedes drove into the hotel's circular driveway twenty minutes later. The last benevolent sheen of afternoon light had drifted over the world and was gone, and Rosenthal felt a faint chill in the air as he stepped out of the hotel's lobby and walked toward the car. Rachel, a tanned woman Rosenthal's age, smiled at him from the driver's seat and extended a hand for him to shake once he was in the car. "I've seen your paintings at the Jewish Community Center," she said in a faint, neutral voice. "They're interesting, and I had a question I wanted to ask you about them." She pulled out into traffic.

Rosenthal waited for her to go on, but nothing followed. "Well, it certainly is nice that you flew back East like this," he said after a moment, then added, "Your dad told me all about you, your sister, your brother."

"He told you about Randy? Did he mention the Italian boys?"

"Uh, no. I don't remember anything like that."

"Randy's got a lot of friends—they all happen to be good-looking Italian guys. My dad's still puzzled about it; he'll be the last to know. For the rest of his life he'll be sitting around saying, 'So when's Randy going to get married?'"

Neither of them made much of an effort at conversation during the drive to the Sperlings' house, a route which wound through hushed neighborhoods, stately homes set on lawns as lush and manicured as expensive toupees. At last they swung around a corner and pulled into the driveway of a mustard-colored house with a pillared entryway.

The front door of the house swung open and Bernice Sperling appeared, flanked by the massive pillars. She stood frozen between them for a moment like Sampson in Gaza, and though she was petite and silver-haired, Rosenthal immediately noted something oddly massive in her demeanor, a stern, predatory cast to her chin that made it possible for him to imagine her toppling those pillars with two good shoves.

Then the tableau came to life and she approached him, arms extended. "Ken! So good to meet you," she said. "Congratulations on winning the Rivka Hirschorn Kissner Prize. *Mazel tov!* I hope you realize what a great honor the Kissner Foundation has bestowed on you." She fixed him with a shrewd, puckered smile. "I've spent quite some time with your paintings," she said, then she stopped short, as if trying to hide another sentence that was trying to peek mischievously out of her mouth like a second tongue. The smile faded. "Maybe you can explain them to me over dinner. Well, come in, come in." She linked an arm through Rosenthal's and led him inside.

As they walked inside, a timer went off in the kitchen, and Mrs. Sperling clapped a hand to her throat. "Amuse yourself, Ken, for just a minute or two—I've got some last-minute preparations to attend to." She scurried back toward the kitchen, leaving him to roam on his own.

The house was decorated in an amazing array of Judaica. In the large, formal living room, a Chagall lithograph hung over the fireplace, flanked by two large brass menorahs. The Chagall was shamelessly whimsical, lit with all kinds of iridescent splashes and flying cattle, so *shtetl*-sentimental it might as well have come complete with canned Klezmer music blaring from a hidden speaker. Around the room the walls sagged with Jewish art; there were several reproductions of Rembrandt's etchings of Amsterdam's Jews, and most of the wall facing the fireplace was given over to posed group portraits of bearded, black-robed nineteenth century rabbinical students, all of them stern as corpses. Jewish literature crammed built-in bookcases everywhere Rosenthal looked.

A small woman with an aging ballerina's taut face and a wide, expressive mouth approached Rosenthal as he perused the bookshelves; she waved a long, bony hand out to him, palm down, as if she might be expecting him to kiss it. "Naomi Glick," she said. "We spoke on the phone. I simply adore your work."

"Oh, thank you," Rosenthal said. "I'm so glad you're here."

"I'm still amazed that I've never heard of you," she said. "It was thrilling to call you and tell you you'd won. The high point of my year. Oregon. Oregon! What an ironic place to live! You're a darling painter. I love what you've done with the plagues; the judges all got together and met several times and reviewed a number of other possible choices and no one had the slightest difficulty in settling on you, you were our favorite, our absolute unanimous choice, you lucky boy." She leaned into his ear like a conspirator and whispered, "Sit next to me at the table. I've got to have *someone* to talk to. The Sperlings are sweethearts, but they're a bit too . . . *devout*, shall we say, for my taste."

Naomi Glick led Rosenthal into the dining room, where an elderly couple were chatting with Mr. Sperling. "Ken, this is Milton Steinhaus," she said, and Steinhaus, a stooped, balding fellow, impeccably dressed, shook Rosenthal's hand. "Call me Milton," he said in a heavy middle-European accent. "Eighty-three years old last Thursday, and I've still got my sense of humor. That's why Chub and Bernice still like me—I'm a lively, irreverent old guy with an appreciative eye for the ladies." He ran a finger across his pencil line moustache, then delicately jerked at the bottom of his shirt cuffs, extending them a fraction of an inch beyond his sports coat.

Naomi Glick put a hand on Rosenthal's arm. "Isn't he something? Eighty-three years old. A lively old guy." She turned toward the elderly woman standing next to Steinhaus. "And here's his adorable wife, Harriet."

"I'm Bernice's oldest friend," Harriet Steinhaus said. "I love her like a sister. Like a *sister*. We've been in the same artistic appreciation group over forty years. Is that some kind of record, or what?"

At that moment Rachel and Bernice Sperling burst into the dining room, both of them laden with platters. The table groaned with food: roast chicken, potato pancakes with applesauce, carrot tsimmes, and a large spinach salad crowded in among the plates and glasses. "Sit, everyone—sit!" Bernice cried, and Naomi Glick planted Rosenthal firmly in the seat next to her, at the end of the table farthest away from the Sperlings. The process of passing platters began. "I always get a little emotional at the start of a Kissner Prize dinner," Mrs. Sperling began. "I tell you, I don't mind the cooking, the baking, the cleaning that always goes into this dinner. No amount of work is too much to revere the blessed memory of Rivka Hirschorn Kissner—a gifted Jewish artist, a painter of immense promise."

"She finished three paintings, all of them bad," Naomi Glick whispered in Rosenthal's ear. "My dog is more artistic when he's taking a crap."

"She died too young, may she rest in peace," Mrs. Sperling continued, nodding sadly. "In Palestine, fighting with her last breath for the establishment of a Jewish homeland."

"An incompetent terrorist, too," Naomi Glick added, tickling Rosenthal's ear with her whispers. "She blew herself up trying set the King David Hotel on fire."

"So as you can well imagine, this is all a labor of love," Bernice Sperling said with a sigh, and nodded to Rosenthal with a noticeable quiver in her chin. She raised her glass. "To the memory of Rivka Hirschorn Kissner, *olev ha sholom*." Everyone drank. "Eat, please. Go ahead," she said. "Enjoy. *Ess, ess gesundheit.* I have to ask Ken a question or two before I get started, just out of curiosity. You don't mind, Ken?"

Here it came. "No, of course not," Rosenthal said, bracing himself.

"First let me explain something to you. Chub and I don't judge the competition, and we don't judge the judges, either. We're not experts. We're just the donors. Am I making myself clear?"

"Of course."

"Good. So humor me," Mrs. Sperling said. "Let me have a minute." She inhaled deeply before beginning to speak. "In the Bible," she said, "there were only ten plagues, not twelve. Ten was enough for God, Ken—you had to add two more. God made the rivers run with blood, he set plagues of frogs and lice and hail upon the Egyptians. But Pharaoh's heart was hardened."

Naomi Glick leaned into Rosenthal's ear again. "He couldn't help it, the poor man, he had hardening of the heart," she whispered, and pounded a fist hysterically on Rosenthal's thigh under the table. He stared at her. Who was it she resembled? And then of course, there it was: Spencer Pelovsky, the clown prince of Rosenthal's Hebrew school class, remembered most vividly for farting into the microphone the day of his Bar Mitzvah. Naomi Glick's flat prankster's face, the wide, idiotic mouth—it was Spencer Pelovsky reborn, thrumming with impish delight. Staring at her, Rosenthal suddenly realized that he'd never really liked Pelovsky worth a nickel.

"So God sent three days of total darkness," Bernice Sperling continued. "He sent locusts, he killed all the livestock of the Egyptians and saved the livestock of the children of Israel." She looked around the table. "How many was that?"

"That's seven, dear," Mr. Sperling said.

"What am I leaving out? Rachel dear, you were Bat Mitzvahed, you can answer this one."

"Flies?" Rachel offered. "Mosquitoes? Gnats? I don't know."

"The money we spent on her religious education," Mr. Sperling grumbled.

"What else? Anybody?" Bernice Sperling called out.

"Boils," Naomi Glick said. "Lovely plague. Heathen though I am, I remember my Bible."

"Okay, so flies and boils, then finally the climactic plague, the killing of the firstborn. That was enough for God, but not for you, Ken—you had to add a couple of your own. Why? What for?"

Rosenthal sat silently, sucking in a chest full of air.

"And the two you added? What was that, some kind of statement? *Call waiting?* That's a plague? That's something God visited upon the

Egyptians in order to free his people? We're talking about *our* people here, Ken. The children of Israel. Call waiting—what is that, some kind of joke?"

"Well, no, not really," Rosenthal said in a mild voice.

"And the other one—the other plague, what was that one again?"

He sighed. She *knew* what it was, and he knew that she knew. She was just doing this to prolong the moment. "Lack of available parking, Mrs. Sperling," he said in a tired voice.

"Right! That's it. *Lack of available parking!* What is that, anyway? That's a plague?" Bernice Sperling looked down at her plate and pushed some food around with her fork. Then she put the fork down and raised a hand to her forehead.

"Bernice, don't let it upset you," Harriet Steinhaus said. Under her breath she muttered, "Expert judges. Feh."

Rosenthal leaned back in his chair and turned his head toward Naomi Glick. She'd been sitting primly, her head lifted high, her hands folded in her lap. He waited for her to say something now, something in her own defense as well as in his. But she said nothing.

"I went over to the Center and I looked at those paintings," Mr. Steinhaus said. "I'm a lively old guy, but I don't know much about art. So I said to myself, Milton, this is Jewish art? Because if this is Jewish art, I'll stick with *goyishe* art, thank you very much."

"Well, enough of this," Mrs. Sperling said with a sniff in her voice, and abruptly arose from the table. "Some of us connect with the story of our people's deliverance from slavery into freedom. Some of us feel that connection, some of us share the pain our people have suffered throughout the ages. For others—well, there's no point in belaboring it," she announced, wiping her hands together as if scrubbing away a stain. "Now, you'll forgive me if we don't have dessert. Normally I would have made something fantastic—I'm known for my desserts."

"She makes an angel food cake you'd kill for," Harriet Steinhaus said.

"But there's going to be food at the reception at the Jewish Community Center," Mrs. Sperling continued. "So we'll have our dessert there. I'll just clean up a little and we'll be off," she said, and walked into the kitchen.

Naomi Glick leaned over to Rosenthal and whispered, "I've got to smoke a cigarette or I'm going to do something I'll regret." She slid out of her chair and was nearly out of Rosenthal's reach before he grabbed her wrist and stopped her. "Where were you?" he asked. "Just then, when they were beating me with baseball bats—what are you, deaf?"

"But they're the *donors*, dear boy. The donors! They bought the *right* to beat you up a little. Why do you think people give money for prizes?"

He let her wrist slide through his fingers, and a moment later he heard her sneaking out the front door. Mr. Sperling and Milton Steinhaus made their way around the table removing the dinner plates, and Rosenthal stood up and began to help them—but Harriet Steinhaus leaned across the table and clutched his sleeve.

"Sit a minute," she said. "I want to talk to you." She waited until he was seated, then fixed him with a steady glare. "More than forty years Bernice and I have been together in the art appreciation group. I'd do anything for that woman. She's like the sister I never had. If it wasn't for Bernice Sperling, would I know about Chaim Soutine?" she said. "Would I know about Jacques Lipchitz? Could I tell you the difference between a Modigliani and a plate of linguini? Would I know Jack Levine's work like I know the back of my hand? Would I have an original Saul Steinberg hanging over my piano if it wasn't for her? Whenever there's a show, an exhibition of Jewish art anywhere within a day's drive, our group is there, thanks to Bernice. Did you know that Rembrandt was Jewish, by the way?"

"Well, yeah, there's some theory about that," he said vaguely.

"It's no theory! The man was Jewish! I'm telling you, I know something about art. The Soyer boys, Raphael and Joseph—our group met them when they were nothing, when they couldn't sell a painting to buy breakfast. Harold Rosenberg gave a lecture—we were in the front row. Clement Greenberg offered a three-week seminar—all of us were there, taking notes like crazy. We were talking about Barnett Newman and Mark Rothko before *anybody* was talking about Barnett Newman and Mark Rothko. Not that that's my idea of art, mind you. Very disturbed people. All that depression! Did you know that Jackson Pollock was Jewish, since we're talking?"

"He was?"

"A self-hating Jew. The worst kind. A *shanda*. As far from Chagall as you can get. Now Chagall, there was a Jewish artist. Better than Rembrandt, for my money. Chagall—there was a person—a *mensch*. He painted like an angel—it's like *Fiddler on the Roof* on canvas."

So that was it, Rosenthal told himself—artistic value could be measured by the quality of your Zero Mostel impersonation. He understood now; once again he'd failed to pass muster. He'd live with it—he'd been living with failure, artistic and personal, for so many years already—another season of failure wouldn't kill him. Lenore, his ex-wife, should have been here—she could have been taking notes on another treatise for his benefit: *The Value of Ethnic Identity, or Why You Shouldn't Be Such A Smart-Aleck All The Time.*

But another thought crowded Rosenthal's mind, puffing up like a balloon in his imagination and pushing Lenore and her treatises into the shadows. He'd never realized it before, but it was plain to him now, as plain as a sign stencilled on the wall: whatever else happened to him, no matter how miserable his existence, he'd be a painter the rest of his days.

"I know why you did it," Harriet Steinhaus said, leaning toward him with her eyebrows arched imperiously.

"Did what?"

"The extra two plagues. I know why you did it." She cocked her head at him. "You can't fool me. I have you figured out."

Rosenthal was about to protest when he felt Naomi Glick's bony hand on his shoulder. "What did I miss?" she whispered in his ear and she slid back into her chair. "I didn't hear any explosions. Did anything happen?"

He shook his head, determined to ignore her, and smiled at Harriet Steinhaus—a conciliatory smile, he hoped. At least the rest of them, the Sperlings, Harriet and Milton, even Rachel, for that matter, *believed* in something, he told himself. Even he believed in something. He'd forgotten that, or had stuffed it away somewhere in his attic, but now, under attack at the dinner table, he recalled it.

"Okay, everybody, we can't be late for the awards ceremony. We've got the guest of honor!" Mr. Sperling said. He rubbed his hands together in an exaggerated show of enthusiasm. "Rachel, you ride with your mother and me. Naomi, why don't you come with us, too? We can talk about next year's competition. Milton, would you and Harriet mind giving our winner a ride?"

"For you, darling, we'd do anything," Harriet Steinhaus said.

"Milton knows the way to the Center," Bernice Sperling said to Rosenthal. "We'll see you there in fifteen minutes, tops. Practice your speech!"

It would have been a fine plan, except that Milton Steinhaus didn't, in fact, know the way to the Apawamis Jewish Community Center, and Harriet didn't either. It took twenty minutes for this to come to light—twenty minutes of turning and twisting through unlit streets. "Are you sure we're going the right way?" Rosenthal asked at one point, sure that they'd passed the same corner three times already.

"I'm living in New York seventy-eight years," Milton Steinhaus said. "I was just a kid when I come over here. Believe me, I'll get you there." He flipped on the windshield wipers, though it wasn't raining. "All the money in Westchester County, you think they could spring for some streetlights." The car sailed through a four-way stop, and Rosenthal decided it might be better to handle this situation with his eyes closed.

Finally, after they'd cruised up and down every street in Apawamis, plus most of Rye, Port Chester and a portion of Scarsdale, Steinhaus pulled to the side of the road and shut off the engine. He pounded the steering wheel and said, "Son of a bitch. Son of a bitch."

Harriet, in the front passenger seat, blew out a ragged breath and bowed her head. "Bernice is going to be very upset about this," she said softly.

"That's okay," Rosenthal said, patting her arm. "Don't worry. We'll find a phone, we'll call, we'll get directions, we'll be there in no time."

"You have to understand, this woman is my dearest friend," Harriet Steinhaus continued. "I'd put my hand in a fire for her."

"It's not that bad," he crooned to her. "We'll find a phone, we'll get directions. It'll be okay—we just have to find a gas station."

"I know why you did it," she said suddenly, lifting her head and wagging a finger at him. "I've thought about it. I know something about Jewish art, let me tell you. Some people, you know, they say 'I don't know much about art, but I know what I like.' Not me. I say I do know something about art, and that's why I know what I like, Kenny. And what I don't like."

"Don't start," her husband advised her. "Your blood pressure."

"I could go look for a phone," Rosenthal suggested.

"Sometimes I think I could write a *book* about Jewish Art. You don't spend over forty years in an artistic appreciation group and come away from it not knowing a thing or two about art. Our group discussed your paintings at length, you'll be glad to know," Harriet Steinhaus said. "When we heard that the judges had given you the Kissner Prize, we all got out slides of your work—we hadn't seen it before, you understand—and we looked. I'll be honest with you, some of us were a little angry. But I figured you out. I know why you did it." She turned to him and smiled; he saw her eyes gleam in the darkness of the car.

"Mrs. Steinhaus, maybe we could talk about it while we're driving. We're going to the Center, right? Because if we are—"

"We're having a conversation," she said. She took the keys out of the ignition and plopped them into her purse.

"Harriet, sweetheart, is this a good idea?" Mr. Steinhaus asked.

"Okay, fine," Rosenthal offered. "We're not going to the Center. We're having a conversation. You figured me out. You got the goods on me. So tell me, why did I do it?"

"You did it," she said, her eyebrows raised, "because you wanted to shock people—you wanted to be a bad boy."

"No, that's not it," Rosenthal said.

"You did it because you hate the culture that produced you. Because you're angry, you're bitter, you're ashamed. Six million of your people died, and you make jokes. Ten plagues were enough to free the children of Israel from their bondage in Egypt, but ten plagues aren't enough for you. Call waiting! Lack of available parking! Joker! Criminal!"

"That's ridiculous."

"I know why you did it," Harriet Steinhaus said after the briefest of pauses, the note of triumph still ringing in her voice. "Okay, you ready? Don't tell me why you did it. I *know* why you did it. You did it to get back—to get back at your parents, and at your people. You did it out of spite, you did it to be vicious."

"Mrs. Steinhaus—"

"That's it, isn't it," she said, nodding in victory. "I hit it on the head, didn't I. Of course I did. Milton, didn't I tell you? I *knew* I knew why he did it."

Rosenthal opened the passenger side door and got out. He shut the door and leaned in through the open window. "Look, stay here, keep the doors locked, I'm going to look for a phone," he said. "I'll be back."

"Mr. Spite. Mr. Vicious," Mrs. Steinhaus spat at him. Her head rose higher on her neck and she looked at him haughtily.

Rosenthal stood by the car musing silently for a moment, running a hand carelessly through his hair. Then he took two steps away, and as he'd half expected, the engine suddenly roared to life, and the vehicle sped away into the dark.

The evening air was balmy and benevolent, soft against his cheeks. He put his hands into his pockets and began to walk, first slowly and then with more purpose, towards a vague light he could see at the far end of the street—surely something was there, some kind of store or service station where there might be a phone. After several blocks he stopped at another darkened street corner. Where the hell was he? The lights he'd been headed toward seemed as far away as they had when he'd started. What else was there to do but push on?

Somehow he'd get back to Oregon, that ironic place—back to the splattered gloom of his studio, where his work, his blessed and awful work, awaited him. He'd spend evenings reading Lenore's post-divorce treatises by lamplight, combing their turgid prose for answers to Harriet Steinhaus's embittered questions. Somewhere in one of them —perhaps in *Get Over It: How Ken Rosenthal Needs To Shape Up and Stop Being So Angry*—he might find what he was looking for. Or perhaps— yes, he liked this—perhaps the answer lay in a painting he had yet to begin, a blank canvas standing in a corner, waiting to catch his eye.

Rosenthal looked carefully to the right and to the left, and then, as he stepped off the curb, he began to deliver his acceptance speech. What the hell, he told himself—why waste the only speech he'd ever written? And besides, he'd rehearsed it so carefully that he felt he knew it by heart. He walked briskly through the shimmering dark-ness, declaiming as he went to an audience of fire hydrants, stray dogs, parked cars; soon he'd left his memorized speech behind, and was thanking everyone he'd ever known in his life.

Gerald Shapiro is the author of a collection of stories, *From Hunger,* from the University of Missouri Press.

FAMILY REUNION/*Daniel Halpern*

What you haven't said for forty years
comes back at you
all at once: long distance,
static-free but clinging
nonetheless. Distant voices
tied to your soul with cords of blood
from all the days you lived out
in seamless childhood, hourless,
but moment by moment,
a boy-child irreversibly growing toward time.

What you've never said, so many occasions
passing without response—postcards, a dime
after nine when the rates were down,
simple terms of endearment that became
forbidden words impossible to utter
even in solitude—passes over tonight.
Together now we have
what we've lived and what
we live now. Two lives, additional families.

I keep as private mantra the required words
of commitment, the speech of
endearment: formula, language
of the spell—the censored
vocabulary bringing us together, holding
us under the stars
as no bonds other than our being here
could keep us, bound, knowing
beyond what we can each say,
even though we say it. Even though we don't.

ART / *Daniel Halpern*

In the *cinéma vérité* of the sixties the beautiful
        protagonists always came so close,
so close to the everlasting

        sunset they were so desperately scripted
to ride into. And we, passives, onlookers,
        pressed forward in our collective seats

and rooted for them, individually
        and collectively. In the end it went poorly
for those we cheered. As if in imitation

        art led us down its artificial path,
every branch blossoming, the thyme walks
        kicking up the herbal scent, the insects insane

for the goodwill so well distributed.
        Good news has the metabolism of a hummingbird,
its instrument not long attuned to this world.

        Bad news won't extend the prognosis, but time
slows down at its intervention.
        The news, because it's finite, is never good

for long. But when the sun rises over the hills,
        the colored scents of August, the autumnal months,
find current and pass on the air. We're okay.

        It's the most we can expect, the temperature
of objects in various weathers, the satisfaction
        of things fitting together, whether in the hand

or the mind. We're happy to sit down, properly attired
        to a meal at day's end, knowing the days
are numbered, but the evening is long.

THE LONELINESS OF BEAUTIFUL WOMEN /
Daniel Halpern

> *The definition of beauty is easy;*
> *it is what leads to desperation.*
> —Paul Valéry

for Steve Dunn

The burden of beauty for beautiful women
is loneliness, the loneliness of being watched.

For those moved by beauty
the burden is simply *the burden of beauty*—

a configuration seen suddenly
that clings for a long time—

like something so grotesque
it can't be dislodged from the figurative

eye of the mind—that lingers
with the uninhabited narrative

of meeting, eventual exchange,
the fruitless pursuit of passion.

If the beautiful are lonely
I want to abandon them

to their solitude,
however beauty inhabits it,

free myself of the burden of beauty,
set it down and simply move on,

available again to what comes along—
why go beyond the recognition of beauty?

I'm thinking of the famous story
of two Zen monks

who, arriving at a river's edge,
find a woman waiting to cross.

The older monk lifts the woman
to his shoulders, carries her

to the other bank and continues walking.
The two men are silent now,

both reflecting but one burdened.
You know it is forbidden to carry women,

the younger monk says. And the other replies,
I left her at the river, but you are still carrying her.

THAW / *Daniel Halpern*

We wondered where the headlands were,
if we were meant to follow one
of the various rivulets north, back up

through rock-base and bird-perch,
to come upon a gentle pasture,
a grassy breach above rock

and the rook's nest, beyond the tight,
speedy passage of water gaining
momentum in the thaw and flow, detachment

of recent winter—seasonal loosening,
distilled fish rising
to surface bait, to hook and eye

of the wanderer, eye of the sun, opaque
lunar tooth. And down, the water gravity-
driven, so long bestilled, winter-gripped,

frozen to place and now, in the gradual
heat-rise filing down again
the ancient river-groove—down river-seam,

rock-gouge along moss-bank. The melt
now at headland pasture, so long under
white, cow-grass and base-wood bud firing

the pre-bank sprawl settling into early spring,
the drape and lank of a sultry summer,
the languid opening, the delicate twigs

of Swedenborg's angels exploding to blossom
as the truth played the obvious
and we took the moment to think back.

We were wandering there and I remembered,

or was it you who said it? It was a path
we pursued, the two of us blinded by scent—

but it might merely have been casual destination,
to be among what opened. What did we call it?
The river-run and wild thyme. The shore-chive.

Ebb and flow.
Keepers

Judged by the inch,
those falling

short
live another day,

those beyond
the limit pay

for their sins,
if sin

is what it is.
Greed or

subsistence, hunger
in any form

looking
for satisfaction—

something
of substance to take

home, something
whole to keep.

THE PLANES / *Daniel Halpern*

[A]

Our red-haired Professor of
The-Shape-Of-Things told us, *To read it*
you have to touch it,
place our fingers
lightly around the straight
angles of the walls
constructed for the sake of
companionship, of relation
one line to another, an [in] answer.

There are circles that choose to hover,
transparent, fluid,
turning on no fixed axis,
but tilted, reflecting
the blue light of autumnal midnight,
the light of midday, late
morning, the hour before
and after sunrise.
Shapes that float, catch light
and turn, reveal and absorb,
display what lies behind, a mirror
or surface through which
to look back on yourself.

[B]

The Professor of What's-Not-Seen pulls down
the colored map of basic elements,
a scrabble of annotated squares, colored,
standing in for the invisible,
the never seen, the air we breathe,
the atmosphere, the unreal
that keeps us real, the surreal,
the substance of what we are,
the ethereal, what we used to call,
in the days of simple, *the ethers.*

You notice lanyards of light
intertwined in a braid of
white light refracted, broken
into a wardrobe of color, a closet
opened suddenly displaying
out of unrelenting non-light
the colors of our daily tours.

Or in August, if you lie on your back,
find in the dark a midnight summer sun,
a disk, unilluminated and muted,
and follow the globe of heated light
in whatever ways your thinking requires,
as the rimmed dime rides
the acreage behind-closed-eyes.

[C]

It was the Professor of What-Was-To-Come
who explained the nature of wood
by warning us on the last day,

If you remember only one thing remember
that what you make
you will by turn ruin
with the finishing touch.

MIDNIGHT: TRIADIC GHAZAL/
Daniel Halpern

Let the night be the one place of darkness.
    Drinking water passes
        to those without appetite.

In the dark we walk through rooms
    familiar as questions
        asked of us, over and over.

We know hope, light of the single star
    shed from the dying body,
        traveling, released. On its way.

Their arms outspread. A smile
    pulling back their lips.
        Gravity, sacrifice, giving over

the sweet wafer of consciousness. Nails,
    straps or ropes, methods of support
        for this one portrait everlasting.

And for us the diminishing night
    if the domestic star blooms once more
        over the farthest shore.

Awake? Whatever you say.
    Part of the past is that night.
        And then, too, what lies ahead.

Daniel Halpern is editor-in-chief of The Ecco Press and was founder and editor of *Antaeus*. He is the author of seven collections, including, most recently, *Selected Poems*.

SWIMMING IN THE DARK / *Nancy Zafris*

LIFE IS STRANGE, isn't it? A hotel pool in Rome, the china plate of blue water, fifteen other girls in the company-issue swimsuit. We're stewardesses from Japan. Yesterday we went shopping. Tomorrow, Singapore.

Our lounge chairs surround the pool like a fence, like a red fence with splashes of white paint. Next to me Michie talks of wanting to wear a bikini. She is the one who wears the most makeup in our group and that is saying something. When we're primped for a flight we look more like a troupe of Kabuki actors. Too much makeup and somehow you begin to look like a man. It's the layers of foundation on our faces—chin and cheeks—but that's how they like us, painted in white, the post-adolescent pimples hidden. The cosmetics clog the pores, causing further pimples, then more layers to cover up, and voilà! in no time I'm admiring a pretty transvestite in the mirror.

Makeup free, I turn my face up to the sun. I have my eyes closed and I'm getting hot. Beside me Michie sighs. *"Omiyage,"* she laments.

"Such a constant trial," agree the others.

Already I have three shopping bags of calfskins and Gucci from Via Condotti, presents for family, in-laws, and friends, but hidden in one is a secret treat for myself: miniature yellow post-its with an inch of Paloma Picasso leather binding, on sale for fifty dollars. There are so many presents to buy for others, and so many international trips, each trip requiring another round of *omiyage*. But the Paloma Picasso post-its are for me; they made the laborious day of shopping worthwhile.

Even now, relaxing beside the pool, money spent and obligations fulfilled, we are still waiting to enjoy ourselves. The blue pool is untouched, a sheet of glass, brittle when we look at it, deadly if we dare to shatter its surface. The only ripples come from the murmurs that begin to rise like heat shimmies from our sunbathing bodies.

"Let's dive in," suggests someone.

I don't immediately recognize her voice so I open my eyes. Of course. It's Hisako. Typical. She's the mischievous one, a hostess in the third cabin.

A couple of others concur. "It's so hot," they say. "She won't mind."

"Do you think she is sleeping?" asks another.

"I could call her on the phone," suggests Michie. "Ask if she is coming down?"

"Not you, Michie." We laugh, then turn quickly around, spooked and fearful, half-expecting an apparition of Ishihara-san to waver before us. Everyone knows our supervisor cares least for Michie though she is diligent and obedient. Michie comes from the north, a small village in Hokkaido. Her skin is like an icy blue pearl; she seems different, a product of the cold. I don't know why Ishihara-san dislikes her; perhaps it is her country upbringing, perhaps it is her large mouth neoned in a prostitute's oxblood lipstick.

One would think Ishihara-san would disapprove of the mischievous Hisako, but Hisako, it is well-known, comes from a wealthy Tokyo family. She is a member of an exclusive tennis club, and Ishihara-san is salivating for an invitation. In another ten months Hisako will quit. She is to be married next May. Having been courted by so many suitors has made her a little arrogant, fearless of consequences. Now that the airline has loosened its rules, almost a quarter of the stewardesses are married like me. But it is still hoped that we abide by the former rule and retreat into housewifedom.

Boredom. I am bored. It's hardly a violent experience—then it would at least have something to recommend it. It's more like being waterlogged and drowning from the inside out. Inside me lives a stranger but I've never met her. All I know is that she isn't married.

The sun heats our conflict about whether to jump into the pool ahead of our supervisor. Our disagreement wanders aimlessly, like a victim of heat stroke. "Ishihara-san is so old," says one of the girls. "I know she's already thirty."

"No, she's twenty-eight," asserts another girl in a peevish tone.

"Let's not argue," says Fumiko, the leader of our pep talks. "Our lack of togetherness will show on tomorrow's flight." Fumiko's zealous dutifulness shows on her face, overshadowing any attractiveness. Her features are suffused with good intentions. How annoying she is!

"I still have *omiyage* to buy," whines Michie in misery.

"We all have *omiyage* to buy," says Fumiko. "It's a blessed obligation to show our appreciation to family and friends."

"I don't need to appreciate them every two weeks," says Michie with a frigid blast of Hokkaido wisdom.

"She's right," one of the other girls says. "This present-giving is a painful chore."

"No one likes it but we have to do it."

"They just tuck the presents away into some cranny with hardly a glance. And our apartments are so small! I have nowhere to put the presents I receive."

"Admit it," says Michie. "You rewrap them and give them away."

Embarrassed silence.

"We are complaining too much," Fumiko admonishes. "And you, Michie, you like buying presents for yourself, why not others?"

That heats up the argument even more. It is silly to discuss such a thing since the custom of present-giving will not change. But this is the sort of useless squabble we carry on all the time. The argument is orderly, each person taking a turn while the others listen attentively. The next speaker is careful to allow an appropriate gap of silence before speaking, so that no one appears to be jumping in out of turn. The very tradition of this squabbling is comforting—or at least it puts me to sleep. I lie back, their words fueling the rhythms of oncoming dreams as I begin to drift off.

Amidst the steady ebb and flow of Japanese comes the rushed slur of English. This intrigues me. I am anxious to see what my dream holds.

All of a sudden several of the girls squeak in horror and my pleasant dream is interrupted. I open my eyes. Above me a weather balloon is floating fast, floating downward, plummeting toward the glassy surface of the pool. How long have I slept? Funny, this is what confuses me. Not the question, Why is a weather balloon floating into a hotel pool? That seems perfectly natural.

The horrified squeaking of some of the girls turns to chortling as the brass ballast of the weather balloon pierces the surface of the pool and sinks to the bottom. Flood warning! flood warning! signals the little balloon. Italian weather reports—hmmph—now I know why not to trust them.

But I wasn't dreaming the English I heard. I hear it again, clearly spoken. A group is rushing up the hill through the bushes, destroying, by the sound of it, everything in their paths. They arrive breathless, leaves and twigs pasted onto their wet faces, the sweat pouring like tears down their cheeks.

"Oh my god!" a woman in the group cries, covering her mouth at the sight of the sunken balloon.

"Don't worry, don't worry," a man calms her, blocking her passage with an outstretched arm. "I'll get it."

The girls turn to me to translate. "Well, there's nothing much to translate so far," I tell them.

"They've lost their balloon," Michie explains to the group.

"Buy another," Hisako says sarcastically, emboldened somehow by the Americans' presence. Everyone shushes her. Spoiled rich girl, the Americans might say if they could understand her. But they're probably rich themselves. Why else would they be in Rome?

In my hotel room inside a shopping bag are Paloma Picasso post-its for fifty dollars. What kind of message is worthy for these yellow squares? *Watanabe-san called. Please call him back.* Calligraphed in brush and ink, my miniature red seal in the corner.

There are five in the group of Americans. The woman who has spoken is blonde, now quite a dirty blonde; perspiration has darkened her roots and flattened out any hair-sprayed body. The man comforting her is handsome and I am moved by his good looks as well as by something else, a gentleness. There is one other woman and two other men.

"Hello, ladies," the handsome man addresses us.

The women of his group are wearing dark dresses and high heels. The men wear white shirts and ties and ironed khaki pants.

"Hello. How are you?" we reply in unison.

Yellow paper squares for fifty dollars. They were on sale. Use them up, I tell myself. They're cheap, half the usual price. Use them up without a care.

"Would one of you, since you're already suited up that is, mind diving into the pool and retrieving that canister?"

"What?" the girls ask me blankly.

I will never use them, I realize. I will never let anyone else use them.

"What?" the girls demand.

"Nothing," I tell them.

The man regards our mute stares. How strange we must look to him, in our matching bathing suits arrayed on a chain of matching lounge chairs. I think of the coffin hotels for commuters—in Tokyo everything, everywhere, is somehow an arrangement of identical cubicles. Does he find us laughable? A handsome, gentle man like him—what could he be thinking of us?

"We are waiting for our supervisor before we go in the pool," I finally explain. "If you would like to wait . . . ."

"Oh my god," the blonde woman says, holding back a sob. Mascara runs down her face, and her black eyes match the collapse of her hair. "What is it?" I ask him. "A weather balloon?"

"Uhh, a weather balloon . . . . No, not exactly."

Michie is tugging on my arm. "What, what!"

"Nothing," I tell her.

The handsome man begins to loosen his tie and slip it over his head, loop intact. He hands it to the second woman. Next he takes off his shirt. "Sorry, ladies," he says as he begins unzipping his pants, but as for me I'm saying, Go on.

He wears blue Calvin Klein briefs. His socks are the last to come off, and then he dives in.

"American men are hairy," Hisako says with disgust.

"At least they're able to have beards," one of the girls remarks.

"Who would want a man who could grow a beard?" another protests. "They scratch."

"You would shave it every day."

"Some don't."

This is threatening to develop into another of our pointless squabbles, but then the man surfaces with a belching gasp and we fall silent.

"It's because they eat so much meat," one of the girls ventures, but the argument has fizzled. All eyes are on the man. He pulls himself out of the pool, hands the brass canister trailing a shriveled balloon to the blonde woman, who is sobbing noiselessly, and then he turns to us. His eyes are wet, they are blue, and his lashes sparkle.

Keep your clothes off for a while, I think.

"Could I dry off with one of your towels?" he asks. "I'm very sorry to bother you."

We gape at him, wide-eyed, without response.

"Someone so hairy, on my towel . . . ." Hisako sucks in her breath, as though in pain. Ever since her engagement, she has become more vocal against Americans, leaving me to wonder if she didn't have a secret wish to marry a rich, good-looking Californian with a nice nose and big eyes, someone, in fact, who looks exactly like the man addressing us.

"Just stand there, you'll dry," the second woman in his group tells him.

"Well, what do we do now?" one of the men asks. "Let's just scatter him over the Piazza Navona. He always liked that place."

"He did not," the second woman says indignantly.

The blonde woman's head dips over the brass canister, her shoulders droop, and it looks as though she might drop to the ground and fold into herself. She is still crying convulsively, making no sound. The veins are starting to show in her forehead.

"It didn't work," says the handsome man, dripping wet in his briefs. His voice is low and sympathetic and he touches her elbow. "We'll have to scatter him."

"No!" the blonde woman cries.

"You could save him," the second woman suggests. "On a nice shelf or something."

"What is going on?" Michie asks.

"Quiet," I tell her.

"Tell me, what is going on? Why is the woman crying?"

"Nothing."

"She's crying because the balloon is popped," Michie explains to the others.

Now I've missed part of the conversation. The man is tugging his khakis over his wet body, saying, "All right, Freda, we'll get some more balloons."

"The woman's name is Freda," I tell Michie.

"The woman's name is Freda," she tells the others.

"But how will we know where it lands?" the second woman asks.

"It's not supposed to land," Freda says.

"Which woman is Freda?" they ask.

"The blonde one."

"Not very pretty, is she?" Hisako says.

"Hush!" the girls say.

"Well, you know it's going to land somewhere," one of the men is saying.

"It will never land!" Freda cries emphatically.

"Freda thinks the new balloon will never land," I tell the other girls.

"She's nuts," Hisako says. "A hag."

With that the group of Americans marches off, a glum, grief-stricken brigade, not down the hill where they came from but through the hotel garden, leaving me to translate this sorry absurd event into something my co-workers can handle.

Sunbathing by a pool in the midday heat, my mind dulled by dreams, I have just watched a man's burial urn sail from the sky and land at my feet. What should I tell the others? That they've witnessed a poolside exhumation?

I decide to ask them what they think has happened. "It was a type of toy helicopter," one of the girls suggests. "Yes, that was it," they all immediately agree.

Consensus creates a new reality, a reality sealing a tiny whirlybird motor in a brass container rather than the ashes of a dead man. Is it any less real? If it satisfies their curiosity, then isn't it just as good?

It is good enough for me. I simply want to go swimming.

I know no one will enter a pool contaminated by a burial urn. I'm queasy enough doing it myself. But I'll do it. I'm becoming desperately hot, and now I see Ishihara-san marching toward us, officious even in a long hotel robe that covers her red bathing suit slashed with white. She is quite a bit taller than average and wears her hair short, parted on the side. It's a business style, without adornment. On our flights she wears less makeup than the rest of us. She is not there to please the passengers; she is in charge of us, towering a head above, her business hairstyle ordering us about without words. Already I can feel myself breathing the artificial air. Tomorrow I will be packed into a 747 cylinder, my whole being pounded with the sonic white noise of silence. We'll feed the passengers, then pull the window shades and let them sleep. The fresh air I breathe every five minutes will be mixed with recirculated air; only my corpuscles will ever know the difference and they're not telling.

Ishihara-san unties her robe, apologizing for the delay. She is all smiles, with an extra beam directed to wealthy, tennis-playing Hisako—until she notices the pool. Someone has jumped in before her: small circles still spread lazily across the surface despite the man's exit several minutes earlier, and on the far side a suspicious trail of wet spots on the cement catches her attention. Ishihara-san immediately scans our bodies, giving Michie an extra hard look, an icy glare right out of Hokkaido. But here we are, everyone dry as burdock. So she jumps in, and with glee the rest of us follow. No water has ever felt better.

Only once could I ever use them. *Paloma Picasso called. Please call her back.*

I return to the pool after dark. I lie back on the lounge chair and look up at the sky. The city lights ignite the horizon, not in a fiery way like Tokyo, but softly. Still, it's enough to do the damage. I can't see the stars.

I think of this haiku:
Everyone is asleep
There is nothing to come between
The moon and me
It isn't true. There is plenty of interference.

In the pool two lovers kiss. They splash daintily, like birds in a birdbath. One could sit for several minutes without realizing they are there.

A man lies on his back along the diving board. He appears to be asleep. A couple sit on a bench in the garden, gazing into each other's faces. In the darkness they look like statues.

Interrupting this peaceful scene is the American group again. They are making plans. Their beer bottles clang noisily against each other. "I owe it to him, man," says a male voice.

"Let's fucking send him off."

As though vexed by the bad language, the man on the diving board rolls over in troubled sleep. He plops into the pool.

"That woke him up," one of the American women says.

"Let's do it." The voice belongs to the handsome man. "What do you say, Freda?"

"Fuck, yeah," says a giddy Freda.

Another big splash, right on cue.

"Watch it, you'll drown the poor guy."

Loud American laughter. Their grief has vanished, their glumness replaced with an exhilarating love.

I was in love with someone once. He was not a college graduate and he wasn't the man I married. The man I married I met in an *omiae*. The meeting was arranged by my father's brother who worked in a large bank as supervisor to my husband-to-be. All I heard about my fiancé was that he had gone to Kyoto University—straight—in a single try of the entrance exam. He was quite a catch. My mother was shrill with excitement, my father nearly dictatorial after the fiasco with my brother, whom they now seldom spoke of. My brother had barely started his first year of post-high school preparatory school, having failed all his entrance exams, when he dropped out and took a part-time job. My parents would never say what the job was.

The boy I was really in love with was an actor. His roles were on the stage, not television, and to get to the theaters you had to wind through narrow streets far from the major subway stops, calling into a public bath or soba shop to ask directions. One evening I saw him perform dressed only in a G-string and painted white. Everyone on stage was naked except for their G-strings, and the white paint covered even the women's dark nipples. In the middle of the performance the actors stepped down from the stage and sidled up the aisle, using the arrested stealth of No dance but adding a modern touch: they stared down a certain member of the audience until the victim began to squirm and shift; his neighbors soon began to do the same, and the discomfort passed down the line, until finally a long, brightly-clothed row was rippling like a Chinese dragon. Then the actors crept on to someone else. My heart pounded as the white bodies stole up the aisle, and like everyone I wanted to flee. The boy I loved approached my row. He was so close I could see the cracks in his white paint. He pointed, and his eyes fastened onto me, but they were blank, staring through me, and it was then I realized he was only acting.

Not long afterwards I was walking with my future husband, still trying to talk myself out of love with the boy who painted himself white. We strolled along Kabukicho, past the illicit theaters, Turkish baths, and pachinko parlors. In front of the shows stood young men dressed in cheap tuxedos who called to the passersby about the merits of each of their stage presentations. They competed with each other, yelling as loudly as the vegetable and fish vendors in marketplaces; sometimes they came out and grabbed the men, trying to win their interest by pulling them inside. Calling in front of one of the theaters stood someone I knew despite the outfit and the hair teased back in a pompadour: my brother. He was approaching my future husband to lure him inside, but in an instant he turned and clapped the shoulder of someone else. His glance had been brief and empty. We walked past. I didn't look back, and we never acknowledged each other. When I saw him for New Year's, I introduced my future husband as a Kyoto University straight graduate and he asked my brother what he did. My brother said, "Part-time job" and that was as far as the questions went. Had anybody asked me, which they didn't, I would have said I had no idea what he did for a living. And why should it matter? Does the American in the brass canister care about my brother's employment? And do we care about his? Is there a gold inscription on the canister that says, *He had a good job?*

He was a banker who graduated from Kyoto University and never made anybody happy.

There they go again, the Americans winding through the garden and back into the hotel. I hitch onto their swaying Chinese dragon and follow them across the lobby and out the front door. I congratulate myself on my impulsiveness. Fumiko and the others are safe in their rooms. If they only knew what I was up to!

The men in the group are dressed in Bermuda shorts and polo shirts. They have on sneakers without socks. The two women wear sleeveless blouses tucked into linen shorts, and white sandals. Freda carries a large, hippie-type handbag that looks like two prayer rugs sewn together.

They stride full-tilt into the first bar they come to. It takes me several minutes to get up my nerve to follow. As I'm about to enter, out they come. Then it's full tilt into a second bar. This time I'm right behind them. I go to the other end of the counter and order a limonata to cool myself off. It's cooler than it was this afternoon, of course, but it is still a very hot night. The handsome man's shirt (the Americans' backs are to me so I can stare) reveals a splash of droplets between the shoulder blades. A splotch of perspiration rises from Freda's beltline, from the other woman's as well. I can hear Hisako complaining about this aspect of Americans, too. In our job we are not allowed to sweat. We're a Kabuki troupe of actors with exaggerated femininity who can perform a flight safety demonstration like a dance. Without sweating. Try to get an American stewardess to do that.

Our routine is this: my partner and I stand side by side in front of the passengers. All our gestures are perfectly synchronized, the oxygen masks pulled out like twin trombone slides. We even look alike, down to the lipstick, the exact same shade, identically applied with lip liner. (Poor Chieko, Michie's partner, oxblooded to match her Hokkaido roommate. The two whores in cabin four, we call them).

In the third bar, before I can order, a glass of red wine is set down before me. I was thinking more of an espresso, something to keep me awake. When I try to pay, the bartender grunts and gestures toward the group of Americans, none of whom are glancing my way. I take only a sip or two before the Americans move on, but in the fourth bar I down my whole drink, and it hits me.

They don't waste any time. Already they're out the door. A sleepy aimlessness thickens their walk. They stagger along, draped over each other's shoulders, but the appearance of comradeship is false. I sense them growing further and further apart, becoming the very thing each one is seeking to avoid: alone.

They are way ahead of me in terms of drinks, but after the fifth bar I feel the same clumsy lethargy seeping through my limbs. I'm afraid I'll lose them. And I have no idea where I am. In the sixth bar I rush in ahead and order my espresso. Better. More alert. But I still don't know where I am.

In the seventh bar I long to sit down. I don't dare take the chance and besides, all seats are taken. The bar is jumping with excitement. Jump jump jump. Here I am, standing still.

She owned Paloma Picasso post-its and was able to demonstrate how to use an oxygen mask with the grace of a synchronized swimmer.

By now I don't even try to order. I stand at the counter, just another mute Japanese, and in a second a drink is plopped in front of me. I lean over the wineglass and rest my head in my hands. *She never loved her husband even though he worked for Mitsubishi bank but she was faithful to him. Rest in Peace.*

"Drink up," a voice tells me. "We're about to go." His hand is on my neck. It's the handsome man.

To show off I take a gulp that involves two large swallows. But I don't turn around. I don't want him to acknowledge that I'm actually following them.

"Wait a minute," he says. "Freda's going to the bathroom. You've got a couple of minutes. Two more wines," he calls to the bartender. He finishes off his wine, then waits for me to do the same.

"Hits the spot," he says. "Though at this point the spot is so big and empty anything could do it. It's a dark night for this little troupe of merrymakers. None of us will ever be the same. Each of us, in one way or the other, will be changed irrevocably. 'Irrevocably.' Jesus, it's hard to say that word after a few drinks. Maybe we won't even know it, but we will be. Changed, that is."

I wait politely for him to continue.

"You don't have to bow," he says.

I clear my throat. My heart is thumping. "He was your good friend?" I ask nervously.

The handsome man nods.

At a loss for what else to say I blurt out, "And he had a good job?"

"The best," he says. "You're bowing again."

"I'm sorry."

"So tell me," he begins. "What are your talents? Because each of our merrymakers has a specialty and we need to know how to slot you in. I don't suppose you sky-dive and compose New Age bird calls on a synthesizer? Because as of Tuesday, we're missing a musical sky-diver."

What are my talents? I can play the oxygen mask like a trombone. I can say in English, *The temperature in Chicago is fifty-three degrees* without making any of the American passengers laugh.

"Whoops. Come on," he says. "Time to go."

We're walking again, but I can hardly hold myself up. I find a wall and collapse against it. Then a street sign appeals to me. I grab onto it. It's the only thing that can rescue me from the ground.

I look up to see in which direction they're heading. They're not off to another bar. They've congregated at a fountain in the square. One of the men holds a bottle of wine upside down over the fountain. He saves a gulp for himself, then finishes pouring. "For you, honey," Freda weeps. From her tapestry handbag she pulls out the brass canister and hands it to the other woman. "Open him up for me."

As they pour him into the fountain they produce a second bottle of wine and pass it around. The handsome man is right there at the fountain with the rest of them. This man I have seen half-naked, muscular as the statues girdling the fountain, is on all fours lapping at the water. His head hangs between his shoulders.

"Hey," says one of the men. "Come on now. G.T. didn't like dogs, remember?"

I drop my hands from the iron stake and stand unsupported. After a moment of weaving I steady myself and then shuffle toward the fountain. In another second I'm there beside him, on all fours myself, to offer him comfort. My head drops into the water and it is only someone's hand grabbing my hair that pulls me out of it. The handsome man's fingers stroke my face clean.

"Well," one of the men remarks, helping to wipe under my chin, "he gets around."

"He always did," says Freda.

The handsome man begins to weep. I put my arm around him.

"You loved him too," the handsome man weeps to me. "You loved him, didn't you?"

"Yes," I tell him. "I loved him."

I discover this small belief, I say hello to the stranger I find under the water. Tomorrow, Singapore.

Nancy Zafris was the winner of the Flannery O'Connor award for her collection, *The People I Know.*

LIFE WITH THE EASTER BUNNY / *Daniel Akst*

The first person to answer our ad wasn't suitable at all. Under "last residence" on the form we made up for these prospective room-mates she put down a place with "Manor" in its name, and during the interview Mother seemed airily indulgent, almost humoring. She didn't even take any notes, which told me the woman had no chance. "Manor my foot," Mother said later, and I could see jutting from her mules the sharp, painted nails and the toes crabbed from years of cut-ting-edge footwear. She was sure that the "manor" had been a mental institution, and her judgment in such matters was usually good.

The next person wasn't much of a fit either, it turned out, although she actually moved into my old room for a couple of weeks. She ran an elevator at Lord & Taylor, white gloves and everything, and Mother's instincts about this straight-backed individual turned out to be right, or if not right, then they simply got sufficiently in the way of things to cause trouble. It wasn't all our fault; I admit our housekeeping wasn't up to the standards of someone in a position like Miss Butterman's, what with the tub and all ("so many rings you'd think it was Saturn," she wrote to her sister in Providence, on a postcard I was sure she wanted me to read), but she was someone who let little things get to her, like the café au lait the three of us drank, Mother and I and the cat, that is. We never offered her any, but we felt, Mother and I, that that would be crossing some line between family and tenant. Miss Butterman's remonstrations about the evil effects caffeine was sure to have on "young ladies and dumb animals" fell on deaf ears. "Well now it seems that Miss Butterman, a complete stranger to man, child or beast, is going to tell me how to raise a family," Mother said with haughty surprise, as if the notion that she needed any advice of this kind was so preposterous that you just had to laugh. Miss Butterman didn't approve of our smoking together, either.

I'm not even sure I approved, for that matter. It was confusing. Like any adolescent,I wanted to hide some things from Mother, the usual stuff at least, but there was little that she minded except the air of nor-mality that I craved. We were supposed to be co-conspirators. She cut holes in my bra cups, tried to sponsor my exploits, explained all about boys. They sounded dumb in her telling, but I was still pretty leery and went to school with my books firmly clasped to my chest, flanked by a bodyguard of girlfriends and gossip.

I became a project for Miss Butterman, who tried to get me to stand up straight and wear white gloves to school. The gloves part wasn't so bad, actually; I created quite a stir in those things, touching someone's arm in a show of intimacy and noblesse, or fingering an earring to show off my jawbone. A couple of other girls started wearing them, and then one added a pillbox hat, until it got too hot out and we gave the whole thing up. It was true, we were without discipline. In the early Seventies, nobody had discipline. We'd never even heard the word. Anyway, the gloves couldn't save Miss Butterman. When we finally got rid of her she said I was the one she really felt bad for, but I think by that time she felt bad for herself. She was a born aunt, I concluded, and for almost a full minute I lamented the tragedy of her thwarted destiny.

Then we had to pay for another ad, and this time Mother said she was going to be more accurate in describing us, so as to spare everyone disappointment "down the road." In retrospect I see that Mother didn't want a roommate, she wanted a man, and in the age before personal ads were common (Mother would have called them common anyway) our economic straits provided a golden opportunity. She had excuses; she felt the place needed a man, there were things to be fixed, items to be "put up," a certain earthy fragrance missing. "The place smells too flowery, too ferrous with just the two of us." She was always sending me to the dictionary with her high-toned pronouncements. "You know, I think we'd be *safer* with a man," she'd say all of a sudden, as if she had just thought of it. "In case of an intruder, or a catastrophe of some kind."

Mother worried about such things, I knew, but she worried most that her worries would etch themselves on her smooth features and she would lose the girlish quality she most prized in herself. As a matter of fact she was starting to look a little worn to me, and since the economic climate in our apartment had required us to double up in bed, Mother's worries had a very direct impact on me. Not wanting to get fret lines, she'd sleep with her palm against her forehead, her elbow sticking straight up, to keep herself from frowning all night and ruining her looks. She never did get a wrinkled forehead, but sooner or later she'd fall into a deep sleep and the elbow would come crashing down, often striking me in the face. Sometimes this would happen three or four times a night, leaving me sleepless and grumpy the next morning. Once she came down squarely on my nose, and when I woke up unable to breathe I was sure she had broken it. I think the bleeding finally made her stop.

With the very first man who showed up, we seemed to hit the jackpot.

"You see?" Mother said later. "With a man things are different." And they *were* different. Peter was an orator, a polymath, an enthusiast, a sufferer of the world's sorrows, and as it turned out, penniless. He showed up that first day in a black beret, bronze-bearded, blue eyes shiny in a way we'd later call twinkling, shoulders back, pot belly thrust cheerily forward as he surveyed the world before him with never-ending surprise and amusement. His speech was stentorian, his smile cat-like and wide. We thought he was adorable.

Peter moved in and, like a tomcat who delineates his turf by spraying, enveloped our little cloister in his maleness. His room (formerly mine) had a sourdough smell that seemed to waft out into the hall; you'd pass through it as if through a cloud on your way in or out of the apartment. Or you'd walk into the bathroom after his shower and know. The whole apartment really did smell different, of soap and musk and cheap after-shave. The effect on Mother could only be described as aromatherapy. She became even more careful about her attire, wearing shoes and stockings even in the house. Her preparations reached a sort of apogee in the late afternoon, when she knew Peter would soon return from his three-day-a-week job at a library not far from home.

Peter made money this way, but he was mainly an author. He was writing a book on how to use Post-Its to organize the material for writing a book, and before long there were Post-Its all over his room, covering the walls, climbing up the desk lamp and down the legs of the table, as if an avant-garde artist had moved in and shingled his room with yellow slips of paper. Sometimes I'd catch him in there with his head in his hands. I felt he was getting an inkling that PostIts were not ideal for organizing your thoughts in order to write books.

"Dostoyevski didn't have Post-Its," I needled at dinner one night. Unlike other tenants, Peter was invited to take meals with us. "Darwin didn't even know about Post-Its."

"Genius does what it must," he answered, grandly indulgent. "Talent does what it can."

"I don't understand."

"You will someday," Mother said with a knowing smile, which I recognized as a cover. She didn't understand either.

"Dostoyevski wouldn't have needed Post-Its," Peter explained patiently, giving my Mother an irritating look that said something like, what do the young know? "But the rest of us mere mortals often find it useful to have a little help from technology. And I daresay old Charlie Darwin would have taken a trunk full of Post-Its along on the Beagle had they existed at the time. Didn't Leonardo make the earliest drawings of the things we now know as 'Post-Its'?" His eyes got that shiny look—that twinkle. "Didn't Einstein postulate that a piece of paper that sticks again and again was entirely within the realm of mathematical possibililty?" Mother, staying on the safe side, arranged a blank face.

We chalked up Peter's pedantry to the Y chromosome that seemed to explain so much else about him. His behavior struck us as quintessentially male, even though we had not cohabited with a member of this strange tribe since I was the tiniest of babes. Peter drank six-packs of Schmidts, for example, "because it is beer, and because it is cheap." When he grew comfortable with us, he belched, albeit with a kind of intentional, post-modern relish, as if it wasn't so much a venting as an ironic comment on the need to vent.

He lacked our prickliness. I'd seen Mother with one of her friends at times just bursting with umbrage, taking every comment as a personal affront. "Well I don't know what you mean by *that,* Mother would say, in a kind of Margaret Dumont impersonation, only serious. I'd do it myself, sometimes, to her. Peter wasn't like this at all; he didn't take much offense, even when he ought to have, and he had the ability to shrug things off, or brood right through them, I could never tell which.

He was balding, too, although very hairy elsewhere, and he wore heavy shoes, in which he sauntered up an down the long hall between his room and the kitchen, as if to regale us with the clomp-clomp-clomp on the old wood floors. I think he sensed that we were fascinated and impressed by the deep maleness of him. He screwed the lids onto jars so tightly that we couldn't get them open, and when we noted this, marveling more than complaining really, he laughed and kept right on screwing them down the same way. It got so I wouldn't think of eating peanut butter unless he was around to get the lid off.

I called him Peter Rabbit, but he charmed me too. When spring came we were all getting along pretty well, despite the emergence in Peter of a few unfortunate habits that tried Mother's limited patience. He was typically behind on the rent, and therefore became sheepish about his appetites, which in our abstemious household ranked as Brobdingnagian. He ate more than Mother and I put together, and he went through tons of soap, toilet paper and other disposables. Mother held her tongue, but I would emerge from the bathroom in a rage when that new bar of special bath soap I'd just unwrapped was reduced to a sliver in a puddle on the sink. I knew where the soap was going; we were doing *Macbeth* in English class, and I had seen Peter wash his hands. He would lather them extravagantly up to the elbows, breathing hard through his nose, splash water all over the place rinsing them off, and then hold his arms with his fingers pointed skyward like a surgeon who's just scrubbed, until he could nudge the door with a hip and get his hands on the towel hung behind it.

Peter's lack of a grip on this problem became clear when he came home one day with a dozen eggs, emptied them into the door of the refrigerator, and then marched the styrofoam carton into the bathroom. In the days ahead, he filled each of the depressions in this egg carton with slivers of soap that he had compressed into balls about the size and shape of an egg, until before long he had a dozen such soap eggs, one or two sprouting curly little hairs from Lord knew where. Mother tried to make him get rid of the carton but he argued that it was a perfectly sensible measure gleaned from a book of household hints perused in a second-hand bookstore downtown. Although she didn't let on, she was shocked—I could see an eyebrow starting to levitate before I looked away in embarrassment—to hear me take his side. By then I was in love with him.

It was those ablutions of his that got me. In the morning I pretended it was really interesting to watch him shave around his mustache and goatee, although mostly I watched the hair on his thick arms and the subtle movements of their sinews as he dragged the razor across his skin. The sound made me shiver a little, like a nail on a blackboard, but I didn't care. I loved the way he splashed water on his face, and the sound of it against the old tiles all over the walls and floor, pieces of the ceiling hanging down in strips like stalactites from the roof of a cave. He shaved in a T-shirt, which was not a bad look for Peter, though the V-neck drew attention to his belly. Still, it was better than the towel I'd occasionally catch a glimpse of him in, his wet hair plastered down over his forehead as he hastened to his room, looking like some Roman caught in the baths just as the barbarians arrived. He was such an odd duck, I was coming to see. It was fascinating to be in love with him.

I took to lounging in Peter's (my old) room when he was out, reading his books and soaking up the faintly doggy odor of the pill-covered woolen blanket with which he made up his bed, as perfectly as if some drill instructor had bounced quarters off the fabric until he'd got it right. It was the only made bed in the house, and I liked that he had brought this martial tradition into our lives. Peter had never been in the military, but he acted as if he had. His heavy black shoes were always luridly polished, and he possessed worn leather kits for this and for his toiletries as well. In my kid-sister role, and as the daughter of the landlady, I could get away with hanging around his room. Besides, it was a refuge from Mother, who had forbid me to bother him—only to have Peter insist he didn't mind. I thought of sticking my tongue out at her, reasserting my girlishness this way in order to throw them both off the trail, but decided against it. One could push Mother too far.

One warm afternoon as I drowsed through biology, our class was interrupted by a bomb scare. It was late enough in the day and in the term that the principal didn't insist that we all hang around the schoolyard in the heat. I went home an hour early with a balmy breeze in my skirts and just that slightly nervous feeling I always got toward the end of a school year as each day came to a close. I slammed the door as usual to announce myself and started toward the kitchen when I heard a lot of rustling in the room I shared with Mother, who usually lurked elsewhere in the apartment by day.

"Mother?"

"It's all right, dear," she said airily. "Peter was just helping me with the latch on back of the door. We'll open up in a minute."

"If only we had a drill," I heard him say loudly.

In the sepulchrally lit bathroom, I ran a hot shower, noticing how no one ever cleaned the white deposits from the metal showerhead; with the water pouring out, it looked like a sunflower. I undressed carefully and beheld myself for a long time in the mirror over the sink, looking at Peter's straight-edged razor and the shelf full of pills and rubbing alcohol. Then I looked down at the yellow styrofoam carton on the sink, with its farmhouse and giant silo etched in blue on the lid. With a nail-on-a-blackboard noise, I opened the carton and, selecting with care, withdrew one of Peters soap eggs. It was a variegated one that must have been made of several kinds of soap—white Ivory, green Irish Spring, pink Dove, all molded together so that it looked like a remnant of the Easter we had just passed. Wielding it like a rock, I scrawled SO WHAT on the mirror.

"Lily?" I could hear Mother calling faintly. The shower was noisy. "Lily?"

I took Peter's little egg in with me and soaped myself with it. It was dense and hard like some essential thing, and didn't lather up easily, but I worked at it until I was covered with fragrance and suds, washing under my arms, between my toes, in my ears, all the private places I often skipped on a daily basis, until I was all clean and on edge and then, stopping the drain, could sink into a steaming tub full of water, and drowning my sorrows, immerse myself.

Daniel Akst is the author of the novel *St. Burl's Obituary* from MacMurray & Beck. This is his first published short story.

TERMITES/*Ned Stuckey-French*

THE SUMMER BEFORE ninth grade, the summer of 1964, we collected insects. During most of the summer we assumed termites would be easy to find so we didn't look very hard for them. Lepidoptera—butterflies and moths—were not only bigger, flashier and more interesting, they were more fun to catch. Chasing a swallowtail across a meadow or touring street lights late at night for big moths was more romantic than kicking apart rotten stumps or dismantling woodpiles, which was what you had to do to find termites. But August arrived and found us without termites. I was the one who proposed the short cut. One of the exterminators around town must have some. My friend Bill Harrison, in particular, was not sure this was on the up and up, but we all needed termites and I prevailed. I checked the Yellow Pages and started calling exterminators. The first five thought I was crazy to imagine they kept any termites, but finally, on the sixth call, I had some luck. The man said almost apologetically that he only moonlighted as an exterminator, but that he did have some termites. He put them in an old terrarium and watched them just like he'd watched his ant farm when he was a kid.

"My queen is something when she's pregnant," he said. "She puffs up to about the size of your little finger. I can give you all you want."

He lived about five miles south of town. "Just beyond the Eli Lilly plant, where they make the pharmaceuticals," he said. The ride would be long and hot but that was okay. In a way, we would be working for the termites after all.

The next afternoon Mike Dobbs, Leonard Johnson, Bill Harrison and I set off on our bikes to get the termites. Dobbs had a ten-speed with thin, hard tires and as we worked our way up the Ninth Street hill I heard the click-click-click as he downshifted to his lowest gear. He pulled next to me, stood on his pedals, churned them hard and blew on by. Almost as if he was riding on level ground he swept past Bill and finally Leonard. Once in the lead he slalomed back and forth, flashed a grin and threw a taunt back over his shoulder at Leonard. "Come on, lard butt. It's only a hill."

Leonard was working his old Schwinn as hard as he could, but it had big, balloon tires, and even from where I was I could hear them sticking to the squishy asphalt. They made a muffled tearing sound, as if an endless strip of Velcro was being undone. While Dobbs scooted about like a water strider, Leonard huffed and puffed and cussed to himself.

Dobbs and Leonard were next-door neighbors and best friends, but totally unlike. Leonard was the biggest, slowest kid in class. He had freckles everywhere, and his hair was all cowlick. The next spring, he would drive to school, the first kid in our class to get his license. Dobbs, on the other hand, was short and quick, a halfback who used the holes Leonard opened for him at right tackle. Dobbs's father was the head of Army ROTC at Purdue University, where my father taught agricultural economics. Dobbs had jet-black hair, laughed at everything and chattered constantly. For Leonard words were the enemy. He could talk about a few topics—his family, cars, his girlfriend Vicki, sports—but even then it was a struggle. When his sentences started to tangle his eyelids would flutter and drop shut. Then he'd raise his chin and trembling lips, and stutter out what he could. I rarely knew what he was going to say and I found it hard to watch him try. Once, when a few of us were playing poker, Leonard drew two cards to a full house. He raised a quarter to open the next round, the limit in our penny-ante games, and then, uncharacteristically, tried to hurry the betting.

"Do . . . do . . . do you . . . ah . . . do you . . . ?"

"No," answered Dobbs to the question that hadn't been asked. "I don't see your quarter. I fold."

Everyone else folded too, and Leonard won eight cents with his full house. This time, Dobbs's "help" cost him, but more often there was a kindness and nonchalance in the way Dobbs finished his sentences that Leonard seemed to appreciate.

I considered Dobbs and Leonard good friends, but I was closest to Bill. He and I had known each other since kindergarten. We'd done chemistry sets and short wave radios together. At my house we made bombs that never exploded and rockets that didn't really fire. The bombs sizzled and burned blue and green flames, and the rockets tipped over and skittered across the driveway. At heart Bill was compulsive and orderly, but he was also willing to be reckless. In that sense he was like his father, a surgeon who chain-smoked Camels. I enjoyed spending time at the Harrisons'. My parents' marriage was falling apart and Bill's house offered some sanctuary. The Harrisons were wealthy and had a big yard with a pool, but the attraction for me had more to do with the easy sociability I found in their house. The radio was always on. Friends of all three of their kids were usually around. Dr. Harrison was home a lot, though unobtrusively so, showing up from time to time during our afternoon-long Risk games to see who was conquering what continent and bring us a tray of Cokes. When Bill had sleepovers and we played poker, Dr. Harrison sometimes sat in, making sure to lose back anything he'd won before he went to bed. He and his two sons always had projects going. At Christmas, they strung lights along their eaves, fastened a sleigh and reindeer on the peak of their roof, stuck Santa halfway into the chimney, put four-foot candles and a crèche on the lawn, and always got their picture in the paper. Bill and his father built a series of soapbox derby cars, each one more sleek and shiny than the last, employing the latest in graphite lubrication and fiberglass bodywork. One year over Christmas vacation the family spent five straight days completing a big, round, all-white jigsaw puzzle. Though Bill shared this penchant for hobbies with his father, he looked more like his mother—blonde, tall, skinny and serious. She kept busy with her own projects, though you could hardly call them hobbies—wall-papering, weeding, cleaning the pool.

My own mother had already been hospitalized once with manic-depressive illness. These were the days before lithium. She was bouncing from one shrink to another, and each one prescribed something different. None of them knew what the others were doing and the prescriptions piled up. My mother lived in a haze of Thorazine, Seconal and Valium that left her helpless, watching television all day in her bedroom with her sunglasses on and the curtains drawn. Meals were usually up to me. After getting lunch for my little brother and sister I'd fix my mom something—maybe a grilled cheese sandwich, of which she'd eat half, or some Campbell's soup. Later, before we finally rousted ourselves to meet Dad somewhere for dinner, a delivery often arrived from Arth's Drugs. I signed for it, always leaving the receipt on my dad's desk so he could deduct it at tax time.

In seventh grade I came home from school one day and saw our minister sitting with my parents in the living room. None of them got up. "Your parents and I have been talking, Ned, and they have something to tell you," said the minister.

My father spoke first: "Your mother and I have decided to get a divorce." I didn't know what to say. I looked at my mother. She wasn't even crying. "Everything will be okay," she said. It all seemed planned out and weird.

In fact it had been planned. My brother and sister weren't there (I found out later that some of my parents' friends had picked them up at school and taken them to their houses). My parents had been fighting more and more, and my mom had been sad since she'd had a miscarriage, but still, I hadn't expected this. Usually I was the little man, but I lost it and screamed, "No! No! No! You won't! No!" As my father started to get up, I jumped away from him past the piano bench and crawled behind the sofa where I balled up underneath a print of a Utrillo street scene. I stayed there and yelled and hit my parents when they tried to get to me. Finally they called my mother's psychiatrist. When he arrived, all four adults went into the family room for a minute to consult. Then the psychiatrist came back into the living room. He sat on the couch and leaned over the back of it to talk to me privately. I'd never met him before. I was surprised to see he wore a hearing aid. He said he knew it was tough, and maybe I could come to his office sometime and he could help me figure out what to say to my parents. I was getting tired and even a bit embarrassed by the commotion I'd caused. "Okay," I said, and came out and sat on the couch.

When my parents and the minister returned, my father said that he and my mother had talked and they were going to stick together after all and keep working at it. I was shocked. I had hidden behind the couch because divorce terrified me. I had not imagined that going behind the couch would give me the power to keep my parents together.

But in reality, it didn't. After the day my parents announced, then retracted their plans, my father began to spend more and more time at his job. He went back to his office after dinner and didn't come home until eleven or so. Once he was home, I tuned in WLS out of Chicago or WLAC, the "home of soul" in Nashville, Tennessee, hugging a pillow against the black plastic headphones of my short-wave radio so that I didn't have to listen to them fighting in the next room.

On the day we went after the termites, I put my parents' problems out of my mind. Bill thought we ought to take our nets with us, figuring we might see some good butterfly fields on the way. Dobbs and I talked him out of it. The ride was going to be long and hot—at least three miles of it would be gravel. The termites, we argued, would be bugs enough for one afternoon.

As we passed the county fairgrounds and headed out of town, the road flattened out, traffic thinned, and soon, in every direction, there was nothing but corn and soybeans. It was hot, and we were already tiring a bit and getting quiet. Dobbs must not have liked the silence, because he started us singing "Da Doo Ron Ron" and "Louie Louie"— songs Leonard knew the words to. The slow pace of the bicycles opened up the countryside to us in a way car rides never did. On the electric lines red-winged blackbirds screeched, warning us that we were now in their territory. Goldfinches scattered from some elderberry bushes and flew along a fencerow and out across a corn field. I thought how the surging, the hurry-and-glide, in their flight pattern made them look like they were on a roller coaster. The bottom halves of the corn stalks were brown. Monarch butterflies worked the last milkweed flowers of the summer. On our right was an alfalfa field. I could smell the third batch of hay, which was raked, but not baled yet. In another week, double sessions for football would start. I couldn't wait. I was ready for school to begin again and fill my time.

That summer adolescence hit me. Bill's older brother, John, gave him some inkling of what was ahead. As an oldest child, I enjoyed no such help, but relied instead on Bill for information—locker room reports from his brother about which cheerleaders did it, or the image of a hand inside a swimming suit, described to me by Bill, who had spied on one of John's pool parties. Adolescence arrived at different rates for each of us. Some of us were already riding puberty's locomotive while others were still waiting in the station, checking our watches. One moment you were wearing corduroys with knee patches, and life was all squirt guns and yo-yos. Every day was a happy slide from breakfast to the time when the streetlights clicked on and started to hum, and you begged your mother for another five minutes outside. But now, this summer, the girls had showed up at the pool in their new bodies and their two-piece bathing suits, and everything had changed. At night, I would sneak out of bed and do push ups in the dark.

The insect collections gave to the summer a second, much-needed focus besides girls. They were a big deal because they were our first assignment for high school, but more than that, these collections had become an academic tradition in our academic town. They were part of the post-Sputnik emphasis on science in the schools. The previous spring, the high school biology teachers had visited our eighth-grade classes to explain the requirements for Biology. We would be expected to do a special project, which could be completed anytime before the end of the first semester. Handouts described our options. Besides insects, one could collect leaves or enter the Science Fair. Most of the girls went these latter routes because it was harder for them to get out at night to collect nocturnals like moths and beetles, but my friends and I knew already we would do insects. Collecting gave you an excuse to roam the county, even at night, and besides, most of the older guys we knew had done insect collections. Often that summer we spoke respectfully of the collection Kit Kildahl had turned in the year before—a hundred and seventy-two total specimens, including both a unicorn beetle and a mole cricket. Bill had shown me the five perfect cases his brother had submitted four years earlier. Though he was a senior now, John still kept his collection in his bedroom, and we had to ask to see it. It was legendary and included three entire cases of Lepidoptera, and one of those was nothing but big moths—a perfect royal walnut, a polyphemus, a cecropia, an imperial, several kinds of underwings. Every year in West Lafayette, sophomores-to-be sold their old nets, purple fluorescent bug lights, and mounting boards to incoming freshmen. We bought collection cases at the ag co-op, field guides at the university bookstore, and began collecting with the arrival of the mourning cloaks in late March.

Each afternoon during the summer we walked remnants of the tall grass prairie, rhythmically sweeping our nets for thirty yards before stopping to check them for wasps, leafhoppers and other species slow to rise from their flowers and their work. Each night we checked a regular set of street lights and neon signs for beetles and moths. Every specimen had to be mounted perfectly and labeled correctly—order, family, and common name on the first label, and on the second, eight millimeters farther down the pin, the date and site of capture. Our instructions were explicit: *Pin butterflies and moths through the thorax slightly to the right of center. Center the insect's body between the two sides of the mounting board (the two surfaces raised so as to lift each wing 7–8 degrees above level) and by hooking the bent tip of a dissecting needle under the wing (far enough out on the wing so that you can gain leverage but not so far that it might tear; also, be careful not to puncture the wing or smudge the powder on the wings of Lepidoptera) fan the upper wing up toward the point at which its bottom edge is 90 degrees to body. Secure the wings by pinning strips of paper over them as indicated in Diagram 5. Straighten and spread the legs. They should appear life-like and not droop. Align the antennae (taking care not to damage the feathering if it is a moth). You may find a magnifying glass helpful.*

One night I was pinning a big hawk moth at my desk in our basement. It was a beautiful specimen—gray with some pink and lavender tints, a six-inch wingspan, and a body the size of a field mouse. It had taken me almost an hour to net it. I had to shinny up a streetlight, under which the moth was swooping like a bat, and wait for it to come within range of my net. Now, having mounted the left wing perfectly, I carefully lifted the right upper wing when, to my horror, the moth's abdomen started to contract and slowly twitch.

The respiratory systems of insects are made up of a series of openings, called spiracles, which line the sides of their bodies. The anterior spiracles are generally used for air intake, and the posterior ones for carbon dioxide exhalation. In killing insects, the collector shuts down this respiratory system with carbon tetrachloride or cyanide. Cyanide is more effective, but also more lethal to humans and so harder to obtain. Carbon tet is available in both cleaning and lighter fluids.

I grabbed some lighter fluid and dripped it onto the abdomen, then sat back, took a breath and waited to make sure the moth was definitely dead. I had been moved to act quickly because my specimen might have torn a hole in its wing or broken a leg, but at the same time I hated doing it because I now knew this moth well. I had bent over it for most of an hour already, examining it, learning its colors, feeling the strength of its wings, and I was revolted at having to kill it a second time. In the field, one killed specimens immediately, often while they were still in the net, but even if you removed them from the net and held them in your hand as you squirted the lighter fluid, the kill was part of the catch, done almost without thought. To have to kill the hawk moth during mounting revealed to me the tension between science and empathy that had been there, dormant but real, all summer.

Two very different teachers taught Biology—Mr. Witters and Mr. Bush. Mr. Witters was an academic, a genuine intellectual who as often as not referred to a species by its scientific, rather than its common name. After school, he stayed late working with students on the many Science Fair projects he sponsored. Even at night, when I had a Student Council meeting or was getting back late from an away game, I would see him in the biology labs working on his own experiments, his Ph.D. research. His lab was busy and messy, the air abuzz with Drosophila (fruit flies), the floor littered with cedar chips and droppings from the rat cages.

Mr. Witters had just gone through a divorce, which had followed the deaths of his two children. A son and daughter had died about a year apart from genetic problems caused by radiation poisoning Mr. Witters had unknowingly suffered while working in the Life Sciences Building at Purdue. Now, his work was everything.

Mr. Bush, a stocky man with a crewcut, also served as the line coach on the football staff. He too had been touched by illness. His oldest son, John, who was my age, had been born a blue baby. Open-heart surgery, a new procedure in the '50s, had saved him, and though he was now healthy and bright, John was slight and pale with thick glasses, two hearing aids, and a speech impediment.

The two biology teachers respected each other and worked well together, but they had very different approaches to the insect collections. Mr. Witters offered a chance for extra credit; Mr. Bush didn't believe in it. In Mr. Witters' class, you could earn ten points for each order of insect above twenty you were able to include in your collection. Until school started and you received your schedule, you didn't know which teacher you would have—Bush or Witters—but we all hustled for orders in hopes that we would get into Mr. Witters' class. Book lice are an order, earwigs another. Stone flies and scorpion flies are each an order. There is even a microscopic order called Strepsiptera that spends its life between the plates in the abdomens of wasps. One had to catch and kill a lot of wasps in order to find one Strepsiptera. Termites were an order in and of themselves—Isoptera.

Some orders were especially hard to find in Indiana. Brent Beebe spent the summer at his grandparents' house in Seattle and was able to bring back a dozen earwigs, common in moist, coastal environments but rare in Indiana. He traded earwigs for his whole collection. I gave him a mourning cloak and a giant swallowtail for one earwig, but considered it a good deal because I had doubles of both those butterflies.

Within many orders there are odd or rare species that we especially valued. Hymenoptera, for instance, are simply bees, wasps and ants, but the order includes unusual species such as velvet ants, cuckoo wasps and the cicada killer, a hornet-like creature that captures cicadas in flight, paralyzes them and drags them into underground nests where its larvae can feed on them. Another form of Hymenoptera is the ichneumon fly, which looks like many other wasps except that winding out from the tip of its abdomen is a stinger, or ovipositor, that is three or four times as long as the rest of the insect. The females curl this long, thin tail back up over themselves, bring it down at a right angle to their bodies, and work it into the bark of dead or decaying trees. The wire-like ovipositor chisels deeper and deeper into the tree until it reaches the tunnels of another insect's larvae—tunnels the vibrations from which the female has been able to detect with her antennae. Into those tunnels she deposits her eggs so that when her brood hatches they can live among and on the other insect's larvae. The several species of ichneumon flies are host specific, parasites of the larvae of particular beetles, sawflies, wasps, or more rarely, spiders and pseudoscorpions.

One night, when I came home from playing basketball at Bill's, my little sister, who was then eight, met me at the door. "Dad's got a really big bug for you," she said. I was surprised that she was up and not in her pajamas yet, and that my dad was home from the office. I wanted to see what kind of bug they had, but I wasn't going to get my hopes up. I assumed it was some big but common moth—a luna or a tomato hornworm sphinx—and that they had torn it up trying to catch it. My dad had the insect in a shoebox. He was smiling.

"It's some sort of big wasp," he said. "Sara saw it on the window. I couldn't find your net, so I just put this box over it."

I got my net and killing jar from the basement, and holding some nylon netting over the shoe box, I slid the cover back. It was a perfect, very large, female ichneumon fly. The body was about an inch and a half long, and unfurled, its ovipositor would stretch to almost six inches. I looked up at my father.

"Weren't you afraid?" I said.

"I figured all it could do was sting me," he said. "Do you already have one?"

"I've never seen one that big."

I stayed up until eleven-thirty that night mounting my ichneumon fly and reading up on the species. When I was done I went upstairs to sit at the foot of my parents' bed and watch Johnny Carson's monologue with them. It was one daily ritual they still shared.

The next day I called Bill and asked him to check with his brother about how to mount the ichneumon's ovipositor.

John said I could just let the long tail curl out behind the specimen, using one or more pins to prop it up if it was flopping to the side. He said the white space that the tail created in your box where you would normally put two or three other insects could be very dramatic.

The insect collections were designed to teach us precision and accuracy but they introduced us as well to deviation, blurring and individuality. The color plates in the field guides, for instance, bespoke clarity and definition, but the captions and write-ups were more qualified. *Often confused with the . . . easily mistaken for the . . . thought to be a . . . often hybridizes with . . . in our region must be considered an accidental.* Our quest for orders was also a quest for order, but it was a quest that was finally futile, and looking back on it now I see that an acceptance of difficulty and incompleteness was some of what we were supposed to learn. I know now that a species is often difficult to recognize, hard to define. Some moths, such as the catalpa sphinx, are distinguishable only by the host plants they select and on which you find them laying their eggs. Beetles are so numerous, it's been estimated that at least a third of their species remain unidentified. Asked to speculate on the personality of God, the English biologist J.S.B. Haldane replied that the Creator seems to have "an inordinate fondness for beetles." As their rain forest habitat is destroyed, hundreds of species of beetles, the order Coleoptera, are passing away and will probably never be seen, named or known, at least by humans.

Species mix, genes are shuffled. The naming of the animals, Adam's task, remains impossible. And yet, classification has its place. The existence of hybrids, for instance, is testimony to the fact that there are points at which nature draws a line. My grandfather used to tell me stories about farming with mules. They were stronger, smarter, less easily distracted and harder working than horses, he said, but they were also true hybrids and therefore sterile.

While collecting our insects, we learned Linnean taxonomy—kingdom, phylum, class, order, family, genus, species, or "King Philip Comes Over For Good Soup"—and that nature is sly and slippery, and eventually defeats taxonomy. We also learned to look, to really *look*. I learned, for instance, that even within the same species there are individuals. Bill and I both caught female imperial moths—a yellow and brown member of the Saturniidae with a four-inch to six-inch wingspan and a body the size of your thumb—but mine was much smaller and darker than his.

As we rode toward the exterminator's, our habit of looking led us to scan the fields for swallowtails, even though we were without the nets to catch them. But after a while we ran out of asphalt, and the country road turned to gravel, loose and treacherous. Just to pedal was difficult and required all our concentration.

At the Wea Creek bridge it was time for a break, and everyone but Dobbs headed down to wade, get a drink, and see if it might be worth coming back later to hunt for scorpion flies. Dobbs said he'd stay up top to keep an eye on the bikes, but really he was worried about poison ivy. He had spent half of June sitting in a bathtub with blisters the size of grapes between his knuckles. At the creek we saw only green darners and the little blue and black damsel flies that everyone had caught weeks ago. It was cool and dark under the sycamores and cottonwoods, but alive with gnats and mosquitoes. The path was lined with shoulder-high stinging nettles.

When we got back up to the bridge, we mounted our bikes and rode slowly up out of the ravine and back onto the prairie. After ten more minutes of pedaling, we came upon the first of the Shadeland Farm feed lots, where a herd of maybe seventy-five white-faced Herefords looked at us as they stood and chewed. Dobbs yelled at them to stop staring. Up ahead of me, Bill stopped his bike along the shoulder of the road. I pulled up next to him. He said, "We ought to check out that pasture for dung beetles."

"Perfect place for 'em," I said.

Big beetles fascinated us both, almost as much as big moths, and dung beetles were a type of scarab beetle neither of us had yet, though we both knew them well from our field guides. They are not as big as water scavengers or even some stag beetles, but they're a nice insect—wide and squat, essentially round, and unique in behavior. Their habitat is very specific—they live in and around cow shit. The adults encase their eggs in a ball of fresh manure. Then, like Sisyphus, though with more success, they roll it and roll it till it is firmly packed and perfectly spherical. Finally, they dig a hole and bury each ball in the ground. The balls are as big as the beetles themselves, about the size of a shooter marble. When the larvae hatch, they feed on the dung ball for protein, conveniently leaving some of it in the ground to fertilize the soil. To the uninformed they might seem like a joke, but to anyone who has seen them at work, they aren't. The Egyptians made the dung beetle a symbol of fertility and rebirth. They're just rolling shit, but the way they do it with their little forelegs is amazing—a wonderful skill, involving as much patience and delicacy as the tying of a surgeon's knot, or the gathering and weaving of strands of spider web for a hummingbird nest.

Dobbs spoke up for Leonard and himself, saying that they did not want to climb into the cow pasture. I could tell that the steers had him spooked. Bill and I climbed the fence and the cattle scattered, loping just far enough away from us so as to feel safe. As we crawled on our hands and knees among the cow pies, I thought about how what we were doing was slightly nuts. We rooted about in the pasture for only ten minutes before each of us had a perfect dung beetle—legs and antennae intact, their shells a deep obsidian with bronze and green highlights, like an oil slick. Having established whose was whose, we put the beetles in my killing jar, leaving Bill's empty for the termites.

We got back on our bikes and took up our ride again. Sunflowers stood tall and still in the ditch along the road, their heads drooping under the weight of their seeds. Sparrows scuffled in the dust.

"You guys probably saw about eighteen gazillion dung beetles in there. But did you get any for us?" said Dobbs.

"You could have climbed the fence," said Bill.

"You two are going to turn into a couple of gigantic dung beetles," said Dobbs. He started imitating, not a dung beetle exactly, but some kind of insect, sticking out his neck, staring blankly at nothing, holding one of his hands up like a claw and swiveling his head in small, mechanical motions. Bill and I were laughing at his craziness when all three of us heard Leonard yelling. He had ridden on ahead of us and stopped about fifty yards down the road where it made a turn to the right. He was calling and pointing. "Hey, you guys, look! Look!" As we approached him it became clear what all the ruckus was about. Just past him, maybe a hundred yards down the hill from where he stood, was the Eli Lilly plant. The exterminator had mentioned the plant in his directions, but in an inconsequential way, saying only that we were to take the second left after we passed it. None of us had been down this road before, and the enormity of the factory brought us to a dead halt.

No one said a thing. We just looked. The plant loomed menacingly on the far side of a huge lawn, looking like the Emerald City gone bad. Painted gray, it shimmered in the heat like a mirage. It was bigger, much bigger, than the Purdue football stadium. A chain-link fence surrounded the compound, and wired to the fence in front of us was a sign declaring "No Admittance. Authorized Personnel Only." Scores of smokestacks studded the plant, and interspersed among them were dozens of gigantic cylindrical tanks. Some of the tanks stood upright like silos, others lay on their sides. The clanging, metal-on-metal sounds of machinery were punctuated occasionally by loud, whooshing releases of steam. The plant included several buildings, connected by enclosed corridors at ground level and by open catwalks above. Past the buildings there was a parking lot of several acres. It was full of cars.

In West Lafayette, where we lived, you could smell the Eli Lilly plant when the wind was from the southeast. Whenever that happened my mother would trot out her tired joke about how at least they were making penicillin. I had seen the plant before, but always from the other side of the Wabash, the West Lafayette side, and then only occasionally when my dad and I drove out to Rumpza's produce stand for fresh sweet corn. From our side of the river the plant's smokestacks, rising above the trees, looked benign, even romantic, like those of an ocean liner just back from Buenos Aires or Monaco.

My mother was right about the penicillin, but only half right. Eli Lilly did make antibiotics, but they also made soybean herbicides and later, the anti-depressant Prozac. During the 1950s and 1960s, before the establishment of the EPA, the Lilly plant buried its waste in underground tanks. Eventually, the tanks rusted and leaked, and the waste leached into the ground water. At first Lilly distributed carbon filters to its neighbors for use on their taps, but the water continued to smell of chemicals, and eventually the company had to buy a subdivision of twenty-two homes because its wells were poisoned. Lilly bulldozed all the houses except one, a brick farm house which dated from the 1850s.

The four of us stood at the fence in silence, when all of a sudden, as if from another world, Dobbs snapped, "Hut to, gentlemen! You have a mission to complete." As we started to ride again, Dobbs organized a game of "catch the leader" to break the tension. Single file and leap-frogging, we headed cross country, following a range line road which scored the prairie in a line as straight as a string pulled across a table, as straight as the X-axis of an infinite coordinate.

The exterminator lived in a little prefabricated house which sat up on a rise, a small heap of terminal moraine left from the last glacier. He was a young man, maybe twenty-five. He wore a DeKalb seed cap, madras shirt and jeans. His cowboy boots were muddy and scuffed, their heels worn. His house, pole barn and yard were surrounded by corn fields. He had planted a windbreak of white pines along the north and west sides, but the trees were only waist high and did not provide much protection yet. The whole effort, both the buildings and the windbreak, seemed to me, even then, to be both pitiful and wonderfully earnest.

He gave us a drink of well water, which was so cold it hurt your head to drink very much, but we were thirsty. He had a beagle which kept yapping and jumping up on Leonard, who talked baby talk to the dog and scratched its ears. The exterminator apologized that he couldn't give us a king or queen termite, explaining that there was only one pair to a colony and they were hard to find. But he could give us as many workers and soldiers as we wanted. Even Bill, who wasn't afraid of wasps or cicada killers, looked relieved when the exterminator put the termites into the killing jar for us. The soldiers, who grow wings only during their migratory, or colonizing, phase, were currently wingless. They had strong, threatening mandibles, or pincers. The workers were a bit less scary, but also possessed a fierce and prehistoric ugliness. Workers spend their entire lives underground, and these were white, sexless, puffy and translucent. Like fish and cave-dwelling crawdads, they had no eyes. The cyanide in the killing jars snuffed them all immediately.

We rode back toward town in pairs about twenty yards apart— Leonard and Dobbs in front, Bill and I following.

I asked him, "What do you think is your best insect?"

"My Strepsiptera took the most work, but I like my royal walnut."

A royal walnut is a member of the Saturniidae family, the largest North American moths. Their wingspans can reach seven or eight inches. The main representatives of the Saturniidae in Indiana are the cecropia, luna, polyphemus and royal walnut, which is the biggest of the four. Bill had all four. I had the first three.

"What's your own favorite?" Bill asked.

"My ichneumon fly is nice, but my dad caught that. I guess I like my hawk moth best."

We talked on like that about our collections, distracting ourselves from the heat and dust, the termites, the Eli Lilly plant and the fact that the summer was almost over. But our conversation wasn't distraction enough, at least for me. I thought about my father and whether he would be home that fall for all of my football games. If he was gone, away to give a speech or do some consulting, I knew it would be hard for my mom to come by herself, though she would do it. The afternoon I hid behind the couch had changed everything. I had backed my parents off and in doing so, realized a power I didn't know I had and ultimately didn't want. I hadn't crawled behind the couch to get that power. There had been no calculation in my scramble, just fear and shock. True, I had started to feel the power quickly, for right away I could see fear in my parents' eyes and hear worry in their voices. But almost as soon as I felt the power, I began to feel embarrassment as well. I was embarrassed that I had been able to manipulate my parents and do it so easily, even though the manipulation wasn't intentional. I had not behaved well and my embarrassment about it was a reminder of the embarrassment I felt when my parents fought in public. They fought in restaurants and at church, and in the other room while I watched television with my friends. I'd hoped that my new power would be enough to stop this kind of behavior and keep them together, but even then I knew that it wasn't enough and that I would be embarrassed for a long time to come.

Besides the breeders (the king and queen), the workers and the soldiers, there is a fourth caste among termites—the nymphs, who constitute a kind of reproductive reserve. They resemble the king and queen, with eyes and wing buds, but assume sexual and physical maturity only if the original king and queen are killed. In that event, the nymphs complete their metamorphosis, pair up and begin to reproduce. The new queen becomes a full-scale egg producer, laying up to

4,000 eggs a day and growing so enormous she can't move at all and is completely dependent on the food brought down through the tunnels to her by her blind, white workers. But if the parents don't die first, the nymphs live out their lives as nymphs, lords and ladies forever in waiting.

In the 1970s, when my sister went away to college, my parents finally divorced. A few years later Bill's father fell sick. I called Bill when I heard. Now a physician himself in Indianapolis, he told me how his father, who had lost seventy-five pounds, claimed to have hystoplasmosis, a fungal disease that is endemic in the river valleys of the Midwest and can sometimes look like tuberculosis or old pneumonia scars on a chest x-ray. Bill had examined his father's x-rays himself and knew better. It was clearly lung cancer, though his father denied it. Our phone call was sad but good. It showed me that we were old enough now for our parents not to embarrass us, and that Bill's parents, or his father at least, could be as stubborn and foolish as mine.

The life cycle of the termite nymphs seems fully figurative to me when I set it against the summer I first learned about them; for it was then that I first saw my parents' weakness, sensed my teachers' frailty—and began my own metamorphosis.

The fall of 1964, the fall after we got the termites, Bill was assigned Mr. Bush for Biology. Mr. Bush, with his firm rules, scorn of extra credit and immaculate, well-organized lab, was intimidating, but after school on the football practice field, he revealed a sense of humor and a willingness to muck it up with us. His own frail son was the team manager, and when John received his letter sweater at the team banquet that year, his father cried.

I was assigned to Mr. Witters, who always arrived for class smiling and excited. I loved his class, but I could never look at him without thinking about his lost family and how hard he must have had to work in order to maintain his optimism and energy. In a fundamental and tragic way, his curiosity and his intellect had failed him. He was a brilliant man who worked hard and lost his family because of it. He couldn't salvage his home life, but he remains my model of a good teacher, full of lesson plans and knowledge and a complete devotion to his students. His insect assignment, with its strict instructions and Linnean taxonomy, taught us the importance of method; yet his extra-credit policy said that rules and method aren't everything. A bigger part of learning is simply finding out as much as you can.

I misidentified one of my two species of scorpion flies, and lost two points, but because I had twenty-two orders, I ended up with twenty extra-credit points and a total score of one hundred eighteen. Bill had three perfect cases and the better collection, but because he had Mr. Bush, he only scored one hundred. His prize catch ended up being not his royal walnut, but an Embiidina, a little-studied web-spinning insect that is rarely found in Indiana. He caught it one night late in August when he and I were checking bug lights out in the county. His particular specimen was a winged male. Embiidinae normally live in colonies (though without a caste system like termites), but the one Bill caught was alone and at least a hundred fifty miles north of its normal range. The Embiidina was Bill's twenty-third order. Neither teacher had ever seen one.

Ned Stuckey-French is a graduate student at the University of Iowa.

"I'm your agent, Kong, so trust me when I say that a jungle cookbook is not what the public wants from your pen."

William Maxwell

© Brookie Maxwell

William Maxwell is the author of six novels and five collections of short fiction, most recently *All the Days and Nights: The Collected Stories,* published in 1994. His 1980 novel, *So Long, See You Tomorrow,* won the American Book Award. He is also the author of a family history, *Ancestors.*

Maxwell was born in Lincoln, Illinois where he lived until the age of 14, when his family moved to Chicago. After graduating from the University of Illinois and a brief stint in graduate school, Maxwell went to New York to seek his fortune as a fiction editor and occasional essay reviewer. The writers he edited include J.D. Salinger, John Cheever, John O'Hara, Harold Brodkey, and Delmore Schwartz.

This is the second installment of an interview conducted by Kay Bonetti in November 1995 for the American Audio Prose Library, which has recordings of readings by and interviews with 131 contemporary writers. The first part of this interview appeared in the most recent issue (Volume XIX, Number 1) of *The Missouri Review.* For more information about AAPL listings, write P.O. Box 842, Columbia, MO, 65205, or call 800–447–2275.

An Interview with William Maxwell / *Kay Bonetti*

Interviewer: You've said you learned from E.B. White that the "I" should always be a real character in any piece that you've written. Have you ever had a sense in your writing life that you were flying in the face of current convention, or being old-fashioned, by adhering to that principle?

Maxwell: I never worried about being old-fashioned because the books I've continued to read all my life have been the Russians. I wanted to write about people, men and women. What's old-fashioned about men and women? They are just as they are. E.B. White taught me to use the "I" unself-consciously. The thing about White is, he is essentially an egoist—not an egotist, but an egoist. He has to start from himself as the center of his observations. But that self is never tiresome, usually amusing, always likable, always acceptable. I remember when I was younger, trying to write stories in the first person, or even novels. They went on and on and on, and were so garrulous. I couldn't somehow rein them in because I hadn't discovered how to treat myself in a way that wasn't the total interior life. The answer is to treat oneself as an outside person, as a character, who therefore is manageable. And also not the center of the action and of attention, but somewhat on the side, visible and sometimes an actor, but only momentarily. To find a place for you that is very much like the place you must find in social life, where you are not tiresome, but agreeable socially. Give other people a chance to talk, too. When I could finally use the first person I was happy, but it was like venturing into cold water.

Interviewer: There's a strong streak in your work of the disparity between the inner self and the outer self. Are you saying that in using yourself as a narrator and a persona, that this is the sort of thing you're also doing fictionally to deal with the material?

Maxwell: We're all so many selves, a whole cast of characters. Now

I'm one person, now I'm another. There's a committee, and somebody is in charge of the committee. That's the person that the outside world knows. But the interior life is more or less bedlam.

Interviewer: It sounds like in the writing process if you're going to insert yourself as the "I" of the piece, you're creating that same duet, or dialogue.

Maxwell: You have to create something that somebody would recognize as a person. But not the whole person in the sense that you get from Joyce, or Virginia Woolf.

Interviewer: You've spoken and written of having been in analysis. With respect to the work, you can certainly see, in *So Long, See You Tomorrow* and *They Came Like Swallows* the aspects of Freudian psychology. Was this Freudian analysis that you went into?

Maxwell: Oh, yes. It was Theodore Reik, who had been a pupil of Freud. When he won a prize in Vienna he was living in an attic and Freud climbed up god knows how many flights of stairs to tell him. He was, I think, a very good analyst. He made me feel that he cared about me. I don't think I could have done anything with him if he hadn't. I think often analysts don't do that, or don't feel they ought to, perhaps. But he did. He had a strong sense of literature, and he was ambitious for me. I think he saved my life because I had a strong tendency toward self-destruction.

Interviewer: This is what drew you into analysis?

Maxwell: No, I don't suppose I would have gone to him or to anybody if some friend hadn't pushed me into it. But in my early thirties I was haunted by the image of a tree; you know what happens to trees when you cut the main stem, and they grow out quite large on the side but they don't grow very tall. I felt that was happening to me, that my center had been cut out, and I couldn't assume my proper shape. I tend to think in metaphors rather than direct, abstract ideas.

Interviewer: What was the center that you felt had been cut out?

Maxwell: I didn't seem to be growing. I didn't have anybody to love, nobody to love me, and I had no wife, no child. I was just an incomplete person. I was only in analysis with Reik a short time. When I got

"You can't write novels based only on why."

married he said, "Now you're on your own. You can come back and talk if you want to, but you better live through this yourself." I did go back for a short time, but after that, not. The effect of the analytic hour was to find that I was focused on why things happened, not what happened. You can't write novels that are based only on why. You have to say, this happened, and this happened, and then and then and then and then. It took a little while to escape from the preoccupation with motivation, back into straight human behavior. But in time it fell away and I forgot about it.

Interviewer: When you speak of turning yourself into a character, it seems to me that you do that with everything. You turn houses into characters, you turn furniture into characters, you turn the dog into a character. What part of that just arises organically from the vision and what part is something you have learned, in terms of craft, about how to tell the story?

Maxwell: I was an extremely imaginative child. But I think what happened was that when I got into my thirties, I became preoccupied with myself too much, too exclusively. What Theodore Reik did was make myself less of a problem to me. Made me accept myself. Therefore, and because of the theories he was presenting me with, I suddenly found myself intensely interested, not in myself but in other people. That interest in other people is just by a kind of poetic transposition done to furniture, to houses, to dogs, to anything. I found that the world around me, the people around me, were so interesting. From that time on I was interested in myself but only as one of them, not as the center of the world.

Interviewer: It seems to me too that what you show in your work is that as a child you weren't a victim, you were a survivor. Have you been conscious of a survivor element, an existential element in your work?

Maxwell: Brendan Gill wrote a preface to an interview in the *Paris Review* with me, in which he said I was an odd combination of somebody who was highly sensitive and hard as nails. That is to say, as an editor, when I had to say "This doesn't work," I was able to say it. I think that hardness was really acquired by surviving. And also because my belief in the perfect thing, the right thing, the right story, was so total that I didn't want to accept something that wasn't right. I *couldn't* accept something that I thought wasn't right.

Interviewer: You've brought up the word "love," and other people have too with respect to William Maxwell and the vision out of which he writes. Do you have a sense that in many ways you've been extraordinarily blessed? It's apparent that the woman your father married after your mother died was somebody you must have loved very much. She was very wise. She knew not to presume to replace the mother you had lost, but instead to be just who she was and what she was. It strikes me that this in fact was a great blessing for you.

Maxwell: I think also now that I'm such an old man, what delights me is the friendships with the children of my friends or with people of that age, people around forty. These new, affectionate, marvelous relationships that make my life like a blossoming tree.

Interviewer: From whence comes the comfort and the acceptance, in William Maxwell, of being able to hold two apparently contradictory emotions simultaneously: the anger at your father for having the nerve to remarry, to tear down or to move out of the old house, sell it. To then uproot you and move you to Chicago. And yet, as you put it very succinctly in one place that I'm trying to remember, you've said that simultaneously, even though you quarreled and had a conflict kind of relationship with your dad, at the same time there was no other model that you could envision.

Maxwell: The only person I trusted so completely. These dualistics are the very essence of life, don't you think? Things are not simple. They shouldn't be made to appear so.

Interviewer: Speaking of double lives and other existences—in a letter to you, John O'Hara asked you how you were coming with your "double life." He was feeling sorry for himself about things that were going on—"And then I think of you, and this double life you lead, that you go home on off-hour trains and try to do your own work, and yet you're carrying this baggage with you of all of us gypsies, and all these writers, and all the manuscripts." Let's talk about the relationship between William Maxwell the writer and William Maxwell the editor. How did you balance that? What did you learn from your editing that you brought to your writing? Or did you try to keep them separate?

Maxwell: I tried to keep my writing life invisible to the people I was editing. I wanted them to think I was their editor and that was all. Of course it wasn't totally invisible, but on the other hand I was not so successful as a writer that it was a problem. During the second half of the forty years that I was an editor I had a fair number of writers whose work I loved, and I loved them as people, the relationship was very close. I was deeply involved in their work, as I was in my own. But when I went home I didn't think about them. I thought about my own work.

Interviewer: Did you ever worry about borrowing from writers whose manuscripts you'd read?

Maxwell: There was nobody who was at all like me as a writer. I'm sure that my sense of how to write well was tremendously sharpened by working with such writers. So it was not a problem, it was a great help. If I imitated I wasn't aware of it, and they certainly didn't imitate me. They were fully crystallized. On the days I had to work at *The New Yorker*, I always shaved with pleasure, thinking, "I'm about to take the train and go be an editor." Whereas, when I was going to be a writer I sometimes said, "It's not going very well. This novel is really a travel diary. I'm in trouble." I never worried about being an editor. I was easy about it, happy about it. I didn't have to worry about money. It wasn't a high salary, but it was enough to live on. That was wonderful.

Interviewer: And it got you out of yourself. You got to go out into the world.

Maxwell: Yes, I stopped being an introvert and became an extrovert three days a week. Since I am part extrovert and part introvert that was a very satisfactory arrangement. There is a book by a woman named Beatrice Hinkle, and the subject is "the subjective extrovert." I seem to answer to the description.

Interviewer: There's a letter from John Cheever to Alan Gurganus in which he says to Alan Gurganus, "Bill Maxwell is a very fastidious person." By that he meant you were a neat-nik type. He said, "Once he called and said he was coming to tea. Mary scrambled around, she cleaned the house, we got tea ready. And here came Mr. Maxwell; we were having tea; everything seemed to be full of decorum, and in came Harmon the cat with a dead goldfish in his mouth." He said, "That just sums up my relationship with the Maxwells in a nutshell." Is there any story you could tell that you think would sum up in a nutshell your relationship with the Cheevers?

Maxwell: Yes. He asked me to leave the house once. I don't remember the goldfish in the cat's mouth, and I rather think it didn't happen. John was a fantasist. I think it has the higher truth, but I don't think it literally happened. Once as my wife and I were dressing to go to a dinner party to the Cheevers' in the country—I'd had a good day's writing, and I was feeling happy—I said, "I'm just going to be myself tonight, my real self." So I was. I didn't censor my conversation. I said whatever I felt. There was a young man across the table from me who was talking about his father. I understood so well what he was saying. It was the kind of joke that really hides pain, and isn't a joke. Having a couple of drinks in me I leaned across the table and said, "Why don't you kill your father?" A few more remarks like that during the course of the evening, and suddenly John was standing in front of me—I was talking to one of the guests—and he said, "Will you go home now?" I was startled, but I realized he meant it. I got Emmy. It was dead winter, and snow on the ground, and we got our coats and left. I came out and I saw a faint glow on the car lights. I had left the ignition on, and the battery wouldn't turn over. I had to go back in the house and get John, and ask him to push us, which he did. Fortunately they lived at

> *"The reason I have any relationship with Salinger at all is that I've never talked about him."*

the crest of a hill. We started downhill and went home. Our relationship was rather cool for maybe about a year, but I told somebody who I knew would repeat it to him, that I thought he was the best short-story writer in America. After that, things got better.

Interviewer: He says things got better with you after he changed the dedication of one of his novels from "To Bill Maxwell" to "To W.M." and that made you change your tune about the book.

Maxwell: He did dedicate the book with my initials but I didn't change my tune about the book. It wasn't a book I liked, and he knew that I didn't like it. At the end of his life—not the beginning—he was a quite unreliable witness.

Interviewer: His son makes that clear in the letters. He says, "My dad tells this, but I for the life of me don't think that ever really happened." There's another story that Cheever tells in his letters. I don't know if it's true or not. He says he gave a dinner party and greeted everybody without his clothes on.

Maxwell: No, that's not true. Wonderful story, but I don't think it is true.

Interviewer: In what sense did you view your editing, if at all, as a creative process?

Maxwell: It was as if we were in a boat together. They were doing the rowing and I was saying, "Look out for that snag." A very affectionate relationship, usually.

Interviewer: That's apparent from the letters I've read, from John

"Ross felt that The New Yorker *was a family magazine so you should avoid anything salacious."*

O'Hara and from Cheever. One of the things that Cheever claims that he was always saying to you was, "You may have invented Salinger and Harold Brodkey but you didn't invent me."

Maxwell: It's not true. I didn't invent him, or Brodkey or Salinger, but it's not something he ever said to me.

Interviewer: What about Salinger? As I understand, you're one of the few people who really knows Salinger because of your editing relationship. Is this true?

Maxwell: The reason I still have any relationship with Salinger at all is that I've never talked about him. And so I'm not going to now. He doesn't like to be talked about.

Interviewer: Can you say this much? Has your relationship with Salinger been mostly in correspondence, with letters back and forth about the work?

Maxwell: Here is something I can tell you: Once a proofreader came to me and said, "This sentence has to have a comma in it." It was just going to the printer and I couldn't reach Salinger. It seemed clear to me that it needed a comma, and I had faith in that particular proofreader, so I said, "All right." Salinger was very sad afterwards because he didn't want that comma. It wasn't necessary. That's what it was like editing Salinger, really. You couldn't safely put a comma into him, and I made a terrible mistake in agreeing to it.

Interviewer: You took a lot of heat from your writers at *The New Yorker* over their perceived fastidiousness about *The New Yorker*. John O'Hara's letters are full of that. And Cheever's, too. What's your assessment of the relationship of the writers with *The New Yorker* and those accusations that have been made, that writers felt that Ross and Shawn were trying to keep it too prudish?

Maxwell: Ross felt that *The New Yorker* was a family magazine and came into the house once a week, and you couldn't control who saw what was in it. There were children in the house, so you should avoid anything salacious. I think this also reflected his own kind of fastidiousness. I thought it was sometimes confining to the writer. Once John Cheever, in one of his stories—there is a description of a man who had been making love to his wife, and he's outdoors, walking across the lawn—wrote, "He walked across the lawn with love in his heart and lust in his trousers." I thought it was wonderful. Shawn thought it wouldn't do, and I argued—I seldom argued with Shawn, but I did the best arguing I could—and failed. It distressed me very much. But now, of course, think what's happened.

Interviewer: There were two things that came up in the letters of O'Hara—or the same thing came up in both the letters of O'Hara and of John Cheever. John O'Hara wrote at length about his distaste for Hemingway's *Death in the Afternoon,* of Hemingway's having adopted these two bullfighters, and that here he loved them but wanted to see them dead. What an awful thing he thought that was. Later, in a letter that Cheever wrote about you as his editor, he said, "He loves me, and would love to see me dead." He'd seen you as indecipherable, and it seemed to him—he said it *seemed* to him; I think that would imply that he realizes this isn't true—that you were a man who mistook power for love in your role as an editor.

Maxwell: You've been talking to me for something like four hours. What do you think?

Interviewer: I think that it says more about Cheever than it says about William Maxwell.

Maxwell: Could we leave it there?

Interviewer: It seems apparent in the letters of Cheever that there was a deep, deep friendship there between the two of you.

Maxwell: The problem was, Cheever was really a modernist, moving toward being a modernist, and at a certain point fantasy came into his stories. Usually those stories were rejected. At another point he abandoned the consistency of character. Characters in his stories did things which it was not in their character to do. He released them from this obligation to be consistent, recognizable characters. In doing that he was departing from Tolstoy and Turgenev and Chekov. I couldn't go with him. I think that the surrealistic work that he did is perhaps the most admired by a great many people, so I don't feel I was right and he was wrong. It's just that I couldn't follow him there.

Interviewer: I was struck by the difference in the letters that Cheever wrote you and the letters that John O'Hara wrote. I got the sense from both that there was a deep friendship there on both sides—and yet John O'Hara's letters went, "Points 1, 2, 3, 4. About this comma here . . . okay. Now, this is why I want the characters addressed by their whole name instead of . . ." I thought it was fascinating, what he wrote you about the use of directives and asides, or "he saids" and "she saids" and characters' names, elements which have been touted as *The New Yorker* style, where they make you do things a certain way. He said, "Dammit, there's an aesthetic reason for this."

Maxwell: I remember that letter vividly. What I was objecting to was that every time a character spoke, O'Hara wanted always to use the character's name. "John Hopkins said, John Hopkins said, John Hopkins said." I thought it was in danger of becoming a mannerism. Couldn't he just alternate with a few "he saids"? And OíHara said, "No, that's the way I do it." I think I was right, it was a mannerism. Editors always think they're right. But he thought I should just shut up about it. That wasn't the way he wanted to write. It's the only time I remember a disagreement of any kind between us.

Interviewer: I was struck by the distinct differences in those two writers, between John O'Hara and John Cheever, and how those differences were reflected in the nature of their correspondence with you. John O'Hara's is full of bills of sale: "If you want to get a good coat in London, here's where you go." John Cheever is talking about the cats and the dogs and trying to assure you that he's been treating this one cat all right, even though he doesn't like cats. And he talks to you about your children and about his children, and summer camp.

Maxwell: O'Hara had been a very difficult young man, especially when he was drunk. For example, Robert Benchley was the most good-natured man in the world, and O'Hara, for no reason whatsoever

"I had no difficulties ever with O'Hara,
but I was aware that I was putting my head
in the lion's mouth."

—they were in a bar somewhere—just hit him in the face. The next day he called up to apologize and Benchley said, "Oh, that's all right John, you're just a shit," forgiving him. I was aware that he had been Gibbs' writer; and Gibbs particularly admired him; he had been Gibbs' favorite writer. I inherited him, and he was half a generation older. I didn't try to push him around. I treated him with great respect, and I really had no difficulties ever. But I was aware that I was putting my head in the lion's mouth. In fact what really happened was that after his wife died—he'd loved his wife very much indeed, his second wife—and after she died he said the most beautiful thing about her. He said, "The only bad thing she ever did was die on me." After her death his doctor said to him, "If you want to see your daughter come of age you have to stop drinking." He never touched another drop. That's why I could safely put my head in the lion's mouth. If he had been drinking I would have lost my face sooner or later.

Interviewer: That's one thing I wondered about, too. How you managed all these personalities—people coming at you with their complaints about money, "aren't I due for a raise?" or "how dare you take this comma out!" You must have some kind of real skill with people.

Maxwell: I had two loves. One was literature and the other was them.

GENERATIONS "I": The Future of
Autobiographical Poetry / *David Wojahn*

"When I speak of keeping the human image, I
am speaking of keeping, not selves, but the
value of selves."
—Allen Grossman
from *The Sighted Singer*

ROBERT LOWELL, CIRCA 1962 or '63, is looking at the camera
with the sort of fixed intensity that's displayed in so many of his
photos. He's wearing the black owlish hornrims which were the uniform of the myopic early sixties, a time when the rose-colored granny
glasses of the Byrds' Roger McGuinn and John Lennon's oval
wirerims, shading acid-dilated pupils, were still unknown. In this particular photo Lowell looks uncharacteristically calm, his hair neatly
brushed; there's none of the eerily dishevelled gawkiness of his more
famous photos, no Einstein-wild hair, no sense that he possesses a
body always shambling and awkward, too large to fit the rooms that
contain it. When the photo was taken he had recently released *Life
Studies,* possibly the most influential book of American poetry published in the last half-century. I don't know the name of the photographer, for the photo was rescued by a friend of mine one day while
she worked as a secretary at Harvard, and was asked to clean out and
throw away some files. On the back, in faded pencil, are the words *Mr.
Robert Lowell.* The photo came in the mail a few months ago, a gift from
my friend, and now occupies a space on the wall above my desk, along
with various other icons—Akhmatova, Louise Brooks, Bob Dylan,
Stanley Spencer, Frank O'Hara, Miles Davis. And of course the family
photos: my father in his corporal's stripes circa 1944, my mother waving from the Perisphere at the '39 World's Fair, and the photo which
would eventually find its way to the jacket of my wife's posthumously
published book of poetry. In profile, drop earrings and a scarf pulled
halfway back and turban-like, she looks uncannily like Akhmatova;
profile to profile, they face each other as I look from them to the leaf-
less March trees beyond and back to Robert Lowell. The living have no
place here, it seems. The mothers and beloveds dead. And the fathers.
When my father posed for the photo before me—somewhere halfway

up the boot of Italy—it was nine years before my birth. And when Lowell looked up from his podium at the Woodbury Poetry Room, facing some now unknown photographer's flash while reading, perhaps, his new poem "For the Union Dead," I was nine years old. It would be another decade before I would hear of Lowell or read his work.

Clearly Lowell is the other dead father, as he is for so many of the poets of the last two or three generations; he has bestowed upon us a complex and troubling legacy. He is both model and pariah, and his tics and mannerisms have been incorporated into our psyches so fully that we scarcely are aware of their presence. Without *Life Studies*, the careers of as diverse a list of poets as Plath, Sexton, Merrill, Levine, Heaney, Bidart, Pinsky, Glück, Hass, C.K. Williams, Sharon Olds, Frederick Seidel and Charles Wright would be impossible to imagine. One could also make a case for Lowell's considerable but less obvious influence upon writers such as Jorie Graham, Paul Muldoon, Carolyn Forché and Allen Grossman. Lowell's impact on these writers manifests itself in many ways—in a prosody which mixes various elements of traditional and free verse, in a sense of public history's intricate connections to personal history, and even in the use of imagery. The most crucial aspect of Lowell's influence has been his creation of a particularly influential form of autobiographical lyric. The self in the world, and the self in relationship to its past are Lowell's principal concerns after *Life Studies*, and most of the significant movements in contemporary poetry can be seen as deriving from Lowell's approach to such concerns. The intensely introspective lyrics of neo-surrealists such as Merwin and Wright owe something to Lowell's attentiveness to the self; and similarly, though less clearly, the quirky subjectivity of Ashbery and his disciples nods to Lowell in this regard as well.

True, the sort of autobiographical lyric that *Life Studies* contained was also being practiced in the fifties by several of Lowell's immediate contemporaries—by Ginsberg in *Howl*, by Snodgrass in *Heart's Needle*, as well as by O'Hara in the jauntily nervous *Lunch Poems*. But *Life Studies* spread its influence everywhere, far beyond the cliques of would-be Beats and New York School followers who modeled themselves on Ginsberg or O'Hara.

What has *Life Studies* wrought? Most significantly, American and British poets of the last four decades have found permission for the first time in literary history to speak in unguarded terms about their own lives. The self who speaks in the typical contemporary poem is considered the poet him/herself, not a persona, not a character. While fringe movements such as Language Poetry have rightfully questioned the aesthetic presuppositions of the autobiographical lyric, there is no question that it is the prevailing period style. The March, 1995 issue of *Poetry* might serve as example, for its poems' subjects are ones which would have been impossible to imagine before 1959. This particular issue's twenty-five poems treat a familiar litany of personal subject matter: one miscarriage, three dead parents, three unhappy childhoods, one husband on his deathbed and one contentious divorce. The poems are all quite competently written and heartfelt, and their authors range from well-known poets such as W.S. Merwin and William Matthews to writers publishing for the first time. The thirty-five-year-old computer programer from Decatur, Illinois, who writes of his bitter divorce in a community college poetry workshop, and the twenty-year-old undergraduate trying to confront the memory of her mother's death or her uncle's repeated molestations both owe something to "Waking in the Blue" or "Skunk Hour"—even if these tyro poets may never have read Lowell. One of the reasons why poetry's audience has expanded greatly in recent years is that several generations of aspiring writers have emerged who seek, simply, and often poignantly, to write about their lives. Robert Lowell, posed with his locked razor at McLean's, or "tamed by Miltown" on his marriage bed, has proven the most enduring model for this horde of scribblers. The situation is certainly not Lowell's fault, for the effect of any period style, once it has been widely disseminated among writers, is to dilute its virtues and turn them into mannerisms.

The following poem appears in a recently published collection, and serves as a particularly interesting example of this process:

Of My Father's Cancer, and His Dreams

With those who love him near his bed
seldom speaking any more,
he lies too weak to raise his head
but dreams from time to time.
In one, he says, he sees his wife,
so proud in her white uniform,
with other nurses trooping by,
their girlish voices aimed to charm
the young man lounging there.
Then eyes meet his and hold.
A country courtship has begun.
They've been together thirty years.

Now, she watches over him
as she tries to hide her tears.
All his children are at home
but wonder what they ought to say,
or do, either when he is awake
or when he seems to fade away.

They can't always be on guard,
and sometimes, if his mind is clear,
he can grasp a whispered phrase
never meant for him to hear:
"He just seems weaker all the time."
"I don't know what else to cook.
He can't keep down anything."

He hears the knocking on the door,
voices of his friends, who bring
a special cake or fresh-killed quail.
They mumble out some words of love,
try to learn how he might feel,
then go back to spread the word:
"They say he may have faded some."

He'll soon give in to the rising pain
and crave the needle that will numb
his knowledge of a passing world,
and bring the consummating sleep
he knows will come.

This isn't a particularly notable piece of writing but it has some modest virtues. The handling of the meter and the inconsistency of the rhyme scheme strike us as a bit awkward, and the final stanza comes very close to sentimentality, but it is a thoughtful and sensitive effort, by no means doggerel verse. Two other aspects of the poem are worth pointing out, and are more remarkable. First, the author of the poem is a former U.S. President, Jimmy Carter. Second, readers familiar with contemporary poetry will hear in the poem distinct echoes of two of Lowell's best-known *Life Studies* poems, "Terminal Days at Beverly Farms" and "My Last Afternoon with Uncle Devereux Winslow." When ex-Presidents mimic *Life Studies*, and in their efforts achieve reasonably passable results, we have reached a curious situation. How are we to read Jimmy Carter's poetry: as an indication of his sensitivity, or as an example of the utter exhaustion of a particular style of autobiographical verse?

In an era when many poets are primarily concerned with self-disclosure, sometimes poetry seems merely another form of the various self-therapy movements which have had such a huge vogue in recent decades. Some would say that such movements foster a kind of substitute dependency just as imperilling as any of the problems that prompt their creation, but I am by no means one of these critics; the value of the self-help movement seems to me considerable. And who is to argue that poetry does not sometimes give the very sort of specific personal solace offered also by AA, Al-Anon, Rolfing, Zoloft or Sufi dancing?

Where does this leave poetry, however? Three of our more astute critics of contemporary verse—Marjorie Perloff, Mary Kinzie and Alan Williamson—have all recently addressed this question. The trio have little in common. Perloff, a champion of the avant-garde tradition deriving from Stein and Cage, borders on sometimes tireless cheerleading for this camp. Kinzie promotes a sort of neo-New Criticism: lots of close readings, an exasperatingly obtuse style and a rather schoolmarmish and moralizing tone. Williamson, a student of Lowell (and a good poet himself), practices psychoanalytical criticism, although he is by no means a Freudian party-liner. Perloff and Kinzie view the contemporary state of autobiographical poetry with alarm; Williamson, in his book *Eloquence and Mere Life* (University of Michigan Press, 1994), takes a more balanced approach, but acknowledges the problems inherent in the "peculiarities" of a situation in which it has grown "very hard to draw a clear line between work whose main value is therapeutic or inspirational and work that really addresses and expands the possibilities of art itself."

Perloff regards mainstream poetry's involvement with self-disclosure as an example of social commodification, and her method of illustrating this is witheringly effective. In a fascinating essay entitled "The Changing Face of Common Intercourse: Talk Poetry, Talk Show, and the Scene of Writing," Perloff argues that the "packaging" of self on television talk shows such as "Oprah" and "Donohue," with their emphasis on intimate disclosure (usually centering upon what were once called shameful secrets—infidelities, transvestism, drug addiction, various sorts of criminal activities), differs little from the similarly ritual gestures packaged as self in contemporary poetry. She is especially concerned with debunking what she sees as the myth of "authentic speech." If the tearful confessions of secret lives and shortcomings among Oprah and Phil's guests represent the media's crass commercialization of human suffering, confessions become merely a formal device, a component of the package, and "authentic" only insofar as they facilitate the needs of programmers and sponsors. A similar packaging, both of the author's sense of selfhood and of a language meant to convey that sense of selfhood through a transparent free-verse diction, is seen by Perloff as a major component—and shortcoming—of contemporary mainstream poetry. She builds her case by debunking certain neo-Wordsworthian notions about "primacy of feeling" and "earnestness" as expressed by Louis Simpson in defense of poetry.

Unfortunately, Perloff is better at fighting battles than anything else. Once she has sheathed her sword and surveyed the battlefield of dead "talk show poetry" and poets, she introduces us to the new emperor and his court: Language Poets Steve McCaffery, Susan Howe and Leslie Scalapino. We are then given some standard Language Poet bromides: word-consciousness over self-consciousness, the questioning of self-referentiality, and so on. Towards the end of her essay Perloff quotes admiringly a passage from a long poem by Susan Howe which begins, "Posit gaze level diminish lamp and asleep (selv) cannot see," and continues in a similar vein. It makes one wonder when Oprah or Donohue will devote a show to recovering Language Writers. ("I've been there! A graphomaniac! An addict to syntax!")

What Perloff terms talk show poetry Kinzie, in *The Cure of Poetry in an Age of Prose* (University of Chicago Press, 1991), defines as "applied poetry," a term she borrows from C.S. Lewis' characterization of certain minor Elizabethan poets who cast advice about crops and animal husbandry in verse form. Where the age of Wyatt had its couplets describing beekeeping and bull-neutering, we have Ann Sexton, whose failings represent a trend to "supplant other notions and kinds of poetry with an exclusivity of therapeutic discovery." Although Sexton strikes me as a better poet than Kinzie regards her, Kinzie's description of Sexton's baneful influence is instructive. Kinzie derides Sexton's "enormous reputation as a victim-seer": her proto-feminist concern for invective, in which "anger is a curiously over-valued enterprise" and her partial responsibility for an atmosphere in which "a *persona* extrinsic to the making of poetry has been mistaken all the way around for an excellent *poem*." Thanks to Sexton, Kinzie implies, there has been a kind of dumbing-down of autobiographical poetry, a loss of the aesthetic gravity which it possesses in writers such as Berryman and Lowell. Self-exploration is replaced by a tedious and unevenly written litany of victimhood. Although Kinzie makes these observations in a fashion both simplistic and alarmist, she has a point. She sees "applied poetry" as not so much an approach to subject matter as it is a form of environmental disease, the poet's version of black lung, afflicting us all to varying degrees.

Williamson, in a ground-breaking essay entitled "Fictions from the Self," describes an alternative to talk show and applied poetry, the emergence of a new sort of autobiographical verse. Like Perloff and Kinzie, Williamson is aware of the problems inherent in most contemporary autobiographical lyrics, and he knows that our better young poets are aware of them as well. "All the negative attention," he writes, "may have stimulated poets to approach the self's story with a tact, a self-awareness, an eye to exclusions and thematic 'figure in the carpet,' that fiction writers have taken for granted for generations. . . . One reads the best of the newer narrative poetry with a sense of point of view, of strategic timing and delayed exposition, that makes the great poems of Lowell and Plath seem raw lyric by comparison." Williamson sees the new autobiographical poetry as essentially narrative, but fractured by flashback and flash-forwards, by cinematic jump-cuts and ruminative asides. It differs from the confessional lyric of a generation or two ago because it emphasizes the speaker's actions with a more expansive regard to the play of consciousness over time. More so than confessional writers, the new autobiographers are concerned with the meaning of memory, and thus we have the long and troubled meditations on adolescence and young adulthood which comprise C.K. Williams' *Tar*, and the yearning and disjointed struggles with family history found in Frank Bidart's *Golden State*. Williamson would add to this list younger poets such as Tom Sleigh, Brenda Hillman and Alan Shapiro. Such poets enact, as Shapiro remarks in *In Praise of the Impure*, (Northwestern University Press, 1993), "the complicated drama of perspective between a recollecting and experiencing self." The immensely long but often highly spondaic lines of Williams, and the idiosyncratic lineation and use of italics and boldface in Bidart can be seen as attempts to more acutely render the elasticity of consciousness. The new poetry of self, in other words, is seen as expansive and inclusive in ways which confessional poetry decidedly was not.

In examining some of this new autobiographical poetry, I want to explore some issues that Williamson and Shapiro only touch upon—specifically the new poetry's stance toward self-disclosure, and how it differs from the often self-lacerating aspect of talk show and applied poetry. How does the truth of self differ from factual truth? One of the mysterious legacies of confessionalism is the reader's implicit belief that poets tell the truth about themselves, and that this activity is not only good, but sufficient in itself to create a good poem. If anything distinguishes applied and talk show poetry from the new autobiographical writing, it is their differing attitudes toward the purposes and possibilities of truth-telling.

The following poem by Bruce Weigl treats a subject that is sadly fashionable on the talk-show circuit, and there are reasons for classifying it among talk show or applied poems as well.

The Impossible

Winter's last rain and a light I don't recognize
through the trees and I come back in my mind
to the man who made me suck his cock
when I was seven, in sunlight, between boxcars
I thought I could leave him standing there
in the years, half-smile on his lips,

small hands curled into small fists,
but after he finished, he held my hand in his
as if astonished, until the houses were visible
just beyond the railroad. He held my hand
but before that he slapped me hard on the face
when I would not open my mouth for him.

I do not want to say his whole hips
slammed into me, but they did, and a black wave
washed over my brain, changing me
so I could not move among my people in the old way.
On my way home I stopped in the churchyard
to try to find a way to stay alive.
In the branches a redwing flitted, warning me.
In the rectory, Father prepared
the body and blood for mass
but God could not save me from a mouthful of cum.
That afternoon some lives turned away from the light.
He taught me to move my tongue around.
In his hands he held me like a lover.
Say it clearly and you make it beautiful, no matter what.

There is much to admire in this poem: the elegant precision of the writing and a reportorial insistence that nevertheless permits several shifts into a more formal rhetoric. The transparency of Weigl's language is especially successful as he relates the specifics of the speaker's recollection of his sexual abuse. The horror of the scene is neither down-played nor sensationalized, and this furthermore permits Weigl to perform the delicate task of characterizing the speaker's abuser as be-lievably complicated in his ambivalence: Weigl refuses to demonize him.

The main shortcoming of the poem is one typical of many contem-porary poems, especially autobiographical lyrics: the poem refuses psychological perspective in favor of mere rhetorical substitutes for it. In the beginning of the poem Weigl's speaker chooses not to explore the compelling question of why he has chosen a particular moment in which to recall his trauma. We are instead given a kind of plain-style telegraphy: "Winter's last rain and a light I don't recognize," and sud-denly the memory holds the poem completely at siege—until its final lines, which are equally disappointing. What are the consequences of the speaker's sexual trauma, and of his need to relive it in his poem? Merely that on the day of the event "some lives turned away from the light." The final line is a regular-guy rewrite of Keats—"Say it clearly and you make it beautiful, no matter what."

What is troubling about this statement is not merely its logical dubi-ousness, but also Weigl's apparent belief that we are to read the poem's narrative as a form of fable, to which the writer has appended this moral. The poem fails at its moralizing purpose because of an inherent contradiction typical of many recent autobiographical lyrics: art may make experience "beautiful," but the form of the contemporary auto-biographical lyric is more frequently designed to convey the illusion of reportorial *fact* than to emphasize the complexity of psychological truth—or beauty, if we assume that beauty is more than meets the cam-era's or the journalist's eye. The desire for transparent and "clear" writing, one of the main goals of the plain style, brings with it the problematic notion that clarity is truth. Weigl links himself in "The Impossible" to applied poets and talk show poets because he appears to operate within an aesthetic that in subtle ways confuses self-disclo-sure with the more resonant poetic artistry which Weigl's best efforts display. "The Impossible" is a good example of Kinzie's contention that the applied art "tic" affects even our better poets.

Susan Mitchell's "Leaves that Grow Inward" makes for an interest-ing contrast to Weigl's poem. Mitchell is one of the better repre-sentatives of the new school of autobiographical writers because of her inventive approaches to narrative, and for a linguistic richness that is exceedingly refreshing in an era of dressed-down minimalism. Rather than build her poem around a single emblematic anecdote, as Weigl does, Mitchell braids several narrative strands and imagistic leitmotifs. Her method of self-disclosure—and by extension her very stance toward memory and catharsis—differs significantly from Weigl's. As with Weigl's poem, "The Leaves that Grow Inward" centers upon a memory from childhood, but it focuses upon this memory only after some circuitous meditation. Here is the poem's first stanza:

> So you see, it was my favorite time
> for walking, toward evening, when the lights came on
> all together like candles on a child's cake.
> I would yawn, as if just leaving a movie.
> The better part of the day was over, no longer
> the chance of doing anything worthwhile.
> The relief of it. This was the hour
> I took a bath as a child,
> not always alone, sometimes with a friend, Clara,
> whose left arm ended abruptly at the elbow,
> as if she had managed to draw up
> inside her the hand, its fingers, even
> a small object the fingers had been holding
> at the time this miracle occurred. If
> I had known Holderlin's poem about the leaves
> that grow inward, I would have recited it
> to her, *hängen einwärts dei Blätter,*
> as she splashed water in my face
> with that budding stump of hers. Once
> at this hour my mother plucked a snail
> from watercress, a black glistening that sweated
> across my palm. Clara held it too
> with her eyes, the way I held her
> in the school playground until all at once
> I heard the train, still far away, that brought
> my father from his office, its wind
> blowing on the lights of our street.

Around the core memory of the speaker and the crippled Clara, Mitchell builds a more elaborate narrative structure; the opening conveys the sense of intimacy and the relentless pace that will characterize the poem. Yet the pace does not preclude a lavish attentiveness to detail—for example, the almost baroque description of Clara's damaged arm or the snail as a "black glistening that sweated across" the speaker's palm. If these descriptions possess a hugely charged eroticism, so too the strange image of the father's commuter train's return conveys a sinister repressiveness.

This sense of the repressive continues in the poem's second stanza, with the speaker's childhood "burning like a fever." The act of memory, which in the initial stanza had seemed bucolic and sensuous, is here likened to a fever, a cry, to "pulling hairs from the tenderest parts of the body." These menacing descriptions seem amorphous and free-floating, until suddenly the speaker makes a startling confession:

> Only, to tell the truth, there
> never was a Clara, a point I might confess
> to a psychiatrist. Instead,
> I confess it to myself, waiting
> for illumination, eyes closed,
> but still as if through leaves, through the sap
> of my cells . . . At school, there was
> a girl like her, but her arm
> terrified me. I withdrew
> from it. Which is quite another thing,
> isn't it? Though in the safety of my bath
> she sometimes entered my life as a possibility
> of future loss. So, you see,
> I am not the person you thought I was,
> the one you had grown comfortable with, maybe
> even liked a little . . . .

More is happening here than Mitchell simply playing the old "I'm lying—do you believe me?" game. What makes the passage impressive is the rigor of the speaker's self-analysis, her insistence on exploring the contrast between authentic recollections and the wish-fulfillment of the imagined ones. This contrast troubles and even frightens the speaker. To explore it, she must jettison several of the period style's more familiar methods of seeming to tell poetic "truth." Autobiography, she implies, is a chronicle of the inner life—"of the leaves that grow inward"—more than it is a truth which can be captured by mere description and anecdotes, which, as Mitchell has reminded us, can be easily false or misleading. Mitchell's narrative drive and urgency do not permit her to merely leave things thus; post-structuralist notions of slippage and the exploded self which the Language Poets embrace are acknowledged by Mitchell, but have little to do with the self-transcending romanticism which the poem's final stanzas bring forth. Now that Mitchell has established her goal of eliminating the line between truth and fable in order to achieve self-knowledge, the poem can grow expansive and Whitmanesque. The speaker describes herself waking to hear "the high rise in which I live / talking to itself like the sea / or like someone stumbling in and out of sleep . . ." This does not, however, mean that Mitchell is about to "contain multitudes"—not yet, at least. First she must return to Clara:

> What
> would it have been like to be the one who played
> with Clara, whooping down to the neighborhood
> bakery, mouth stuffed with strudel, not caring
> if my tongue scorched and blistered? What would it
> have been like to hold
> the sticks of dog shit, the purified chalk
> they scrawled their names with? At the edges
> of memory, Clara glimmers, beckoning
> as if into a forest. Striped with desires
> more bruising than prison bars, she leans out of
> herself . . . .

Clara is a memorable embodiment of the Id's capacity to be liberating and self-annihilating at once. And the poem's final passage builds upon these qualities, removing them from fantasy and placing them in the real world, a world, moreover, that is now charged with a sort of intense sensuality, a visionary landscape:

> Well, life
> is better now and sometimes I consume
> four movies in a day, surprised, as I drift
> to the street, it's dark outside too, surprised
> to see people waiting to see what I have just seen.
> This is the hour when two men
> kiss in the elevator, a long kiss
> which stops only when an old woman gets on,
> then they hold hands. Half asleep,
> I hear them kissing and the sky
> darkening, washing out to the Hudson
> where the freighters kneel in the sailors' shadows
> and the kids tripping on acid come
> to watch the men knotting
> and unknotting in their ecstasies.
> Even from here I follow their brief spurts
> of pleasure, the tides of clouds, until I feel far
> as someone drifting in a boat

or waving from a train a paper
hat, while the dark snails of my flesh slide
toward some heaven of their own.

The conclusion of Mitchell's poem is convincingly exultant, yet it
also refuses—in contrast to Weigl's poem—to reduce the struggle between the self and the world to a well-intended truism, or to draw
from its examination of the speaker's inner conflicts the implication
that these struggles have now somehow been solved. Fittingly, her
self-questionings do not resolve themselves in a rhetorical flourish, but
in a vivid recapitulation of the poem's motifs, imbuing the landscape
with the self rather than claiming to define or map the nature of selfhood. It is this stance, highly exploratory and obsessive in its urgency,
that has created a new sort of autobiographical approach. A small but
growing number of younger poets share with Mitchell these concerns,
among them Mark Halliday, Mark Doty, Deborah Digges, Rodney
Jones, Dean Young and Brigit Kelly. Of course the values I have iden-
tified here are not new ones, and are in fact the values that have
continued to attract me to the searching and flawed heroism of Robert
Lowell—not the Robert Lowell whom even retired Presidents can
ape, but the Lowell who will continue to look down on my desk, who
questions relentlessly and who sees the self in all of its tricky complexity—and in all of its elusive preciousness.

David Wojahn is a widely published poet whose new collection, *The Falling Hour*, is due
out in 1997.

October 31, 1996

All Humanities Department Members:

There will be a Department Meeting Tuesday, November 12, 3-4:30 p.m. No emergencies, as far as I know, it's just time to have a meeting. Apologies to those who teach at this time—it's a time of fewest class conflicts. An agenda will be distributed by Wednesday, November 6, and will include location of meeting. Please leave any suggested agenda items for me in writing in C120 by Tuesday, November 5, at 5 p.m. Thanks!

Karen Keener

LOVE, A DARK, UNTITLED COMEDY /
Jesse Lee Kercheval

I see my love for you
as a tin cup full of feathers,
a kit for making angels
to deliver non-believers.
I love you, you write back,
but that won't save me.
You see yours for me
as a book lent
to an infant in a basket
when language is what's missing.
Surprise, I write you,
I know a goldfish
buys you nothing.

Our love always
the stranger with someplace
else to go, a coat, a gown
walking down the road,
feet following,
while we sit, each of us
beside our mailboxes
hoping for a picture postcard,
blissful ration
of words from one another.
Words to draw the sting,
to numb the swings of the body's
brief duration
to take life in its teeth,
dirty string,
and tie a lasting knot.

DEATH, A SECOND TRIP BY SEA /
Jesse Lee Kercheval

No matter how much we love
our skin, life
will finish its work
and leave our bodies,
poor dead things.

Leave them underground.
Box turtles
listening to insects,
their small short breathings,
feeling the green grow
in our bones, the black
around us dense as licorice.

Above us, landscape.
If Florida, sand and thistle,
heat, long, generous
and Southern.
If Wisconsin, a field
on which snow sits all winter
like a white, still swan.
Over us, limestone angels,
bored and nearly human,
their wings folded,
killing time.

Unless our families
have us cremated,
bring us home
in the kind of tiny box
that holds expensive presents.
Imagine being sprinkled from a plane,
feeling vertigo,
the best of us transformed
into small and floating clouds,

the rest, white hail,
falling on the farms below.

What will it feel like, death?
Sudden, cold,
each life a fish caught
and thrown down on concrete.
Or will we be like children?
playing hatless, gloveless
in the snow,
not feeling cold,
not knowing of the world
or its significance.

All I know is this—
on our second trip together,
the boat becomes the water,
the ocean of all time.
From the shore, our families wave
and we wave back,
smiling billboards,
already only pictures of ourselves.
Down below in the cabins,
in stacked bunks,
strangers sleep,
dreaming of some god, good heart,
who will take us all in hand.
And if there is none?
Then we will have to help each other
and there, perhaps,
the good begins.

AUGUST IN MY NEIGHBOR'S GARDEN /
Jesse Lee Kercheval

1.
Fluff from the cottonwood
floats past your old roses,
lost wishes,
turning the lawn
into a feather bed.

Clouds come to earth
just for a visit.
We made skies like this
in kindergarten
with blue construction paper,
glue, little dabs
of cotton.

Take a picture,
you said. Keep it.
Next year
in it, we will look so young.

2.
You said Enid and Lou
didn't ask to be born starlings.
You, who were up
every night for weeks
feeding them worms
and fish meal. Remember?
I tucked a five
in your wallet
to buy crickets
from the bait store.

Outside, in your garden,
there are crows
big as cats. Black cats.
The kind of black
that makes me

want to say *Raven*.
But are they?

3.
Now, in your garden,
green apples fall,
turning the picnic table
into a drum,
startling a chipmunk
sleeping on your sundial.
They hide in the grass,
perfect, useless,
children who won't grow
up or old.

Where are you now,
I wonder?
The wisteria is blooming.
Only you could tell me,
*Oh honey, it always does
this time of year.*

WORLD AS DICTIONARY / *Jesse Lee Kercheval*

Book dog ball spoon
My daughter knows two dozen words,
common words,
and they are everywhere.

Up is her word for motion
up is up and down the stairs
up with her arms raised
is *carry me, Momma.*
And I do pick her up
make her part of me again.
From the seventh floor she sees
her father bundled pass below.
Hat, she says, *coat.* She's right.
He's hardly ever home.

Ope is her other verb,
Ope for open
doors, bottles, cans.
In the store she hands me
an apple. I turn it in my palm, faking.
No Ope, I say, shaking my head.
She looks at me,
one eyebrow raised—
All things ope.

And at home I do open it,
cut the apple with my knife,
give my daughter
the white true heart of it.
Her father isn't home yet,
hasn't called.
Ope ope ope, I say,
we live in hope.
My daughter claps her hands.

SINGING FOR UNCERTAIN SINGERS/
Jesse Lee Kercheval

Who am I? Your mother.
And who are you
but someone soft
slung across my chest,
puzzled by the sight
of breasts, smaller whiter
beasts than you,
clockfaces,
moonphase chronographs,
seeming to you as pointless
as they always have to me.
Until your mouth opens,
takes in a nipple,
purple with the waiting,
and milk takes us both
quite by surprise.
Warm and salted,
the stars should smell like this.
Each breast a moon,
a ladder to the sky,
each nipple a hole
through which the universe
is pouring. How could we
live without this? Happiness
our white garment to put on.
You nurse, you sleep,
and I sleep too,
and dream of tongues,
and dream of eating snow.

IN THE GARDEN WITH GREEN CHAIRS/
Jesse Lee Kercheval

Take this peace
that is offered you,
bird touching strange bird.
In the garden
near your heart
wisteria is blooming.
Huge white peonies,
last night tight as fists,
this morning
stagger open.

What does a garden
ask of you
but to open,
see what colors
you have missed.
To the dovecote
comes the very bird
it has waited for
a hundred years.
Beneath the lavender breast,
a soft heart,
beating.

And why does it beat,
a heart?
Except to close, to open,
each beat
a kind of blooming.
And what has a garden
to give? Except
a chance to rest,
to loose the cord
around your neck
you've been trying so hard
to tighten.

Listen,
your death would break
your poor heart's heart.
Be the bird,
be the garden
blooming.

Jesse Lee Kercheval is the author of two books of fiction and has a memoir, *Space,* forthcoming. Her poetry has appeared widely.

"It explodes at 10,000 feet, spreading copies of my poetry around the world. Beats the hell out of a small press, eh?"

STILL-HILDRETH SANATORIUM, 1936
/ *David Baker*

When she wasn't on rounds she was counting
the silver and bedpans, the pills in white cups,
heads in their beds, or she was scrubbing down

walls streaked with feces and food on a white-
wash of hours past midnight and morning, down
corridors quickened with shadows, with screaming,

the laminate of cheap disinfectant . . .
and what madness to seal them together, infirm
or insane, whom the state had deemed mad.

The first time I saw them strapped in those beds,
caked with sores, some of them crying
or coughing up coal, some held in place

with cast-iron weights . . . I would waken again.
Her hands fluttered blue by my digital clock,
and I lay shaking, exhausted, soaked cold

in soiled bedclothes or draft. I choked on my pulse.
I ached from the weight of her stairstep quilt.
Each night was a door slipping open in the dark.

Imagine, a white suit for gimlets at noon.
This was my Hollywood star, come to be lost
among dirt farmers and tubercular poor.

He'd been forgotten when the talkies took hold.
He saw toads in webs drooping over his bed.
O noiseless patient, his voice would quake.

He took to sawing his cuticles with butter knives
down to the bone and raw blood in the dark.
Then, he would lie back and wait for more drug.

And this was my illness, constant, insomnolent,
a burning of nerve-hairs just under the eyelids,
corneal, limbic, under the skin, arterial,

osteal, scrotal, until each node of the 400
was a pin-point of lymphic fire and anguish
as she rocked beside me in the family dark.

In another year she would unspool fabrics
and match threads at Penney's, handling finery
among friends just a few blocks from the mansion-

turned-sickhouse. She would sing through the war
a nickel back   a greenback   a sawbuck   a penny
and, forty years later, die with her only daughter,

my mother, to hold her, who washed her face,
who changed her bed gowns and suffers to this day
over the dementia of the old woman weeping

mama mama, curled like cut hair from the pain
of her own cells birthing in splinters of glass.
What madness to be driven so deep into self . . .

I would waken and find her there, waiting
with me through the bad nights when my heart
trembled clear through my skin, when my fat gut

shivered and wouldn't stop, when my liver swelled,
when piss burned through me like rope against rock.
She never knew it was me, my mother still says.

Yet what did I know in the chronic room where I died
each night and didn't die, where the evening news
and simple sitcoms set me weeping and broken?

I never got used to it. I think of it often,
down on my knees in the dark, cleaning up blood
or trying to feed them—who lost 8 children to the Flu,

who murdered her sisters, who was broken in two

by a rogue tractor, who cast off his name . . .
Sometimes there was nothing the doctor could do.

What more can we know in our madness than this?
Someone slipped through my door to be there
—though I knew she was a decade gone—

whispering stories and cooling my forehead,
and all I could do in the heritable darkness was
lift like a good child my face to be kissed.

FOR THE OTHERS / *David Baker*

It's almost nothing the way fireflies
flare every foot or so under wings
of grass on the calm lawns, like matchheads
struck down coarse cloth or stoplights blinking
blocks away green to gold on the slick street.
In answer each corresponds to the last.
Once I came to be cheek level to this earth.
I lay among others—still, glittering glass.
Dusk had gone down to dark and the usual,
slight traffic stalled into one strand
of a web dampened and lit like a slip
of moonlight up the long way to the sky.

I was flung from the wreck at the speed
of light. I closed my eyes, spinning with pain,
as I open them now drawn by small wings
from the grasses veined with my form.
They rise shining a few inches on fire.
They slip back on a breeze like a breath
to float through another blank moment
before lifting, before lighting, again—
such nearness to flight, such temptation to go.
How patient they are pulling their weight
from the grass to be ankle-, hip-, branch-
high mounting the treeline to the sky.

Once I wished my way back to the ground.
I belonged to the body asleep, hurt
in the white, crumpled grasses and glass.
So the bow hurls its arrow once again
and the dipper drains its portion of stars.
I stand in the lengthening yard where we fell,
mind and heart, sunset, and the dew
but a touch of damp air at dusk. Here
the first death like a shatter of carlight
speeds through the twilight and rain far away.
Here I am born in sweet grass as the others
take to their wings for the flight.

A RECESSIONAL / *David Baker*

Clear stars afoam
    on a black wave,
  a cold night—

we step from the old
    porch by ones
  and twos

over yards burned
    blue by ice during
  the viewing.

How quickly
    the family turns
  to itself with grief

—and how torn away,
    like ice-flecks
  in the cones

of each car's headlamps
    pulling out
  on the journey.

So soon the city,
    the trees, gone by
  in a blur.

We are
    part and parcel
  of a great recession,

souls in sequence
    bearing our dead
  on our backs

like relic radiation

from creation's
first blaze,

each of us, flung
off like froth,
scorching to ice

down the long highway—
out of the darkness,
into the dark.

THE ART OF POETRY / *David Baker*

This photograph of fog the small clearing gives up
to a late winter sky, gray gauze of exhaustion,

> this heat of old snows suddenly melting,
> or not-melting but given off as emanation,

the day above freezing for the first time in weeks . . .
she has left it here for me to find, the way

> the background trees, the high bleached sycamores
> ruined in snow-grain, hold the fog, will not let go.

It is her way of saying without saying what we know.
She was alone in the house—she went to these woods.

> Later, she lifted print after print to light,
> the fog of each photograph scaling gray to a cloud.

This was before we had exhausted ourselves
of ourselves. It freezes me to think of such care—

> to break through woods, out of haze, backwards,
> footprint by print, so her path fades into trees

as though she has gone there and not come back,
as though she is background, a granular, fierce fog

> the heat of piled snow cedes to hurt limbs.
> Once more I find her desire, to be doubled, to be
> here

and not-here, and not there. Now she steps backwards
out of bare trees, through the snow, and now back

> into the fog of the trees. She has left the picture
> for me to hold. She is fog given up to the trees.

David Baker is the author of four books of poems, including *Sweet Home, Saturday Night*.

THE DIARY OF LORENZO GREENE

Introduction

AT THE CLOSE OF THE 1930 Negro History Week celebration in Washington, D.C., Lorenzo Johnston Greene confessed to his diary that he had experienced a conversion. He said that the events of the final evening made him "a confirmed and dedicated associate" of Dr. Carter G. Woodson, the undisputed father of African American history. He pledged an even higher commitment to the Association for the Study of Negro Life and History, the organization founded by Woodson. "The Association," Greene said, "is indelibly stamped upon me. It is my cause and shall transcend everything else, even my allegiance to Woodson."

Greene was the last of a succession of bright young scholars whom Woodson nurtured and converted to the field of African American history. His life story is one of hardship, struggle, and dedication.

Woodson was born in rural Virginia on December 19, 1875, to parents who had been slaves and who struggled to support their nine children by farming. At twenty, he began high school and completed the work in one and a half years. After finishing high school, he entered Berea College in Kentucky, which at that time was still integrated, where all students paid their way by working on campus. In 1912, Woodson became only the second African American to earn a Ph.D. in history from Harvard University. The first was W. E. B. Du Bois, who received his degree from Harvard in 1895.

Woodson devoted his life to correcting misconceptions about the history of black people. On September 9, 1915, he and five other persons founded the Association for the Study of Negro Life and History (now the Association for the Study of Afro-American Life and History). In 1916, he began publishing the *Journal of Negro History;* in 1926, he began the celebration of Negro History Week, which has now become African American History Month; and in 1937, he began publishing the *Negro History Bulletin.* In addition to editing the *Journal* and the *Bulletin,* Woodson produced an impressive number of scholarly works. Before the publication of John Hope Franklin's *From Slavery to Freedom* in 1947, Woodson's *The Negro in Our History* was the standard general treatment of African American history.

At times Greene's dedication to Woodson the man was severely tested; however, he never wavered in his dedication to Woodson the scholar. Moreover, his devotion to the Association remained unshaken over the next almost six decades of his life. The immediate manifestation of this dedication and devotion was the bookselling odyssey Greene undertook to provide needed funds for the Association and to promote the study of

African American history. On June 21, 1930, Greene and three young men who were students at Howard University left Washington in a Model A Ford to sell books published by the Associated Publishers. Their tour took them through Virginia, North Carolina, a little of South Carolina, Tennessee, Georgia, Alabama, across the northeastern tip of Mississippi, and into Arkansas, Louisiana, Texas, Oklahoma, Missouri, Illinois, and Pennsylvania. Greene left an account of this journey in a diary he kept in a series of notebooks.

This was not a journey for the timid or the fainthearted. The South of the 1930s and, for that matter, of the next four decades, was not a place where four young African American men were expected to travel without encountering serious problems. The black press in 1930 and 1931 headlined lynchings and other acts of violence suffered by African Americans in both the South and the North.

In the diary, however, Greene expressed surprisingly few misgivings about encountering racial violence. He did inquire and record information about the climate of race relations at the places they visited. He also left vivid descriptions of the people, geography, and other attributes of the routes they traveled. Greene's diary, however, was much more than a travelogue. Before leaving Washington, he completed proofreading *The Negro Wage Earner*. Acutely sensitive to economic conditions in the South, he became on this journey one of the most knowledgeable scholars about economic conditions among African Americans at the advent of the Great Depression in 1930–1931.

When Greene and his fellow booksellers arrived in a town or city, their first contact was with black business and professional people. In many places, they could seek potential buyers through names, furnished by Woodson, of doctors, dentists, lawyers, and teachers who were in school at Howard University with him during his undergraduate years. Invariably, these men and women were suffering from the effects of the Depression, but most of them were cooperative.

Greene's life as a protégé of Woodson was not always easy. Woodson served as a role model because of his struggle for an education and his singular dedication to his cause. But various people described him as "arrogant," "cantankerous," and "domineering." While agreeing with this characterization, Greene found Woodson to be an extremely complex man, and throughout his life remained ambivalent in his attitude toward his mentor. He respected and admired Woodson as a scholar, and for the sacrifices he made in his struggle to preserve the African American past and to correct the myths and errors commonly found in American histories. This is what Greene and others labeled the "cause." On the other hand, Greene resented Woodson's patronizing attitude toward him and his failure to ever recognize him as a colleague.

Greene endured Woodson's bluntness and directness, often responding respectfully, but directly, to jabs taken by Woodson. Overall, the relationship was beneficial to both men. Greene contributed greatly to the support of the Association for the Study of Negro Life and History by selling books, spreading the gospel of "negro history," and helping to organize branches and negro history study clubs. In turn, Woodson helped to train Greene as a researcher, provided him with work, awarded him fellowships, and recommended him highly for jobs. Woodson obviously was quite fond of Greene and respected him.

Nevertheless, Woodson refused to give Greene the type of recognition he desired and always kept a certain distance between them. By 1931, Greene was becoming restless in this relationship and resentful that Woodson would not acknowledge him as a colleague and peer. This resentment came to a head over the authorship of *The Negro Wage Earner*. When Greene left Washington in July 1930, the book was ready to go to press, and the manuscript listed Greene as sole author. The published book, however, listed Greene and Woodson as coauthors. Greene wrote to Woodson in September expressing his resentment, and he poured out his bitterness to his friends.

This incident continued to poison the relationship between the men. Woodson, however, continued his usual patronizing behavior, seemingly oblivious of Greene's feelings, and Greene, like an unappreciated son, continued to seek the approval and recognition of the father. He also remained dependent upon Woodson for financial assistance. He confided to his diary, however, his antagonism toward his mentor and idol.

The Greene diary provides a rare case study of an African American who was maturing as a scholar in the 1930s. The teachers in African American schools—whether elementary, secondary, or college—were expected to behave with strict conformity. Those caught deviating from accepted conduct often found themselves without a job. Standards differed somewhat from community to community, but sexual misconduct was universally frowned upon. In most communities, African American women teachers were severely restricted in their social relations. They outnumbered men teachers, and few other men in the community were on their educational and social levels.

This situation was both a boon and a danger to Greene. He was educated, attractive, and adept at gaining the favor of young women. While he was ever aware of the danger to both his and the women's reputations, he developed relationships that went beyond the platonic with several young women. His greatest embarrassment probably came from Woodson's knowledge of his involvement with women while he was on the bookselling tour. After Greene returned to Columbia University, Woodson wrote: "We are getting various letters here from women who express their love in poetry and in fervent song. . . . We are holding these things here because we understand very clearly that you cannot give your attention to women and to song [and] at the same time study diligently."

Much about the South fascinated Greene, but he remained the consummate New Englander. He generally measured things Southern against things New England, and this outlook shaped his view of the South and those who lived there. He was a critical, albeit biased, observer of the black church, although churches were important sources of clients. Almost everyplace Green went he contacted ministers, hoping to be invited to address a congregation or church organization. By and large, Southern ministers were helpful even though, in many cases, they were struggling to survive as leaders of impoverished congregations. Even while profiting from their assistance, however, Greene was strongly critical of black ministers. His ideal minister was Vernon Johns, who was Martin Luther King, Jr.'s predecessor at Dexter Avenue Baptist Church in Montgomery, Alabama. Johns ranked with Mordecai Johnson and Howard Thurman as among the most distinguished African American preachers of the period. Johns was learned but unconventional. He abhorred emotionalism, favored the establishment of black businesses, and was an active opponent of discrimination.

Greene's views on the black church and its leaders received public attention in November 1930, when he went to Lynchburg, Virginia, to speak at Virginia Seminary, where Johns was president. While there, he delivered his speech on "unemployment among Negroes, its causes and its remedies" to an audience at the Court Street Baptist Church. This speech was based on observations made during his journey through the South. He described the displacement of black workers on farms, in hotels, in homes, as garbage collectors, and in other occupations traditionally reserved for them. The audience expected this kind of analysis, but, according to a newspaper account, it was not ready for what followed. Greene "astounded his listeners by asserting that the Negroes' own unreliability, lack of responsibility, want of training, and their general failure to take care of their jobs have all collaborated to drive [them] out of [their] customary employment."

His remedies were less disturbing: returning to the land to truck farm, patronizing black-owned businesses, and the creation of more black businesses. Greene voiced limited support for boycotting white businesses to gain more jobs for African Americans. He also called for restricting immigration.

Then, he again shocked his audience with a discussion of the black church. First, he called for a moratorium on the building of new churches and for diverting the money that would be used for this purpose into "productive channels by erecting factories and stores." Next, he recommended consolidating churches and selling some of the buildings to obtain capital to support businesses. The proliferation of churches, he said, constituted a "financial millstone about the neck of the race."

Although he was loath to admit it, Greene learned much from the African American ministers he criticized so vehemently. As the tour progressed, Greene became more and more adept at "preaching the gospel of Negro History." If he were permitted to address an audience, he was almost certain to sell some books. After an especially exhilarating experience before an audience preaching on the contributions of Africans to world civilization or the causes and remedies of unemployment among African Americans, he would confide to his diary, "I gripped them."

In September 1931, Greene returned to Columbia University to continue work on his doctorate. He completed the course work and passed the oral examination. In addition, he continued to sell books, to fill speaking engagements, and to serve Woodson and the "cause."

As the Depression deepened in 1933, Greene's financial situation became desperate. Woodson reminded him periodically how tight things were economically and informed him that things were also desperate with the Association. "If it were not for the fact that I am sacrificing every thing for the work," Woodson wrote in January, "we would have to close up." The sale of books remained Greene's only source of income. Many of those who subscribed for books were not able to pay the balance due and accept them when they arrived C.O.D. To add to his woes, Columbia University began dunning him for past due payments on a long-term loan the University made to him earlier. Then, in April, Harriet Coleman Greene, his mother, was hospitalized, and the family expected him to contribute toward the hospital expenses. His mother died in June. By this time, thanks to Woodson, Greene was offered a job teaching political science and history at Lincoln University.

Greene accepted the appointment and worked at Lincoln University for his entire teaching career. In spite of his personal and professional resentments against his mentor, he remained Woodson's loyal supporter and was always ready to serve the "cause."

Editors' Note

The following excerpts from Greene's diary of the bookselling trip, as well as the preceding introduction, are taken from *Selling Black History for Carter G. Woodson*, Arvarh E. Strickland, editor, to be published in the fall of 1996 by the University of Missouri Press. Our selection starts with a reminiscence by Greene, written some thirty years after his travels, of the genesis of the bookselling campaign. The actual diary excerpts cover the first four months of Greene's trip, and give a representative sampling of the kind of trials and successes he encountered. They begin with Greene's entries of June, 1930, detailing his group's departure from Washington D.C., and end with a description of his brief reunion with Woodson in Washington, prior to Greene's trip to Cleveland for the annual convention of the Association for the Study of Negro Life and History.

Because of the length and scope of the document, we have cut numerous passages that were repetitive or of lesser interest. What follows is a version of one part of Greene's diary. Scholars should refer to Strickland's more comprehensively annotated edition of the bookselling diary.

A T THE END of May [1930] Woodson suggested that I take a two-week vacation, then come in and talk with him upon my return. Having completed the study of Negro Employment in the District of Columbia,[1] I was happy to leave for New York.

Arriving in Washington at 2:30 p.m., I went directly to the office. Woodson was glad to see me and expressed the hope that I had got some much-needed rest. . . .

He then said he wanted to talk to me concerning the books of the Association, which were mildewing in the basement. . . . He asked whether I had any suggestions for disposing of them. I responded in the affirmative. "But how?" he asked, "I am sending out 2,000 letters a month advertising the books, but few orders come to [the] office as a result. Last fall, I paid Paul Miller $14.00 to train salesmen, but few or no books were sold." I remembered that all too well also.

"Mr. Greene," he went on, "how can we get the public to purchase these books?" I briefly recounted my experience with the Union Circulation Company of New York City three summers ago, when at the head of a team of four students, I sold magazines over approximately one-fourth of the country.

"Well?" he inquired.

In reply, I stated, "Do what the magazine companies do."

"What is that?" he snapped.

"Well, take some of your best books, figure the total price, then cut that price to the bone. Send out salesmen; they will sell books."

"What are you proposing?"

"Choose some of these books," I responded, "which would sell for about $18.50. My proposal is to strike a line through that figure and peg the new price at $9.98."

Woodson nearly collapsed. "Why, that's a giveaway," he exploded, "are you trying to ruin the Association?"

"Well, Dr. Woodson, the books are mildewing in the basement. . . . Paul Miller's plan failed and so did [Thomas] Georges's."

"How will the salesmen be paid?" he asked. "We don't have any money."

"You don't need money. The agents will collect their salary by

---

[1]Actually, Greene had just completed *The Negro Wage Earner* with Carter G. Woodson. The study of employment in the District of Columbia, which is covered in this part of the diary, was not conducted until 1931.

receiving 40 percent of the sales price. If they sell books, they eat; if they don't, they starve. But it will cost the Association nothing."

"Mr. Greene, you mean to tell me that . . . the salesmen will receive $4.00 and the Association will net only $5.98? And what assurance do I have that the Association will receive even that much?"

He bristled up so, I feared he would have a stroke.

"The $5.98 balance due will be collected C.O.D. by the postman when the books are received. In this way neither the subscriber nor the Association can lose. Especially will the Association be assured of its $5.98. It cannot lose."

Whether he was silenced or convinced, I did not know. Whatever the case, Woodson gave me a quizzical stare, then asked, "When can you start?"

"As soon as I can recruit a couple of salesmen and secure transportation," I replied.

Again that stare. "Transportation? What do you mean by transportation?"

"A car, an automobile, Dr. Woodson."

He just glared at me. "Well, I'll see what can be done," he said.

I left him and went to the Kappa [Alpha Psi] Fraternity House. There I was able to interest three students in selling books. [John Wesley] Poe and Noble Payton were glad to find some work for the summer after listening to my tale of the fun we had while selling magazines in 1927. Further, since they had no jobs, they had nothing to lose. The third chap, named [James Cecil] Wilkey, said he had a job on Lake Champlain that would earn him $200 a month. However, I was able to persuade him to forgo that employment for the opportunity of seeing the country, the possibility of making more than his job would pay him, and especially because of the people he would meet and the diversion that would be ours as we met students in the various towns and cities we would visit. Wilkey decided to go with us. All three promised to have surety for $100, which Woodson demanded.

When I returned to the office, lo, Woodson had bought a used Model A Ford. When I thanked [him], he advised me to take good care of it and by all means be careful on the road.

Saturday and Sunday June 21 and 22, 1930. [Al]though I had informed the fellows that we would leave at 3:00 a.m., they actually set the alarm on their clock for 4:05. It went off with considerable racket at that time.

Within five minutes we were off. Filled the car with gas. The trip to Richmond gave us our first thrill. We also had an opportunity to behold the stately Potomac in its most beautiful dress. Dawn was just breaking as we left Washington. And as we crossed the Long Bridge a most gorgeous panorama engaged the eye on every side. Above, the mist was rising, disclosing an azure sky from which the stars vanished one by one. Clouds, varying in color from dark blue to white, scudded heavenly eastward. On both sides spread the green-clad banks of the river, rising in verdant grandeur until they lowered their heads under the weight of the horizon. And between this, the river. Never have I seen it more beautiful. It glistened even though there was neither moon nor sunlight to illumine it. It was placid, calm, silvery. It almost appeared wintry. Whatever it was, it evoked exclamations of rhapsody from us all.

Leaving this behind we attended to the serious business of getting to Richmond. Wilkey, who was driving, not only failed to impress me as a driver, but even frightened me at times. He . . . evinced a marked tendency to run off the road. . . . Once Wilkey dozed, ran off the road, brought the car back, and zigzagged to such an extent that I bade him give over the wheel to me. He assured me, of course, that he was awake, that the fault lay in the unevenness of the road. It reminded me of [Sidney] Wells[2] in 1927.

Trying to pass between a parked car and a bus traveling downhill on his left, he ran into the former. Why he did not stop in order to avoid it is a mystery. The owner of the car, however, a Maryland poor white, was in good humor, evidently, for he assured us that outside of a dent in his fender, his car was unhurt. Did not even ask to see our license. Our fender was bent a trifle. Wilkey blamed the man. True, he was technically at fault because he had parked on a state highway. But I blamed Wilkey.

Reached Richmond without further ado about 7:30. . . . I became conscious of our wretched financial condition. Went to Slaughter's Cafe for breakfast. I ordered cereal, fruit, bacon and eggs, and milk. The other fellows followed suit, Wilkey, however, getting ham instead of bacon. The proprietor had no fruit. Could scarcely believe this was the Slaughter's Cafe of 1927, when we could order almost anything within reason and get it. After the meal three of the fellows, I find, are absolutely penniless. One, Payton, had $2.00. The total bill was $3.15. I had to pay for Wilkey and LaGrone; Payton for Poe. I was astounded, as well as provoked, for had I known that the boys were in such pressing straits, I should never have left Washington until Monday. I was

---

[2]Sidney Wells and Greene traveled together during the summer of 1927 selling magazines for the Union Circulation Company.

---

left with $2.50. By the time I bought gas and oil, only 80 cents remained.

Not only did lack of money plague us but tire trouble was soon added. The rear right tire, we discovered, had a break on the side, evidence of rottenness. Not far from Richmond, it went flat. We had to put on the spare tire, which, if it lasts for 100 miles, will certainly surprise me. In addition, we had no pump in the car. The Ford agent certainly made a fool of us. We ought to have been outfitted with new tires all around.

We reached Hampton without further trouble, tired, sleepy, and hungry, at 2:00 p.m.

It had been an otherwise enjoyable ride through historic Fredricksburg, where remains the only slave auction block in the United States, past the home of [Mary] Washington,[3] mother of George; the spot also where he supposedly threw a silver dollar across the river; the law office of James Monroe; and the beautifully terraced battleground of Fredricksburg.[4] It is as near Colonial in architecture as Alexandria, perhaps even more so.

Richmond on her seven hills reminds me of the Eternal City. Two rivers, the Rappahannock and the James, flow through it. . . . Many of the Negroes have beautiful homes, especially on East Leigh and East Clay streets. There is considerable Negro business here—insurance companies, [a] building and loan, grocery stores, drug stores, and the like. Many Negroes also work in the industries here, especially the tobacco factories. Others find employment in flour mills, iron factories, and in common labor. Most of the women, except those in tobacco factories, are domestics.

One cannot but be shocked at seeing the wretched hovels tenanted by many Negroes in the heart or outskirts of this great city . . . . Their inmates seem coarse, vulgar, and ignorant. Most of those seen by us were black Negroes. They were untidy, unclean, and careless even to exposing their persons. Of course this applies only to the rougher, more illiterate element of the Richmond Negro population. Most of the streets upon which they live are unpaved. In many of them the toilet accommodations and water are on the outside.

[3]Here Greene had confused the names of George Washington's mother and wife. The house in Fredericksburg belonged to Washington's mother, Mary Ball Washington.

[4]The Union Army of the Potomac commanded by General Ambrose E. Burnside was defeated by Confederate forces under General Robert E. Lee at Fredericksburg on December 13, 1862. This was one of the bloodiest battles of the Civil War, with Union casualties numbering over twelve thousand and Confederate losses at about five thousand.

Finally called upon Capt. Brown at his home. Greeted me affably. . . . Told him of the book campaign. Asked whether he could lodge my four men. Replied he would be glad to do so, but the incoming of 300 ministers to their Annual Conference would make it a little difficult. But Capt. Brown is such an excellent man that he made room for the boys by putting extra cots in the summer students' rooms in order to accommodate them. He asked whether I desired a room. Told him at first that I was going to Suffolk. Finally, decided to remain here. Each of us bunked with three fellows.

Frankly, I am disappointed in today's outcome. I had hoped to arouse interest in the work in all the larger tidewater cities such as Norfolk, Portsmouth, Suffolk, and Newport News, by sending a man to each of them. Because of lack of funds, however, I was unable to do this and thus open the way for a good start on Monday.

Incidentally, I went to chapel along with Poe, LaGrone, and Payton. . . . This is a good time to take stock of my companions. Poe is a gentleman, tall, spare, and exceedingly lean of face. He is of a reddish hue. A most agreeable companion, well read, soft spoken, a good conversationalist, and possessing an engaging personality. He is a lady's man; more truthfully, the ladies admire him easily. He has just received his B.A. degree and will study law at Winchester. Is self made. Both mother and father died when he was a child.[5] Is of the irrepressible type.

In contrast to Poe, there is Payton. Noble Payton! What an uncommon name for a Negro. He wears the cognomen well, is tall, reserved, almost to an extreme. Where Poe is buoyant, he is coldly calculating. He is refined, soft spoken, an excellent talker, so I hear, a logical reasoner, and very careful about his sartorial appearance. His reserve is accentuated by the fact that he wears glasses and rectangular ones at that. He comes of a good New Jersey family. Expects to specialize in

---

[5]This statement is contradicted by information contained in entries made in August 1930. John Wesley Poe was from Huntsville, Alabama, and a later entry in Greene's diary has an account of his visit to the home of Poe's mother and stepfather there. Poe completed a Bachelor of Science degree in Howard University's College of Liberal Arts in 1930. Although he left the bookselling campaign before the end of the tour, later in 1930 he rejoined Greene in Philadelphia. He remained in Philadelphia after Greene left in early 1931.

[6]Noble Frank Payton received the Bachelor of Science degree from Howard University in 1931 and the Master of Arts in chemistry from Howard in 1934. He taught chemistry at Howard and several other institutions. He also served as plant manager of the Suburban Chemical Company (Julian Laboratories) in Franklin Park Illinois, and president of PharmChem Corporation in Chicago. From 1953 to 1964, he was director of Development at Meharry Medical College, and in 1964, he became Director of Alumni Affairs at Howard.

law at Harvard. He lacks stick-to-itiveness, according to Poe, and is easily dismayed. He and the latter are good friends.[6]

Still another picture is presented by LaGrone. A fine physical type of fellow such as football coaches would like to grace their teams. Heavily built, strong muscled, and heavy jawed, he could also perhaps be mistaken for a prize fighter. . . . But there are two qualities that stand out prominently in him. He has initiative, plenty of it, he is irrepressible; and he has guts. He ought to make a good salesman under a little coaching. He is an Oklahoman and expects to become a lawyer. Is a junior at Howard U. Complexion brown.[7]

Last but not least comes Wilkey, the fellow whom I persuaded to relinquish a $200-a-month job on Lake Champlain to come with me. Wilkey is the youngest of all. Just 21. Very dark, not good looking, with reddish eyes. He has great initiative and is a hard worker. . . . Lacks polish, but underneath this rough exterior, I believe that there lies true mettle.[8]

Tuesday, June 24, 1930. Rose 6:45. Wrote in diary until 8:00. . . . Had to go to Hampton City, thereafter, for breakfast. Best available place was wretched. Full of flies and, as usual in Negro places, no fruit nor cereal. Just bacon and eggs. Did not even give me butter. When it was finally brought, it cost me a dime extra. May Allah shrive me! Could not enjoy my meal. The flies ate as much as I. Finally, had to go across the street and get a pint of milk and some raw prunes. If my stomach can stand up under this, I'll live to a ripe old age.

The Ministers' Conference is really a nuisance. Some few take it seriously. Most, however, regard it as a pleasure or sight-seeing trip.

---

[7] This and subsequent comments about Clarence Oliver LaGrone show that Greene failed to recognize a kindred creative spirit in this young man. LaGrone was born in McAlester, Oklahoma, on December 9, 1906. He did not return to Howard after participating in the bookselling campaign. He earned a Bachelor of Arts degree from the University of New Mexico in 1938. In addition, he studied at Wayne State University and the Cranbrook Art Academy. He became a teacher, sculptor and poet. He taught in the Detroit Public Schools and at Pennsylvania State University. His sculptures include pieces on George Washington Carver, Langston Hughes and Nelson Mandela. His published works include *Dawnfire and Other Poems* (1989), and his poetry has appeared in several anthologies. In 1992, when the editor interviewed LaGrone by telephone at his home in Hamlet, North Carolina, the octogenarian was still actively exhibiting his works and lecturing.

[8] James Cecil Wilkey was born on September 16, 1908, in Morristown, Tennessee. His father, Thomas W. Wilkey, was a barber there. In 1930 he transferred to Howard University from Morristown College. He remained with Greene to the end of the tour in 1930. In 1933 he returned to Howard for two semesters and took courses in commerce, but he did not complete a degree there.

When Dr. [James H.] Dillard[9] was speaking this morning, fully one-half the ministers were absent. Many were playing croquet, others were visiting or sight-seeing in Norfolk or Portsmouth, while a goodly number of others sat on the lawn either flirting with the summer school teachers or arguing trivial biblical points.

Spoke to the ministers at 2:30. Supposed to have five minutes. Took nine. The topic of the conference, "How to Keep Youth in the Church," afforded me an opportunity to tell them the truth about youth's growing failure to attend or support the church. I gave the findings of our survey of 1928. Told them youth itself was dissuaded from going to church for three reasons. First, that the Negro Church had failed to keep pace with worldly progress; second, that the church still frowned upon such innocent diversions as dancing, card-playing, and theater-going; and third, that the church was giving youth an impractical doctrine—one that's like a brand new suit, [which] could only be used on Sunday. I explained that youth was tired of being taught to die or of being preached into heaven or hell. He wanted to be taught how to live. Told them also that youth should be given a place in the church to demonstrate its talents. This could be consummated by organizing church clubs like Negro History clubs, dramatic clubs, poetry clubs, musical clubs, etc. In this way, youth would be kept in the Church, also, [that] the cause of Negro History would be served. I also explained that the books we were selling were admirably adapted to such uses and exhorted the ministers to see me and purchase them.

Whatever my talk did, it aroused such a storm of debate among the ministers that I feared I had wrecked the meeting. Led by Dr. [A. G.] Galvin of Newport News [pastor of First Baptist Church], a fiery dispenser of the gospel of the Old School, many of the ministers swore that they would not let down the bars in order to keep their young people in the church. . . . Then, others sought to minimize the problem by stating that they had difficulty in getting the old people into the church. . . . Old Galvin, a crusader, if ever there was one, took the floor again and waxed so eloquent against what I had said that I felt like congratulating him (only for his oratorical ability, however).

Against this determined stand of the conservative older preachers stood the younger, more intelligent, and the more liberal older preachers. . . . For half an hour the struggle waxed in intensity. I finally had to leave in order to get a little milk. I had not eaten since early

---

[9] James H. Dillard was president of the Anna T. Jeanes Fund and the John F. Slater Fund. His topic for the conference was "The Kingdom of Heaven."

morning and had a splitting headache. I smiled as I reached the outside, knowing full well that I had precipitated the storm.

To my surprise, however, the argument soon turned out to my advantage. When I returned to the campus, the ministers were just leaving the meeting. Some of them spied me and after congratulating me, asked to see the books. One said, "If these books will keep my people in the church, let me have them." In a half hour, with the aid of Wilkey and LaGrone, we had sold 12 sets of books. For such a result, I would gladly start another argument. Poe and Payton sold two sets each in Hampton. It was a fine day for the exchequer.

Tonight was beautiful. Never have I seen the stars so near the earth. They seemed to be just above the tree tops. There was no moon and the stars were so thick and so clear that they appeared like gold dust scattered over the blue-domed heaven. And the campus, now hidden save for the tower of the chapel, seemed so restful, so quiet. There is almost something inviting in the very atmosphere, something that seems to call to one's soul. It gripped me so until all unawares I found myself stretching forth my arms to the star-bedecked heavens, as if to pluck down a handful of its precious jewels.

Friday, June 27, 1930. Awoke at 6:30 this morning. Beautiful, brilliant morning. Took the car to the Hampton garage. Had it greased, the horn fixed, and [the] flat tire repaired. Went through Hampton tailor shop. Surprised at the fine work done by the students. A German teacher is in charge.

On the way to Suffolk, I picked up two white men who hailed me for a ride as I was going across the James River Bridge. Unthinking of the hazard, I picked them up. One sat beside and the other behind me. It was only after I had admitted them that I felt the imbecility of giving them a ride. So many tales of violence done to sympathetic motorists had reached my ears. And I was alone with them on a bridge 4 1/2 miles long stretching over a vast expanse of water. It was a high bridge and as far as I could see I was the only motorist on it. How easy it would have been for them to have slugged me and thrown my body into the river. I stepped on the gas and traveled at 60 miles an hour until I reached the crossroads going to Norfolk and Suffolk. Arrived there; I presume my guests were as glad to be rid of me as I of them.

Sunday, June 29, 1930. This was one of the busiest days I have yet experienced. At 9:30 I spoke before the Sunday School at the African Methodist Episcopal Church on Pine Street; from there, I visited the Lakeview Baptist Church in Saratoga. The audience ranged from the most illiterate to school teachers. Here I made my best effort so far. Brought forth a series of amens and applause from the audience by recounting the achievements of the race. . . . One man asked me whether I had any pamphlets that I could leave with him. Told me that the books were too long for him to read.

From the Lakeview Baptist Church, I rushed to the First Baptist. Spoke 15 minutes, although Rev. Williams told me I could have only 7 1/2 minutes. The sermon was delivered by a Reverend [P. D.] Price of Danville, Virginia. He is a powerful speaker, philosophical, yet practical. His sermon was so gripping that it fascinated me. Then he spoiled it by an impassioned appeal to the emotions that started the church shouting.

Left soon afterwards for Belleville. Arrived at 6:00 p.m. This is the home of the Church of God and the Saints of Christ. They have a remarkable place . . . . The Bishop, Father Abraham ([William Henry] Plummer), was playing tennis. Told me his son would attend to the business. The latter, Howard,[10] a law graduate, took an entire set and then two extra books, giving me a $6.00 deposit.

Although this colony has its own oyster beds and farms, they will plant no crops this year. It is their custom to let the ground lie fallow for an entire season every seven years. They put aside enough of the crops from the preceding harvest to last over that period. Potatoes are dried, fruits likewise; vegetables are canned; and every means known concerning the preservation of food is taken to enable the colony to experience this seven[th] year non-planting custom without hardship . . . . Not only is this a remarkable plant, city lighting, engineering, and boat system, it has the best buses in Virginia. Here also are located the finest tennis courts owned by Negroes in the state and among the best in the country. So much so that the Negro state tennis tournament will take place here in a few weeks. They have a permanent judges' stand erected, something that the others lack.[11]

Sunday, July 6, 1930. At 5:15 a.m. . . . we were thundering over the

---

[10] Howard Zebulun Plummer (1899–1975) was born the same year as Greene. He succeeded his father as head of the church in 1932 and was succeeded by his son, Levi Solomon Plummer, in 1975.

[11] Bishop William H. Plummer received some unwelcome attention in the press in 1930, shortly before Greene's visit. A disgruntled former minister, E.T. Yancy, charged that Plummer was living extravagantly, while others at the Belleville colony received only the bare necessities of life. P. Bernard Young, Jr., son of P.B. Young, publisher of the *Norfolk Journal and Guide,* went to Belleville to interview Plummer. His description of the operation agrees with Greene's, and Young was equally impressed with Plummer as head of the church.

roads to North Carolina with Rocky Mount our first objective. It lay about 60 miles away.

The morning was cool; the sky overcast by clouds. But the scenery was beautiful and the roads excellent. Extensive farms or plantations stretched along both sides of the road. The fields were green with growing cotton, sweet potatoes, corn, and tobacco. This is especially a tobacco section.

In the midst of these plantations stood the large, well painted home of the planter. Dotted hither and thither, like soiled spots on a white tablecloth, appeared the huts of the Negro tenants—unpainted, windowless in many instances, and most of them containing one room. Where the windows had been, they were effectively replaced by boards, which not only shut out the air but the light as well. It's no wonder these people die of consumption and other diseases. In other cases, the windows are stuffed with burlap, calico dress remnants, paper, or any other material that happened to be at hand.

These cabins are of the "shotgun" type. There are two doors—one front and one rear—and when both are open one can stand in front of the hut and look into the backyard. In front of these hovels grew the gardens of the tenants, for the planter usually allows them a half acre or sometimes an acre to grow vegetables or whatnot for their families.

Living conditions naturally are terrible. These people with no other diversion except sex naturally have large families. In one instance, I saw eight children ranging in ages, it appeared to me, from 3 to 17, emerging from one of these one-room affairs. In another instance, we could see the inmates still asleep in their shack—men, women, and children, lying about indiscriminately, and with only the privacy that one room could give them. Such conditions as these naturally keep the moral tone at low ebb.

A considerable number of Negroes, however, own fairly large farms. Some are well kept; others show lack of attention. Some of these farmers with their families were working their crops on Sunday. They undoubtedly were small farmers, who work on the white plantations during the week and tend their own plots of ground at their only possible opportunities—Sundays and holidays. Their crops are chiefly cotton, tobacco, sweet potatoes, and corn. I saw one or two cows on such farms, but they were thin and obviously underfed. Nine prosperous farmers had well painted houses and some of them sat smoking on their verandas or reading their Bibles.

Left [John Wesley] Poe in Rocky Mount. Consigned him to the tender mercies of the people, for Poe was penniless. And I had naught to give him for I had spent my money buying gas, etc. . . . . Took LaGrone to Tarboro, about 18 miles east of Rocky Mount. Admit the town did not look any too inviting. Put LaGrone in the charge of a deacon of the St. Paul Baptist Church and left him with instructions to meet me in Rocky Mount Tuesday at 6:00 p.m.

Wilkey and I then continued the 27 miles to Greenville, another important tobacco mart, to the south. Arrived in Greenville. We were shown to the reverend gentleman's home by the chief of police. Disappointed in the worthy reverend's dwelling from outside appearances. On a dirt street (Clarke)—a straggling house, one story that smacked more of a store than a dwelling. Down in a hollow, too. Instinctively, I rebelled against such quarters. The worthy divine came to the door. He was fat, black, and sweating profusely. "Sorry, I cannot invite you in. Place not suitable, for my wife is away. Have you eaten? No, then you can find a good place over near my church," pointing across the way . . . . Told him I was tired, hungry, and dirty, after a four hour drive, and desired to wash up. Referred me to a Mrs. Wilkinson, who took in boarders. I was disgusted. Felt like going back to Rocky Mount. Nevertheless, went over to find Mrs. Wilkinson. When I saw her, I immediately knew that I could not stay at her home. She was ugly, black, untidy, ignorant. She relieved me by stating that all her rooms were occupied, leaving nothing but the parlor divan, which I could use. I hastily refused.

In our attempt to find Rev. Nimmo, I happened upon a man who was to mean more to me than anyone else in the town . . . . He turned out to be Professor [G. R.] Whitfield, the supervisor of the rural schools of the county in which Greenville is located.

How hospitable Mr. Whitfield was. Took me to his home and after learning that my stomach did not permit me to eat the sort of fare common here, sent out his son to get me what I desired. He himself boiled the eggs. The first were too hard, but on the next attempt they proved to be just right. He then made me some toast, and with [this and] a glass and a half of milk, my appetite was immediately satisfied. He just killed me with kindness. His wife had gone to her church in the country, and he begged me to make myself at home, which I proceeded to do. Invited me also to stop with him. He has a large home not sumptuously furnished, but clean. There are eight of the largest rooms I have ever seen and all on one floor.

When I finally cleaned up, shaved, and was ready to go, it was ten minutes to twelve. Mr. Whitfield was kind enough to get one of the deacons to take me to the church [York Temple African Methodist Episcopal Zion Church]. It turned out to be a brick affair, about half completed. Church services were held in the basement. The church itself, when completed, will be a good sized edifice capable of seating about 500. When I arrived, the pastor, Rev. Shaw, was in the midst of his sermon. . . . After puffing, blowing, and finally leading up to a crescendo of apostrophes on heaven, Shaw fumbled about in a hymnal until he secured a song to his liking. Having done so, he first recited— as in the old Greek chorus—the words while his rapt listeners chanted the tune after him.

He then attempted to introduce me, but could not remember my name. . . . I merely acquainted the people with the origin, purpose, and achievements of the Association and bade them come out tonight with pencil and paper and I would try to give them something to think about.

Left to speak at Rev. Nimmo's Church. Only a handful at the B.Y.P.U. [Baptist Young People's Union] meeting. After speaking I demonstrated to the young people the various points of interest in the books. Persuaded a young fellow named Norcott to take a set. He plays the organ here. [He] took them for his sister. It was a godsend to sell him, for otherwise, I would have been virtually destitute in this town, with only 50 cents. Rev. Nimmo promised to see me tomorrow.

Returned to Mr. Whitfield's and changed my clothes preparatory to speaking at Rev. Shaw's church. Somehow, I was filled with misgivings. Mr. Whitfield's son, a fine young fellow, accompanied me there. Had to walk since Wilkey had the car.

Arrived at the church, found it dark. [It] had not even been opened. A few people sat outside who assured me that, although most people did not come to church at night, they were sure to get here about 8 o'clock. . . . Finally went in about 8 o'clock. Rev. Shaw, limping and sweating, came puffing in about 8:30, giving me profuse excuses for his delay. There were about seventy-five people in the church when I started to speak. These had increased to 100 before I finished.

Spoke about 50 minutes. What I said about the Negro . . . either must have interested them or they were mighty fine actors. They interrupted me several times with applause. Dr. Shaw then made a stirring appeal to the people to show their appreciation for the information that I had brought to them. I sold several sets of books. Received $12.00 for myself. Shaw embarrassed me. Asked for contributions for me as I sat on the platform. Collected $14.00 for me. [He] later gave it to me wrapped in [a] paper napkin. I put it in my pocket. When I got home, I found I had but 85 cents, mostly in pennies.

Monday, July 7, 1930. It was terrifically hot today. The temperature must have been well over 100 degrees. It was 110 degrees in Rocky Mount.

After breakfast, I met Mrs.[M.P.?] Evans, wife of a former bricklayer, who told me of the extreme poverty of the people here. . . . Many destitute children are forced to resort to eating out of garbage pails. . . . The town, she said, is totally dependent upon work in the tobacco factories, but since last Christmas there has been almost no work.

Some of the owners have taken care of their help since that time, but in what way? By raising the funds from the meager salaries of those poor Negroes who are working and donating it as their own gift. In this manner, Person and Garrett, one of the largest tobacco factories, raised $300 last winter and distributed it among the starving Negroes. The richest man in the town, Mr. Flanagan, who works 500 Negroes, also secured $500 in this manner, yet donated it as his personal gift. Such a thing would be unheard of in the North, where men of wealth know how to give money. They have not only a civic, but a humane spirit.

What a terrible predicament in which the professional class of Negroes now find themselves! With the Negro masses unable to find employment, consequently they lack means of paying the doctor, dentist, and preacher. This was reflected in my attempts to sell these people. Dr. [W. M.] Capehart was not at home. He was playing checkers somewhere. Better this than worrying, or to sit idly in his office, or to attend persons without prospects of remuneration.

Called upon Drs. [J. A.] Battle and [Archibald L.] Banks. The former is a doctor, the latter a dentist. Both were out.

Went home to a dinner of string beans, milk, and graham crackers. After dinner Mr. Whitfield's sons came in. One had worked all day stripping tobacco leaves from the stalk; the other handing tools to a mechanic. The former received $2 a day for backbreaking work, the latter 50 cents a day. Meager wages, but better than nothing.

Wednesday, July 9, 1930. Made preparations for trip to Raleigh. Went to Rev. Battle's [in Rocky Mount] to pay the fellows' bill. Felt he should have had nothing for tricking me in the first instance. Had to borrow money from Wilkey to pay him. Charged them $5. Took boys to hotel to breakfast. En route, Poe showed me fried potato cakes he had taken from the table in order to give the impression that he had eaten them. They were sour, the potatoes having been cooked Sunday. En route to hotel to buy milk, found it impossible to do so. Could only buy it at the drug store, 25 cents a quart. A & P clerk told me this was the first time that a grocery store could not sell milk. Forbidden on account of typhus fever raging. Had to buy shredded wheat, milk, and bananas to help out breakfast. Negro restaurants don't have such things.

Return to house. Went downtown. Relations between races good here.

Friday, July 11, 1930 [Raleigh]. After breakfast this morning . . . I called upon Mr. Trigg. Failed to find him in, however. Wanted to secure his frank opinion upon my talk of last night. Mr. Dickinson, his secretary, took me over to the office of Mr. Newbold, the Secretary of the Board of Education [State Agent for Negro Education]. A very splendid man. His greeting was just as cordial as a Negro could expect to receive from any Northern white man and, if anything, perhaps more genuine.

I congratulated him upon the fine work his state was doing in behalf of Negro education. Told him truthfully that throughout the length and breadth of the country people looked at North Carolina as the foremost commonwealth in its attempt to enlighten its Negro citizens. To this Mr. Newbold responded that the work had not yet reached the goal for which they had set out, but he felt some little progress had been made. Even now he was busy preparing a report for Hoover's Child Commission Study, which is to take place later in the month. He showed me a large collection of data from South Carolina, Mississippi, and North Carolina—all of which he must read and incorporate in his report.[12]

I finally brought the conversation to the subject in which I was most interested, namely the possibility of getting some of our publications upon the North Carolina supplementary reading list. In this connection I suggested *African Myths*. Here, I told Mr. Newbold, was a fine collection of 36 folk tales, handed down by word of mouth for generations by these people. Not only are they charmingly told and carefully selected for children from the third to the fourth grades, but they contain no reference whatsoever as to race and, therefore, could be read and enjoyed by whites and blacks as well.

I asked Mr. Newbold had Dr. Woodson sent him a copy. He did not know, saying that he receives so many publications that he has little chance to do more than acknowledge their receipt. However, upon glancing at his book cases—one of which contained only books dealing with the Negro—I saw that he did have a copy. I took it down and asked him to look through it. He seemed to be agreeably impressed, so much so that he told me if Dr. Woodson could reduce the price from $1.00 to 60 or 75 cents he would urge upon the school board its acceptance.

---

[12] Newbold chaired the section on Negro Schools of the Committee on The School Child.

After such an encouraging beginning I then turned to the only other of our publications that could be used in the grades. This was the *Negro Makers of History*, an elementary version of *The Negro in Our History*, suitable for children from the 6th to the 9th grades. Mr. Newbold agreed that the books ought to be in the system for Negroes, and added that, as in the case of *African Myths*, it would be necessary to reduce the price somewhat in order to bring it within the buying power of the Negro family. . . . I promised to write Dr. Woodson asking his best terms, then to communicate with him. He advised me to do so, stating that he would urge their adoption upon the school board in case the reductions were made.

Thursday, July 24, 1930. After breakfast, we began a systematic canvas of Charlotte. LaGrone, the ambler, was assigned to the district called Brooklyn, where live the largest number of Negroes. Most of them are poor people, yet since there is no exclusive residential section here for Negroes as in Winston-Salem or Durham, he ought to at least make two sales. Allotted the professional men to Poe. He will sell them if they possibly can be sold. Payton, I took with me. LaGrone could not conceal his chagrin at the territory given him, but it was far better than to have him roaming at large, spoiling sales. Instructed him to remain in his territory, yet I assured Poe and Payton that within twenty minutes he would be in the Negro business and professional building.

What a stupid fellow. And just will not accept information. Has an inflated ego that needs puncturing if he is ever to make any success in life. At the breakfast table he entered into an argument with Payton on what is knowledge. It was induced when he began bringing in the argument of the behavioristic school of psychology to settle an argument. . . . He has read a little psychoanalysis by that popular bamboozler, Andre Tridon, and being unable to discriminate the probable true from the false . . . has accepted verbatim what he has taken in. I tried, by analogy, to point out that no man was fit to discuss a subject or to form his point of view until he had familiarized himself with every possible angle from which the subject is, or might be, presented. He then changed the point at issue . . . by saying that any science of knowledge was derived from actual physical experiences with concrete images. Although all of us tried to show him the error in his reasoning, he was finally more silenced than convinced. . . . He just will not listen, always thinks someone is trying to disparage him. . . . Sometimes, I believe he is nothing more than a first class moron.[13]

---

[13] Many years later, when editing a transcription of this entry, Greene added to it: "God forgive me! Maybe *I* am the stupid one."

En route back up town, I noticed white men working on the streets. There was only one Negro among them. In the large hotels and restaurants on North Trade Street, the chief business highway here, white girls performed nearly all of the work as waitresses. In only one large restaurant did I see Negro waiters. Even in the Greek places, white girls are used. These people come in from the hills and work almost as cheaply as Negroes. Yet, they are displacing the latter because the white man cannot generally bear the sight of his own race idling while the Negro works. Then, too, in many instances, white girls give better service, are more reliable and even neater than the Negroes. Moreover, the whites like to be waited upon by them. This situation is truly remarkable and manifests clearly the abolition of racial lines in occupations caused by the necessity of earning bread and butter.

Later in the afternoon, I called upon Dr. C. E. Davis. . . . An elderly man of about sixty-two—small, very fair and a fine conversationalist. He taught chemistry, physics, and biology at Johnson C. Smith[14] here for 35 years and proudly exhibits a physics textbook that he used as a student and that he subsequently employed in his courses. It is an old and rare edition printed in 1813 by an English publishing house. The author was a certain Hulton. The book was used at the Royal Academy in London. . . . In Mr. Davis's opinion, specialization is ruining the young people. . . . I ventured to suggest that they were victims of the present universal demand for men who can do one thing and do that well. In other words, training today is intensive rather than extensive. He agreed but felt that the old fellows could put us to shame insofar as all-around information is concerned. I agreed with him.

He felt that the Negro's salvation lay in developing experiences that would give employment to his own group. Deplored the trend of industrial schools away from the original purpose to become more and more academic institutions. Cited Hampton and Tuskegee as outstanding examples. Felt also, even as I, that manual training in this machine age as taught in Negro industrial schools is a waste of time. . . . Felt that the Negroes should have two great technical schools comparable to Massachusetts Institute of Technology. . . . Told me of the loss of several occupations—such as street cleaning, garbage and scavenger collecting—throughout North Carolina by Negroes.

---

[14] Johnson C. Smith University was founded in 1867 by the Board of Missions of the Presbyterian Church in the United States as Biddle University. The name was changed to Johnson C. Smith University in 1923. In 1926–1927, the school had a college enrollment of 211 and a faculty of fourteen.

Tuesday, July 29, 1930. Immediately after breakfast, Reverend King took me to see some of his members. His theory is [the] "big" Negro will argue with you and always cry broke; the "little" Negro will buy and think you are doing him a favor to take up time with him; the big Negro thinks he's doing you a favor. First one was a Mrs. Powell. She pleaded broke. The second was a Mrs. Bolding, a woman of fair intelligence but who has a son and daughter in school. Sold her on the strength of her buying inspiration for her children that they could not get in school.

Went to a Mr. Rackins, a common laborer. Owns his home. Sold them also, after telling them of the glory of Negro History. These were the "little Negroes." The "big Negroes" . . . gave me much talk. They had books or could not make out check without the consent of husband.

Poe and Kilgore returned at 5:10 p.m. Made nothing. Doctors' offices burned down last night in Spartanburg. Bad roads, bad "crackers." Negroes in condition of squalor. Fine farms worked by Negroes.

Lunchroom expensive. Had to send out for eggs, bacon, and bread as ordered.

I made $10 in Hendersonville. A life saver for me.

Got lonely. Dressed for speech at West Asheville. Went to party. Girls and fellows came by for me. Miss Michael, H____ and Howell. Left. Went by Miss Michael's. Late for talk. People leaving. They returned. Made most effective speech yet. People applauded forever. After that another party. Met charming Miss Howell. Attracted me as no other girl has on trip. Almost persuaded her to leave Wilkey. Charmed by a Miss Hightower of Memphis, also.

Saturday, August 2, 1930, Nashville. Before leaving, I spied Dr. [William Jasper] Hale[15] sitting on his porch reading the morning paper. He was comfortably attired in BVDs and a robe. Went over and thanked him for his hospitality. Told me he was glad to help out in this little measure. Congratulated him upon the fine school of which he is president. . . . I pointed out the many fine buildings and the beauty of the grounds as concrete proof of his great work here. He told me that it had been a difficult struggle; whites and blacks had fought him, the whites because they felt that the school was superfluous since there already existed Fisk, Walden, Roger Williams, and Meharry;[16] the

---

[15]William Jasper Hale (1876–1944) was the founding president of Tennessee Agricultural and Industrial State Normal University, now Tennessee State University.

[16]In 1930, Nashville was an important center of African American higher education. Tennessee Agricultural and Industrial State Normal University (Tennessee State

Negroes because they felt that Hale laid undue emphasis upon agricultural training. Oh, my people, how they endeavor in every way to forsake that which better than any other pursuit would return them a comfortable living if only they prepared themselves even as they train their minds for the ministry, medicine, law, or teaching.

Hale went on to say that the school was founded in 1912, that his troubles began when soldiers quartered there during the war were charged $7,000[?] a month. Forbes, who commanded them, refused to pay the money, and when Hale declined to nullify the expenses of maintaining them, threatened to close the school, have Hale thrown out, and started a general war against him. The struggle reached an acute stage a few years later when charges of misappropriation of funds and immorality [were made against Hale]—in fact Hale said every charge except murder was hurled against him. To such a point did the criminations and recriminations reach that Hale turned to the Governor of Tennessee, who had accused him wrongfully and called him a "liar" right to his face. And this was while the governor sat on the platform at his own (Hale's) school. One more attempt was made to dislodge this fearless and fighting president when the Board of Examiners came to chapel one day and decided that the school would have to be closed, because agriculture, which constituted the main reason for the founding of the school, was not being taught. Now came Hale's capital stroke. He rose, told the student body and friends what had been said, and called upon everyone who was taking agriculture to stand. Marvelous to relate and to his intense and happy surprise everyone stood, male and female, old and young, visitors and students. Even his gray-haired mother who was visiting him stood. The board was discomfited, withdrew in a huff, but [was] convinced that the school could not be closed on that ground.

After this, Hale's troubles largely ended. The school, he confided, receives $600,000 a year from the state, a larger appropriation than any other colored school. I admired Hale; we need other men who can be men when occasion demands and not [men who] eternally surrender all principles and virility when the whites suggest or demand something that the Negro knows to be contrary to the best interests of his group.

Dr. Hale then told me of his interest in me. . . . He asked what was my connection with Dr. Woodson. I told him. He was surprised yet

University) was formally opened on June 19, 1912, as an 1890 land-grant institution. By 1927, it had an enrollment of 422 students, a faculty of sixteen instructors, and a physical plant of twelve buildings, three of which were completed that year.

happy to discern that I could still remain on the ground. The trouble with most young men, he said, is when they earn their master's or doctor's degree or accomplish a little something, they begin to suffer with self-inflation.

He had tried to persuade me to remain for breakfast. . . . It was so near breakfast time that I yielded to his last invitation. He gave me a note to give to the lady in charge of the dining room ordering a special breakfast for five of us.

How the boys welcomed the news of a free breakfast. They even forgot that they had waited for me almost an hour. The dining room, a cafeteria, is located in the western wing of the administration building. The very first sight was a revelation as well as a spur to whet the appetite. It was large, spacious, clean, airy. . . . I have never seen in any Negro cafeteria or dining room such a varied collection of food. For fruit—which very few Negro eating places serve—there were peaches, grapefruit, baked apples, orange juice, bananas, prunes, and cantaloupe; four kinds of meat including chicken and lamb chops (these were the first lamb chops I had seen in a colored lunch room since I left D.C.); cereal from Post-Toasties to oatmeal; rice and four kinds of bread, even brown bread. We all partook with relish.

I was anxious to reach Atlanta before dark, therefore got Wilkey and Mr. ____ to show us the way to the route leading to that city. Filled up with high speed gasoline at a station nearby. When Poe inquired my reason, I responded that it was [an] added precaution so that, if any trouble occurred in Georgia, I could get away from Mr. Charlie (the whites). He laughed but took the trouble to see that the crank and an iron used as a jack handle were within easy distance so that they could be wielded, were we attacked.

Within two miles we were over the Georgia border and it seemed as if everything suddenly changed and not for the better. My attitude changed. Security gave place to uncertainty. Came to roads metamorphosed into bumpy asphalt. Tennessee license plates, with which we had been familiar for more than a week, were now replaced by that of Georgia. All the unpleasant things I had heard of Georgia now rose before me. Each car full of people; each white on the street, about the gasoline station, or stores, were potential enemies. I was filled with a desire to reach Atlanta as quickly as possible. Still, nothing happened.

We reached Atlanta about 6:30. We had experienced no trouble. Only once did we hear the word "nigger" and that by a group of young white hoodlums whom we passed on the road and who perhaps hated to see Negroes riding while they walked. Our relationships with the whites, however, we found exceedingly cordial all the way from Nashville.

What was the economic condition over this route of nearly 300 miles? Very bad in some instances. In the mountain regions of Tennessee the prolonged drought has played havoc with crops. Streams and creeks, upon which the farmers depend in large measures for irrigation for their fields or as water for their cattle, have dried up . . . . Fields have burned up; the grass has been scorched until it is as brown and withered as one would expect to find it in October. Cattle graze patiently on the brown stubble, which cannot furnish them sufficient food, and farmers are compelled to buy feed for them. Tobacco has turned yellow . . . cabbage has burned up; even corn, which thrives on hot, dry weather, has begun to dry up. . . . The only crop that looked encouraging was the cotton of northern Georgia, and God only knows what will happen to that once the boll weevil begins its depredations.

As we drove into Atlanta we at once realized that we were entering a metropolis. Diversified manufacturers met us on every hand. . . . We went directly to Atlanta University, thanks to the piloting of a Negro. . . . Not as elaborate as [at] Tennessee State, but then a nice room with two beds, private bath. We were utterly fatigued. Washed, took a little refreshment, and retired.

This city is still agog over the murder of young Hubert by white hoodlums. One has been sentenced to from 12 to 15 years in the penitentiary, something heretofore unheard of in Georgia.[17] The whites are aroused and Mr. Waldrom [Wardlaw] informed us that he feared reprisals. Negroes are forbidden to buy guns, or at least white storekeepers are not to supply them. The idea is clearly seen. If a riot comes, for God's sake have the Negro defenseless in order that the white casualties will be as small as possible. Nevertheless, many of the Negroes, especially the lower element, are well supplied and ready for any emergency.

Saturday, August 9, 1930. . . . I called upon Mrs. Gatewood to bid her farewell. From there went to Mr. C. W. Washington's office (Urban

---

[17]On June 15, 1930, Dennis Hubert, a sophomore at Morehouse College, was killed on the playground of Crogmann School. A grand jury indicted seven white men for the crime. Two days after a bail hearing for the accused men, the home of Hubert's father, pastor of the Glen Street Baptist Church, was burned. A few days later a tear-gas bomb was thrown by a group of white men into a mass meeting of African Americans. The prominence of the Hubert family caused an unusual reaction to the murder and the incidents which followed. Ministerial groups protested and a movement was launched to raise funds to rebuild the Hubert home.

A jury found T.L. Martin, the first of the seven white men brought to trial, guilty of voluntary manslaughter and set his sentence at from twelve to fifteen years in the state penitentiary.

League Secretary). Told me of case of peonage near Atlanta, where two Negro boys, 11 and 13, respectively, were held on the farm of a white named Peters. He refused to send them to the mother on the ground that they were indebted to him for board and other expenses to the amount of $16.50. Yet, they had worked sawing wood, plowing, picking cotton, and at sundry other chores for nine months. Peters had itemized both the boys' debts and credits, of course, in his favor. The mother, distracted, had appealed to the Urban League, and Mr. Washington, after quite a lengthy battle, succeeded in having the boys returned to her. Peters was illiterate and his letters show his average intelligence being scarcely that of the third grade and his penmanship about illegible.

Could not say farewell to Miss Hall the way I wanted to because of the presence of Mr. Washington. She looked at me so wistfully as if to say, "Is this goodbye?"

We experienced no trouble getting out of town. A beautiful concrete road took us past fields of cotton, which was just beginning to blossom . . . . For hundreds of acres these cotton fields stretched along the road. The fields were deserted, for the farmhands do not work on Saturday afternoon. Of course most of these were Negroes. These plantations, of course, had their small unpainted gunshot shacks sitting haphazardly amidst the cotton field.

Tuesday, August [12], 1930, Tuskegee. To school early. Speak at chapel. Sold books in hall. See many attractive girls. Saw Bea at noon. Make arrangements for ride at 8:00. Sold 12 sets of books. Russell takes me in hand. Promised to give him a set of books if I can sell 10. Takes me to Mrs. Weeks of Mobile; sell her 2 books. Reverend buys nothing, offers good time. But I'm due at Whitley's. Started to party, looking for Bea. Finally find her. Take her for *ride*. . . . Go to dinner and party 1 and 1/2 hours late. Forgiven. Meet Mr.____, a railway mail clerk. No discrimination he tells me. A never-to-be-forgotten evening with Bertha. Oh, yes, during the day, Mrs. Moore took me to see Dr. Carey. Sold him.

Sunday, August 17, 1930. Saw Huntsville after breakfast. Fine little town. Hemmed in by mountains. . . . Could not send telegram to Payton. Office closed. Left for Athens after fun with two girls. Had leak in pump fixed by friend of Poe's. Blowout between Huntsville and Athens. Mr. McWilliams tells me of labor conditions. Laborers $20 a month with board, $25-30 without. Day labor $1.00 to $1.50. Negro peasants in fairly good shape in country. Farm owners have holdings of 20-158 acres. Drought has ruined corn. Cotton better. Domestic service: only one white home hires white servants, Negroes do rest of it. Trades: Negro work at them. Number lessening due to Negroes' failure to make selves proficient, also attraction of trades to white men.

Left about 3:40. Good gravel road to Florence. . . . Terrific storm comes up. Road like glass. I drive from Florence. . . . Stopped in Sheffield at Mrs. Mathews's for night. Wife of school principal. Took us to a Mrs. Taylor. People afraid of lightening. Terrified of putting on light. Stayed all night at Taylors'.

Monday, August 18, 1930. Beautiful Mary Sieveg, attractive, from Sheffield. Saw Negroes going to work. White man had group. As we crossed Mississippi line, [we] see Negroes working in sand pit. Whites carrying gun. Wilkey bends, anticipating shot. Wretched hovels lived in by whites, bed, stove, table, all in one room. Children in excess. Saw about 15 in one house. Cotton in northeast Mississippi does not look so good.

Tuesday, August 19, 1930. Had to fix flat tire this morning. Lodging and breakfast 50 cents. Lovely Mississippi. Large island in center, but water not as muddy as I anticipated.

White tenant homes on plantations are pathetic, 4 families each. Containing each about 2 rooms. None of Negro tenant homes have screens. Flies rampant. Corn burnt up or stunted. Grass looks as if it had been burnt over. Saw rice grow for first time. Done by irrigation.

Whites kind. Exceedingly so in Little Rock. Terrible time getting to Little Rock. Had to come 18 miles on flat tire. Money gave out. Tires not worth spending money for new tubes.

Called Dot Gillan, engagement for 9:30 a.m. . . . Little Rock looks promising.

Wednesday, August 20, 1930. Saw Dot Gillan at 9:30. Left her and went to see Mr. Bush. Fine office. Slim, cultured mulatto. Looks like [Ernest E.] Just. Took first set of books. Referred me to Luther Moore. Went there. LaGrone interviewing him. (Lost sale.) Was able then to eat breakfast.

Sunday, Monday, and Tuesday, August 24-26, 1930, Hot Springs. Left Little Rock Saturday, about 1:30. Original intention to send Wilkey to Pine Bluff. Could not secure car for him, however. I had to take him with Poe and me.

All along the road the ravages of the drought are in evidence.

Brooks, rivulets, and creeks are dry. Some of them fifty feet wide, or-dinarily, show not one drop of water. Trees stand denuded, desolated as if a fiery holocaust had swept over them. Grass is burnt up. Cotton will yield nothing. Farmers are hard put to it to find forage for their cattle, and the cattle wander aimlessly along the road nibbling a little burnt grass here and a little there. Lack of long feed has also reduced the milk supply.

The drive to Hot Springs was beautiful. The road wound about the Ozark hills continuously. The air was fresh, crisp, and flavored with the invigorating aroma of the pines.

Reached Hot Springs in one hour and twenty five minutes (60 miles). What a surprise. Magnificent hotels greeted us on every side of its one extremely long street.

We had been told in Little Rock that all the business in Hot Springs was on one street. So were the residences. What was my surprise to find here a large number of fine Negro homes. And in no case did I see the dilapidated structures such as Little Rock, Memphis, and other Southern towns presented. The reason, no doubt, is that the riffraff are discouraged from coming here because of the absence of any other work than hotel work for the unprepared Negro, and for the large op-portunities for educated Negroes due to the fact that the home offices of two insurance companies are located here. Then too, the Negro res-ident here gets contact from all over the world.

Thursday, August 27 [28], 1930. At 7:45 we began making preparations for leaving Hot Springs. I had only $1.65. And we needed a tube, the oil ought to have been changed long ago, gas was to be bought, and meals purchased; and everyone broke. LaGrone made me especially angry. During the last two days he made $8.50, yet spent it foolishly either on golf or girls and saved but 50 cents as his share for traveling expenses. Yet, I cautioned him several days ago we had to travel 204 miles. I was exasperated. I was tired [of] "carrying" him and Wilkey. I can save nothing.

The effects of the drought were everywhere. The fields are baked, the very mountainsides are parched. . . . The dust was choking. It was as fine as powder. The roads were the worst over which I have ever traveled, worse than those of Tennessee. We finally had a respite from such, however, for five miles of concrete highway loomed ahead of us. It was certainly welcome.

Forest fires as a result of the 91-day drought or the carelessness of motorists or campers were everywhere. The woods on both sides of the road were burning fiercely for miles and miles. The smoke rolled up and across in huge white billows almost obscuring the road. Thousands of dollars worth of valuable pine and spruce timber were being consumed. And no one was fighting it. What amazed me was that, although the flames were gradually licking their way toward the farmhouses, both whites and blacks sat on their porches watching the fires with the most complete indifference. At Smithton, Arkansas, the station manager lay asleep on top of a large baggage truck, while a half mile away, forest fires were crackling and burning over a large acreage.

This entire region is sparsely settled, which accounts, to a large degree, for the lack of roads. For miles at times, we passed through nothing but woods. Before leaving the mountains again, there was nothing to be seen save mountains and the road. There is no crop diversification. One sees corn and cotton only, the great curse as well as the wealth of the South. There are plenty of watermelons, however, but the supply exceeds the demand; hence, one buys them at unbelievable prices. We got two at Hope, which is said by white farmers to be the best watermelon section in the country, for five cents apiece.

We saw other things of interest between Prescott and Texarkana. Near Wheeler Springs, the doors of the Negro farmers were open in some cases, and we could see women stretched out on the floor sound asleep. Near Prescott we saw cotton in mule-drawn carts being brought to the gin. They were driven by whites in every instance. . . . I wanted to go into a cotton gin, but time did not permit. Saw the familiar sight of Negro men, women, and children picking cotton, dragging their huge sacks after them. They are earning from 45 to 50 cents an hour [a hundred?], a white man told me in Prescott. We passed another forest fire. A little farther on, I saw the first all-Negro railroad gang in hundreds of miles of traveling.

Arrived at Texarkana, Arkansas-Texas, at 5:00 p.m. Instructed fellows to canvass the physicians and dentists as quickly as possible in order that we might go on to Marshall.

Met Dr. A[ustin] H. A. Jones. Young dentist. Howard grad (1925). . . . He was the first man I sold. I brought to bear upon him my strongest sales arguments, showed him the great ignorance common to both races concerning the Negro. Informed him of the omission of worthwhile things concerning the Negro in schoolbooks and also recounted some of the deliberate and vicious propaganda circulated in books to demean, debase, and belittle the Negro in order to keep him feeling inferior and the whites superior. For these reasons, I added, these books should be in every home. He looked at me amazed, but I was talking for bread. He finally—after pleading broke—took *The Negro in Our History* and *African Myths,* giving me $1.60 deposit.

Friday, August 29, 1930. After a fine night's rest and a good breakfast, we set forth to interview a Mr. Pendleton, recommended to us by Mr. Hawk. I accompanied Poe in order to help reinforce his sales argument, for he needs to make some money badly.

Following the sale, Mr. and Mrs. Hawk and the latter's mother took us to their farm. The farm is owned by Mr. and Mrs. Williams, Mrs. Hawk's parents.

Farmhands, I was told, received a higher wage here than in either the lower South or Arkansas, $1.50 a day. Of course this is without board. The pickers get from 60 to 75 cents a hundred. Mrs. Williams pays her pickers 75 cents a hundred. According to her, the best pickers can make 300 pounds a day. Most of them, however, fall considerably below that figure.

We finally arrived at Mrs. Williams's farm. They have about fifty acres but are nonresident. Her husband is a hostler in one of the railroad shops.

I met Mr. Wallace, a small, halfway intelligent man who runs the farm. I congratulated him on his corn and cotton. Asked him about wages. . . . Cotton pickers, he confided, were receiving less this year than formerly because of the great abundance of labor due to unemployment. Most of them were glad, he said, to receive 50 cents a hundred. . . . The average cotton picker could pick 150 pounds a day. Some can pick much more.

He also told me that many colored farmers are in dire straits. Many of them, indeed, are giving up farming, and are allowing their land to lie idle. Others remain but are not growing paying crops. Lack of organization and inability to avail themselves of the Farm Loan Act account for this. The white man usually secures the loan, then charges an exorbitant rate of interest to the Negroes. Many of these farmers have quit in disgust, and work in the pipe and other plants about Texarkana.

I also saw my first Mexicans, one of whom was hurrying with his dinner, which consisted of tomatoes and bread. They remind me of the Italians in my home. These people, Mexicans, have swarmed across the border since the war and seriously undermined labor for the Negroes. They live cheaper, hence, sell their labor cheaper and, as a result, they are driving the Negro workers from the farms in the Southwest, from the railroads, and, also, from other fields of common labor.

Saturday, August 30, 1930. On the way to Shreveport, we passed numerous Negro farmers and laborers coming to town where they massed their wagons or autos for buying or selling. Some came by auto; others came in wagons or carts. Still others trudged along on foot. Some of the wagons had been made into rentable carryalls in which sat the entire family on seats, the women in their gaudy red or other fantastically colored dresses and the men in their best coats and trousers. Others came in mule-drawn carts piled high with fluffy white cotton carrying it to the ginneries. . . . These people lived for Saturday. They go to town, gossip, meet friends, buy, sell, get drunk, spend their money, and return home.

Tuesday, September 2, 1930. Beautiful day. Sent Woodson telegram for books for agents.

Left for Dallas about eleven. . . . The land, as we proceeded, changed from brown to white loam, then to red, and finally back to white. This it continued for a long distance. The soil was like cement dust. It was so fine and light that it burned our eyes and nearly choked us.

Passed through Grand Saline—a small Negro-hating town almost halfway to Dallas. Negroes are warned not to stop there, so Dr. Dogan's son and Mr. Hodges, purchasing agent for Wiley told us. The only evidences of their hatred, however, proved to be a few harmless whistles and calls. Wilkey, however, was so frightened that he actually exceeded the speed limit and made me fearful that in trying to escape a mental hazard he might run into actual danger—the hands of the law—and God only knows when or how we could get out of the clutches of these "crackers."

Just outside of Saline we saw a white woman selling watermelons at a stand. They were grown on her own farm. Cost 10 cents apiece. She cut 5 in order to get 2 good ones for us. Was exceptionally civil. Asked us to sit under the trees and eat them. Brought each of us knives; Wilkey was nervous for fear white men would take umbrage at our sitting there eating and talking to the white woman. Many passed but paid no attention to us. Many of the melons, we were told, were small and dry on account of the prolonged drought. No rain to speak of since April.

At Wells Point, we saw idle whites and Negroes laying around the general store or cotton gins. Gins and cotton oil mills are everywhere. Cart after cart of fluffy, newly picked cotton, driven by blacks and whites, passed us going to the gins. The driver usually sits on the cotton. He needs to over some of these roads. Much cotton already baled was lying about uncovered in yards. No provision for covering it in case of rain.

September is the beginning of the rainy season here. There are miles of cotton, however, not ready for picking. What is being picked is being done more by whites, it seems, than by Negroes.

We now came to the region of the . . . Great Plains. From a small rise in the road the landscape stretches interminably before us. Never before have I gazed upon such vast distances. It is a beautiful sight to look about one for miles and miles and see green cotton fields and white farmhouses with the beauty marred only by the ugly tenants' quarters. On one large plantation, all Negroes were working. Men, women, and children of all ages were picking cotton, trailing their large bags behind them. Other men were filling the cart with the newly picked cotton.

The road led into the black dirt section. This soil must be extremely fertile. Again we could see for miles. Church steeples of ordinary heights in towns 10 or 12 miles away were clearly visible. We saw white men using three mule plows in the road preparing an embankment. Again we saw whole families of Negroes picking cotton. None were mulattoes. Very rarely do they work on farms it seems, especially the women. Must be a slave tradition still adhered to. The pickers' quarters are mere shacks thrown up in the midst of the cotton field or near the road. Most have two rooms; many one. The bed is the most prominent article of furniture that can always be seen from the roadside. Cotton, cotton, cotton—it is everywhere.

The outskirts of Dallas were imposing. The street designation here is good, although they are named. The block number is given along with the street at intersections.

Go to new Y.M.C.A. Best equipped building yet for Negroes. Has everything—fine swimming pool, basketball, volleyball, handball, and baseball courts, drying room, best bath conveniences, assembly halls for men and boys. Fine rooms with steel desks, etc. Mr. Stewart, frat brother, in charge. [It costs] $1.00 a night to stay there. Boys could not pay it, therefore, I went with them to Hotel Powell where a Dr. Hamilton directed and took us. Secured rooms for $1.00 apiece, two in a room. As usual, Poe and I stopped together.

Played and beat Wilkey [at] a game of golf and retired about 8:45 in order to be ready for trip to Austin, tomorrow. I shall leave Wilkey here. Pick him up on my return from New Orleans.

Dallas Negroes leave much to be desired upon first impression. Seem to be unprogressive. Wilkey and maid.

Wednesday, September 3, 1930. Left Dallas 6:00 p.m. Wilkey, fresh from the arms of his "ammorata," [sic] leaned over the balcony of the hotel to get final instructions.

Drive to Waco was uneventful. Did not stop nor leave seat until I reached Paul Quinn College[18] in Waco, 109 miles away. En route there, saw the most beautiful and the vastest landscape I have ever been privileged to see. So illimitable were the distances that the very land seemed to merge into the sky. It was grand, inspiring, mighty.

Thursday, September 4, 1930. Left Austin at 6:30 after giving LaGrone instructions to work Austin and then San Antonio. Will pick him up there.

... Received two letters from Woodson. He told me he received requisitions for *The Rural Negro*. Sending them to New Orleans. Sending blanks as I ordered. Wants to know what is being done with them. Angers me when he asks whether we are distributing among children. Mentions the fact that we must be having fine time with ladies judging from letters coming to the office. I shall write him and give him an equal amount of sarcasm in return. This trip is netting me nothing financial. It is being done by me solely because of publicity given the organization. He cannot see that, however, or else every other little thing bulks so large that it obscures his vision. It is such petty things that will impel me ultimately to sever connections with him and tell him to go to hell.

Friday, September 5, 1930. Rose at 6:30. Wrote in diary until 7:30. Dressed. I had 73 cents. Ashamed to meet the landlady because we could not pay her. For breakfast, sat in car and ate a few grapes and remainder of graham crackers I had bought last night. Got gallon of gas. Reduced exchequer to 15 cents.

After dinner, wrote Woodson. Referring to his sarcasm in respect to the use made by us of the subscription blanks, I said: "I am at loss to understand your very excellent sarcasm in this respect. If you expect that for every subscription blank which leaves the office a corresponding order will enter the office, then I see that you know nothing about practical selling in the field. Since you are ignorant of this fact, let me enlighten you. Some people when interviewed by the agent do not find themselves in a position to buy at that time. Some do not intend to buy. However, they will ask that we leave a blank which they will forward to the office with the initial deposit before the sale ends. And

---

[18] Paul Quinn College, an African Methodist Episcopal Church school, was founded in 1872 in Austin, Texas. After five years, the school was moved to Waco, where it operated as a trade school. A college site was acquired in 1881, and the college celebrated its formal opening in 1882. The enrollment in 1927 was 177, and the faculty numbered seven members.

we leave them. If this may be called distributing blanks or souvenirs for juveniles then we plead guilty. And it shall continue until you order otherwise, since we are interested in arousing the curiosity of these people as to our work even if we are not able to sell them. You ought to know what a subscription blank in the hands of an interested person means when a book on Negro History or some kindred topic is needed."

Referring to his ironic statement concerning our advertising the office through the fair sex, I wrote: "Yes, the ladies are advertising the office. And we are having a lovely time. My love letters kindly hold until my return that I might pick out the lady who offers most fiscally!!" I felt better after writing him this letter.

Saturday, September 6, 1930. Went back to Odd Fellows Building. Could do nothing there. Went then to Bastrop Street after securing directions from Miss Henry. Found Mr. [Johnny] Walls. Had been expecting me. Is mailman, president of the Postal Employees' Alliance of Houston.

Told me . . . post office was rotten when he entered 12 years ago. The old-time Negroes had made it difficult for a young, intelligent colored carrier to get a job. . . . Took all manner of abuse and would remove caps when going into office buildings. . . . White superintendent would not take an intelligent colored man. Preferred more ignorant who were more pliable. Walls got in, however. Organized the Postal Employees' Alliance and fought to break the power of the old Negroes and to bring in men who were eager for promotion through efficiency.

Alliance, through his persistence, caused a shake-up in the office here two years ago. Succeeded in bringing the post office inspector to Houston from Washington. The result of his investigation was the dismissal or demotion to carriers of all the supervisors and even of the superintendent himself. Inspector congratulated Walls.

These streets in Houston are terrible. This applies, of course, to the Negro sections. They are unpaved and most of them are as narrow as alleys. The section around George Street is terrible. Sanitary conditions are bad. Water in many cases is outdoors; so are the toilets. The same can be found in all the wards. The homes, of course, vary from fine brick or frame structures to hovels. All in all, the Negroes are more progressive here than anywhere else in Texas. They have a dry goods store, pharmacies, insurance companies, a newspaper, two fine office buildings, grocery stores, a large theater, gasoline stations, etc. There are about 80 physicians and about 15 dentists.

There is a fine school system, the city is well churched, too well perhaps. There is an amusement park for colored and several dance halls. There is no exclusive society here. Houston is too young and democratic.

Wanted to go to New Orleans early today. Poe, however, has sold nothing. Holds me up. I believe he is doing more socializing than anything else. Can't carry him much longer, for I too must live.

Monday, September 15, 1930. After breakfast called upon Dr. [B. J.] Covington, who had given me his card yesterday and asked me to call upon him. An elderly dark man of medium build. Resembles my uncle. Told him so. Marveled but remarked it might be possible, for his father was sold south from Virginia and had no recollection of any relatives. Frequently did happen in slavery.

I remarked that the Houston Negroes had the best potentialities for development of any group of Negroes I had yet seen in the South. Told me he agreed but that there were some things which nullified to some extent these advantages. For instance, he never drives with his wife if he can help it, neither does he ride with her on the streetcar, because he feels that the Negro is so prone to be insulted by any person with a white skin that it is impossible for him to be a man in the presence of his women. . . . Just last week, he told me, a rich Negro woman driving a fine car was ordered by a policeman to take her car off Main Street and leave it on Milam Street (Negro district) where the "niggers" belonged. She was infringing upon no law. . . . It is such things as this, according to Dr. Covington, that make the tenure of the Negro so insecure that it is equivalent to sitting on a volcano.

Wednesday, September 17, 1930. Arrived in Galveston about 4:40 p.m. A beautiful sight across the water as we sped over the bay.

After securing a room at the Orlando Hotel (God help us) where we paid just 50 cents for the night, [Henry Lee] Moon and I went down to get a view of the Gulf at night. We drove along the boulevard that borders the gulf. But just as the pavement usually ends where the Negro section begins, just so were the beautiful lights on the boulevard discontinued in front of the Negroes' property.

After driving along and watching the swashing waves of the gulf from a distance, Moon and I walked down a pair of steps until we sat just above the huge rocks against which the relentless waves rolled and broke unceasingly. The water was beautiful. It was bewitching. There was no moon and the white-capped billows, starting afar out on the black water, appeared like a great light in the distance. Then suddenly they took shape and began their surge landward. As they rolled nearer they seemed to stretch out lengthwise at a furious pace, until they reminded me of legions of enormous snow-white horses galloping madly down the gulf only to swerve and pour their foaming, undulating forces toward the shore . . . .

Thursday, September 18, 1930. At 8:15 I was in the office of Principal J. W. Gibson at the Central High School, where I was to speak to the student body upon some phase of Negro History.

While waiting for the assembly period, Professor Gibson told me some very interesting things about himself. These were reinforced by certain certificates and commissions hanging on the walls of his office.

In the first place, he served as Consul for Liberia at Galveston for 29 years. . . . He was also a four-minute speaker during World War I and bears a certificate of honor from the federal government and a letter of congratulations signed by President Wilson. . . . Mr. Gibson also has the dubious honor of having been the only man to "whip" Jack Johnson, former heavyweight champion of the world. Jack was formerly a pupil of his, went as high as the fourth grade, but would go no further. Mr. Gibson said he had to whip him for fighting, the very field in which he was to rise to world renown. Told me that he regretted doing so many times, for he might have crushed his pugilistic talent.

It was now time to speak. Addressed about 600 students. They gave rapt attention. Perhaps I did well, for one of the teachers, congratulating me afterward, told me that I must have been a Lincoln [University in Pennsylvania] man. They are noted for oratorical ability, which I sadly lack. Mr. Gibson told me that I could have held them there all day. I felt encouraged because I know it is difficult to keep the attention of high school students. . . . Professor Gibson tried to persuade me to stay in town to speak at his church Sunday, but I told him it was impossible. He then subscribed to a set of books for the school library.

Left Galveston at 12:30. Arrived in Houston, after an uneventful ride, about 1:40.

En route to San Antonio, we were accosted by a white man just outside Houston who hailed us thusly: "Say Uncle how far are you going?" I replied just a short distance, not wishing to accommodate him on account of his rough appearance. Asked him where he was going. Told me he was going to pick cotton, or to do anything that he could find. This statement caused me to reflect all the more seriously over this problem, for full well I understood that the entry into these jobs by poor whites meant the corresponding displacement of Negroes.

We also passed Mexicans in droves. These people migrate from the border cities of Mexico in search of employment in the cotton fields, on the railroads, or in domestic service. Whole families were in motion in Ford trucks or in wagons. Near Richmond, what I supposed at first to be a truck full of cattle turned out to be a family of Mexicans with the children peering through its boarded up sides and dangling their tiny hands through the openings. In many cases they had paused for a rest, either under a tree, along the road, or in a vacant field. Some of them traveled with all their meager household effects. Most of them had mattresses only. Near Richmond we passed migrating Mexicans in covered wagons and could discern mothers suckling their babies as we passed. It reminded me of frontier days.

Friday, September 19, 1930. Laredo is almost a Mexican city. [It is] just across the river from Nuevo Laredo, Mexico. Very little prejudice here. The reason is that very few Negroes live here. Indeed they are so rare that people stare at us. The streets are terribly narrow. Spanish, as well as English, adorns the signs and business houses and one beholds hundreds of beautiful dark-skinned, black-haired Mexican girls, many of whom cannot be distinguished from Negroes. They have so reacted to minimize prejudice that the whites allowed us to use their toilets and to go into their offices in order to drink from their water coolers.

Went to a night club. A slick, handsome Mexican introduced us to some beautiful Mexican girls. We danced. Then the Mexican offered us our pick of the girls, who were kissing us and making suggestive and seductive movements as we danced. We could have our choice for dos pesos ($2.00) [$1.00] for an hour and cinco pesos ($5.00) [$2.50] for the night. We broke out of the girls' embraces, gave them a tip and left.[19]

Friday, September 26, 1930. On to Tulsa. Oil wells are everywhere. One just a mile from Main Street in Oklahoma City. Yesterday an oil well was discovered, yielding more than 80,000 barrels a day. Wells are scattered all around in Oklahoma City. Seventeen miles from Tulsa the whole countryside was dotted with wells and storage tanks. In Drumright, oil wells were even in the backyards of houses. The latter frequently are huts, showing the unexpected oil boom. . . . Many refineries here. Passed Sinclair, Texaco, Consolidated Oil Refineries, and also Tydol. . . . Entire country is oil rich. LaGrone tells me that [an] 82,000-barrel oil gusher in Oklahoma City is owned by a Negro. That is, the land. White oil company has leased it. Negro gets one-eighth of the flow as royalty.

---

[19] This final paragraph is missing from the entry in the diary notebooks, but Greene included it in a draft of a transcript he made.

Car gave much trouble en route. Everything goes wrong at one time. Lost my books, briefcase, diary, am broke, have $1.78, and auto is on the blink. Mechanic at Langston worked on it. Told us the steering apparatus needs repairing. Cost 75 cents.

Arrived in Tulsa at 7:30. Went to Century Life Office. Manager, Mr. Wheeler . . . took us to Hotel Small. Expected to see fine lobby. Astonished to find plain water keg in hall with common water pail to catch waste water.

Mr. Small told me that he experienced the riot horror of June 1, 1921, when Tulsa's Negro section was burned by a crowd of infuriated whites. He was suffering from appendicitis. Whites forced him and others to come out of buildings with hands above heads. Assured them they would not be hurt. Even helped him to carry out things. Put them in a field. Then fired homes. Negroes and whites fought one day.

Saturday, September 27, 1930. Dr. [P. S.] Thompson, druggist, tells me that the Tulsa riot was led by city officials—the mayor and chief of police. Latter had to leave the country. In Mexico now. The mayor has been in retirement ever since. Showed me picture of devastated area stretching from Arch[er] Street north to Standpipe Hill and from Hartford east to Boston Street. Not a house or building standing. (85 blocks burned.) Said thirty Negroes and more than 100 whites died.

Dr. Thompson told me Negro uses ballot here to extort concessions from city. Seven precincts out of one hundred entirely Negro. Have just recently secured a hospital, municipal center, library, park, and a police precinct where Negroes arrested may be booked, admitted to, or refused bail without being carried uptown. Balloting entirely controlled by Negroes.

Whites fooled Negroes during riot. Told them all to go to convention hall or ballpark and they would see that they would be taken care of. Negroes did so. Whites then took furniture, looted homes, and burned them. Took Negroes' effects. Later in the fall, many Negroes even found their furniture or clothing in white homes. School teacher found white woman wearing her suit. After the Negroes found they had been fooled, they began fighting. Corner Greenwood and Archer was a bloody ground. Armed Negroes on church tower ran whites from machine guns on hills. Two hours later, whites found it out. Then riddled church.

There are several good Negro schools.

Monday, September 29, 1930. Things were critical financially for us today. None of us, save Poe, had any money. Or rather, I should say the latter was the only one who acknowledged such. LaGrone claimed to be penniless, but we all believed that he was withholding from the fellows. He is peculiarly unethical. Expects one to "carry" him when "broke" but as soon as he gets money refuses to recognize his obligations. We ate, therefore, a very meager breakfast in order to lessen the strain on Poe.

[Later] the fellows told me that LaGrone had gone home. . . . He was in my debt about $20.00 and sneaked home like a common thief in order to avoid paying his just debts. As long as I shall know him, I could not employ him, neither could I recommend such a person for a position. It is appalling to believe that a college man would crucify his honor and his name for just a few paltry cents.

Tuesday, September 30, 1930. My first act this morning was to borrow LaGrone's books and call upon Mr. S. P. Berry, the keeper of the finest service station and garage owned by Negroes and operated by them. Sold him easily.

Next to Mr. Jackson, the undertaker. Congratulated me upon my speech. Had to go to court. Told me to see his wife at 410 North Elgin Street. Fear [he] is giving me the "run around," as we term the attempt of a prospect to dodge us. . . . Went to the high school to speak to the little tots in the adjoining graded school. Met Miss Algerita Jackson, charming teacher. Mrs. [Jean] Goodwin, who had invited me to speak, was surprised to see me. Felt I would not have time. Told her as busy as I was, I could not forego an opportunity to tell these children something about their past.

The proceedings of the assembly amazed me. . . . Here the pupils conduct their own exercises with class president, secretary, treasurer, etc. They are thus taught self-expression and self-confidence, and also obtain the experience of public speaking in this manner.

I spoke for about 15 minutes. No man could have desired a more appreciative audience. I told them facts about the Negro in Africa and entertained them with tales from *African Myths*. Then the teacher asked whether they had any questions to propound. Did they? They just bombarded me with queries, and intelligent ones, too. This is more than any adult gathering has done on the trip. And I must confess that had I not read, comparatively speaking, so much on the Negro, their confidence in me would have been utterly shattered.

My greatest surprise yet came upon my return to speak to the class. When after the preliminaries I waited to be introduced by Mrs. Goodwin, the teacher, something astonishing happened.

A little girl ten years of age rose, faced the class of seventy pupils, and in a manner that would have done credit to many a grown man or woman introduced me to the class in the following manner. "Boys and girls we have with us today Professor Greene. Professor Greene is traveling through the country in the interest of Negro History, and he is going to tell us about the boys and girls of our race in Africa and in other places. I take great pleasure in introducing Professor Lorenzo J. Greene."

I was too dumbfounded at first to move. When I finally rose to my feet it was difficult to find words to commend the class in general and this little girl in particular. Never had such an experience been mine, and I spent almost three minutes congratulating her. As at the other hour, I spoke about 15 minutes and reserved the rest of the time for questions. This second audience of children was just as attentive as the first. They leaned forward in their seats in rapt interest, unwilling to lose a single word. And how they plied me with questions. I enjoyed it, and both the pupils and I were sorry when the dismissal bell rang. Like grown men and women, as they passed by me, they congratulated me and shook my hand. Never have I been more gratified nor more satisfied with three quarters of an hour's toil.

Mrs. Goodwin and Miss Jackson showered me with their thanks. The former told me that last year she was assigned the assembly work and told to teach it. There was no guide. Therefore, she has the children instruct themselves, with her lead of course, in ethics, citizenship, health, cleanliness, and Negro History. It was the most interesting experiment I have ever witnessed in education. And for our children, it is invaluable, for it tends to instill in them that confidence that we as a race are so sadly lacking and so vitally need.

Back to the hotel. Met Lawyer Twine of the firm of [W. H.] Twine and [Pliny] Twine and [Chauncy] Twine of Muskogee. Frat brother. Told me there are 16 Negroes who are lawyers in Muskogee, all doing well. Rich Indian and Negro clients and constant litigation over oil well and claims keep them busy with big cases. . . . Many Negroes have extensive holdings, Twine told me. Before Oklahoma reached statehood, the U.S. allotted lands of 100 acres in size to Negroes and Indians. They were not to be sold. Came statehood. Oil was found. And the whites, in order to get this valuable land, removed the restrictions upon the Negroes which forbade the disposal of their land. Naturally, many Negroes who had been given stony land sold it eagerly only to have oil discovered in this supposedly worthless soil. Hence the buyers became millionaires, in many instances overnight. Those few Negroes who still retained their land also became rich when an oil strike was found.

In order to get the Indians' land, however, a subterfuge had to be resorted to. The Oklahoma legislature declared the Indian a white man and forbade intermarriage between them and Negroes. In this manner, whites could marry Indians and inherit their oil lands, while the Negro was legally debarred from the same privilege.

Thursday, October 2, 1930. Felt aggrieved over the manner in which the group has broken up. Payton and LaGrone took French leave—deserted. Now Poe departs—my friend and the only man on the entire trip, save Payton, with whom I could converse. He goes to Little Rock to see his fiancée. I hated to see him go. Will meet me in Chicago on Monday.

Friday, October 3, 1930. Arrived in Kansas City. Saw thousands of idle Negroes, some lying about on the grass asleep. The population here is about 390,000; 40,000 Negroes.

Most Negroes work in the packing plants. Have lost jobs more so than whites. Much is to be ascribed to the fault of the Negro worker himself. Mexicans doing most of the railway labor. Three-fourths Mexicans on street railways.

Picked up a white man just outside of Kansas City. Brought him to Jefferson City. Was broke. Apologized. We assured him he was our guest. Don't know how he took it. Promised to meet us at the capitol tomorrow to go to St. Louis with us.

We arrived in Jefferson City, Missouri at 7:30 a.m. The capitol is beautiful. Small town. Population about 18,000. Lincoln University sits on a hill. Called on President [Nathan B.] Young. Greeted me cordially. Gave us every hospitality.

Saturday and Sunday, October 4 and 5, 1930. The strain of the past day told upon me so that I was unable to awake before six o'clock. And we were supposed to pick up "Charlie" (a white man) at the capitol building at five. I pitied him out there in the cold. And "broke" too.

Decided to remain until 6:20 for breakfast in the dining room. . . . The meal, however, was wretched—Post Toasties, one sausage, and bread. There was coffee or milk. It even proved unappetizing to me, low as my finances were. I had two dollars. Wilkey nothing.

Went to the capitol to find our "white friend" ("Charlie"). Did not see him, although we drove around the building. Both of us were awed by its beauty.

Failing to find "Charlie," we decided to leave for St. Louis only to pick him up at a gasoline station on the way to Route 50.

"Charlie" was certainly elated to see us. He had waited for us since five o'clock. I knew he was angry, peeved, and exasperated. But beggars must ever suppress their feelings and instead of complaining, he fawned upon us. Poor fellow, he must have been penniless. Told us he would never forget our kindness.

The scenery en route to St. Louis was very impressive. Time after time, as we journeyed through the picturesque Ozark Mountains with their rolling steeps clothed in blue mist, we could survey the country for miles. On one occasion, we reached the summit of a peak, and far below and before us stretched a rolling plain where farmhouses and neatly kept or newly plowed fields stood in deep contrast to the multicolored slopes of the mountains that rose behind them upward, upward, upward, until they lost their green, brown, and crimson colored summits in the low-hanging clouds of blue haze. . . . As "Charlie" remarked, who can doubt the presence of an all-pervading Deity when the puny human tears himself away from the "ant-hill" creation of man and goes forth to feed his soul by contemplating the grand, vast and majestic creations of God?

"Charlie" left us at Union, about 43 miles from St. Louis. Took our names. Thanked us profusely and promised to send us something to Washington, D.C.

I canvassed on Jefferson Street where much of the Negro business is. Just wanted to make one sale in order to get enough gas to get to Chicago. Few professional men were in their offices. Most of them had either gone to the ball game or were listening in somewhere else over the radio. Those who were in would purchase nothing. Some, like Dr. Centre, were even discourteous. Walked away with a curt "no."

We decided to leave with $3.85 between us. Luckily, gas was comparatively cheap. 13 1/2 cents. We crossed the "free" bridge over the Missouri [Mississippi] to East St. Louis, Illinois. This was the scene of the fatal race riot in 1917, when 150 Negroes were killed by whites. The town is dark. The Negroes and whites all look degraded and the whole atmosphere reeks with the possibility of something about to happen. . . . We were glad to get out of town. My dinner consisted of one 5-cent hamburger sandwich. Wilkey ate two. Could not afford to spend any more money for food; needed it for gas.

Arrived in Chicago about 9:36 a.m. Wilkey said that his brother would be able to keep us. Took me there. First he had moved. We finally found him at 4101 South Parkway. And in what a predicament. Penniless, out of work, and expecting us to help him. At first glance, God forgive me, I did not like him. He looked rough. . . . Went to Pilgrim Baptist Church to meet Reverend [Junius C.] Austin. [I] knew if I could get an opportunity to talk to his congregation, my worries would be at an end. Tired and sleepy, I drove up before his great stone edifice, formerly a Jewish synagogue. Waited in his office for him. Choir and ushers came in, sang, and prayed. I sat while they stood singing and praying. Felt like a fish out of the water.

Reverend Austin, a small man, entered. Inquired of me my business. Told him I had written him from Tulsa, Oklahoma. Oh, yes, he remembered. Had communicated with him a little late, and his program was filled. At least it was filled for this morning, but he advised me to come in and sit in the pulpit. I could not do so without first going to wash up, shave, and put on another suit. I went home for this purpose.

On my return, Reverend Austin was just ending his sermon. . . . Three thousand people before and all around him, gazing intensely upon the man that they had come to have inspire them, hanging on to his every word, greeting his fiery and fervent outgushings with equally loud and fervid "amens," rising with the pitch of his voice, descending as he lowered his tone, rocking as he rocked and, in short, blending their persons even as one with him. And he, cognizant of their weakness, and knowing full well the strings of their collective hearts, played marvelously upon them. It was oratory—captivating, seducing, entrancing, formidable as the sea's billows, which swept everything before it and consumed all it did not sweep away. It caught and held me, made me to gaze in astonishment at the power of the spoken word. I yearned to have just ten minutes with the same audience. I felt the urge to speak, to say something to arouse them to another pitch of frenzy, only this time on Negro History. But it was not to be. A Miss Davis, a slight missionary from Africa, had previously been scheduled to speak. She did so in a clear, soft, musical, almost childish voice, telling of her struggles and progress in Christianizing the Africans. She was rewarded by a substantial collection, taken up in a wastepaper basket. Austin asked each one to give her a dollar, and many was the dollar that fell in the plates as they passed around. I might say that Austin takes up his usual collections in wastebaskets. I myself saw half a dozen such receptacles, nearly three-quarters full, sitting almost before the pulpit.

. . . Went to Wilkey's sister-in-law's, who was to have cooked dinner. Did not do so. Gave Wilkey a dollar to take us to a lunchroom. I desired to go to the Y.M.C.A. The older Wilkey vetoed it. Oh, he is so different. His level of values are so much lower than mine that it was almost impossible for me to restrain myself from crying out against him. For dinner I took some kale and rice, with cornbread. It was wretched, but it kept the wolf away. I determined to get out of Chicago as soon as possible.

I went back to the Wilkeys'—the eldest. Went to sleep for two hours. When I arose, the Wilkeys had gone out. Folks were playing cards in the dining room. Liquor was freely flowing. Judging by the carefree speech and actions of the people, it did not take me very long to realize what sort of people I had fallen among. One woman even openly stated that it was getting cold and that she had to find a "sweetie" who would give her a home for the winter. Shocking, yes. But then body and soul must be held together and such immorality is just as great a reflection of unfavorable and low economic opportunity as it is traceable to inherent moral looseness. I played cards for a while in order not to create the impression which I felt.

Monday, October 6, 1930. My first stop was at the office of the *Chicago Whip*. It is located on the second floor of the Phythian Building on State Street at 37th. It is the largest building I had ever seen owned by Negroes.

Met Mr. [Joseph D.] Bibb. . . . Extremely glad to see me and to hear of my travels throughout the South. . . . Congratulated Bibb upon his campaign to open up jobs for Negroes in white business houses here. Told me that it was only a local panacea and perhaps could not be applied to any community indiscriminately. It comes about by the concentration of many white businesses in the heart of a Negro section. Bibb's slogan is "Don't spend your money where you can't work." Through it he has opened up more than 3,000 jobs for Negroes. Asked me to come in to see him at 6:30 to tell Mr. MacNeal about conditions in the South.

Went from Bibb's to the *Chicago Defender* Building on Indiana Avenue at 33rd Street. Met Mr. [Robert S.] Abbott, the owner. He asked an assistant to take us through the plant. I was interested in the linotyping machines. They are almost human in their operation. As one white operator commented, they do almost everything except talk . . . . Whites operated all the linotyping machines. This is in marked contrast to the *Norfolk Journal and Guide* plant, where all such work is done by Negroes. My guide informed me that these workers must belong to the union and that the union distributed these several men around to the various jobs. The same whites, he added, taught one colored fellow. He is in charge of the makeup department. There are 85 employees. All of the mechanics are white. Negroes do not belong to the union.

Next, I was introduced to Dewey Jones, the city editor. He was so struck by my observations on the trip that he asked me to write an article for his paper. I promised to give it to him tomorrow.

Tuesday, October 7, 1930. Returned to Urban League. Met Mr. [Alonzo C.] Thayer, who is in charge of the industrial department. Estimates number of Negroes out of work at 10,000 here. I believe number too low. Perhaps he means those who would work. . . . He referred me to Mr. [Irwin C.] Mollison, an attorney who, he added, was president of the Association's branch here.

Mollison's office is in the Loop district. Young man, very fair. Looked with disfavor upon my speaking. Thought it might compromise the Association. Told me the unemployment situation here had created factions, each of which feels convinced it had the panacea for the labor ills of the Negro. The Urban League, of necessity, since its income is derived from capitalists, counsels caution, and asked that economic bars be let down to the Negro because he is efficient. On the other hand, the *Whip* contends that such will never come to pass (and I must to a great extent agree with them) without agitation. Two hostile camps have, therefore, sprung up in Chicago, each striving to solve the problem in its own way and each unable to find any common ground for action.

Mollison tried to get the Negro History Club together to have me talk to it, but it could not be arranged. Asked me to speak to his Economic Club tonight at 8:30.

Went to dinner at Smith's Cafe on 47th Street. Hungry, yet had only 60 cents. Had to pour [sic] over the bill of fare until I could find something within my reach. Could not, so therefore, took vegetable dinner. It cost 50 cents. Had to leave when the waitress was not looking, for I could not tip her. Forced to walk eight blocks in the rain. Drenched. Almost decided I would not go to Moore's office. But then I had promised to do so.

I arrived at Moore's about 8:15. Mollison arrived about 10 minutes later. After a little preliminary business, they introduced me, or rather Mollison did. Told me that they adjourned at 9:00 sharp, even if the speaker was in the midst of a sentence. I began talking at 8:45. Finished at 9:50. Wesley, a lawyer, told me it was the best discussion of the Negro unemployment problem that he had ever heard. Mollison said he could not stop me, it was so interesting. He told me I was the only speaker who had ever exceeded the time limit.

Wednesday, October 8, 1930. Rose at 8:00, after spending an abominable night. These two Wilkeys were all over me. At one time they had me lying on the extreme edge of the mattress, with one foot dangling over the side. They roll, toss, and tumble, and the younger one takes on the shape of an "S." I have not been used to this and God knows if

I were able financially I should have left Chicago long ago. I have just refused, however, to cash another personal check in order to extricate these fellows from their predicament, and Wilkey's brother had the temerity to ask me when I expected to leave.

Now for breakfast. Grapes, doughnut, and coffee, with a small piece of cheese. For the first time in my entire trip I have been called upon to eat such a meager breakfast.

. . . I stopped at Wendell Phillips High School. Met Mrs. DePriest. She is a junior high school teacher. The school, itself, is too small to accommodate the students. Hence, a double row of portables takes care of the overflow. In one of them, Mrs. DePriest, a pleasant, brown woman of 35 or 36, taught. She greeted me affably and expressed delight in her brother's sending me. She took me to meet Mr. McCarthy and Mr. Williard. The latter, a small, white man about 52, did not incline to favor my speaking. He told me that several times Negroes have spoken from the platform and their speeches have rankled both the whites and some of the blacks there.

I assured him, however, that my talk to the students would be free from anything that smacked of propaganda. He told me to make out an outline, and if it met his approval, all well and good. Williard was satisfied when I showed him the outline that nothing I would say could possibly arouse resentment. However, he still was not inclined to let me speak.

Still not wishing to commit himself, Mr. Williard took me to the dean of the school—Mrs. [Annabel Carey] Prescott. . . . She decided it would not be expedient to have me speak on an entirely Negro subject. The colored students might feel that since they are about 95 percent of the student body they were having things foisted upon them which they would not get if they are attending Hyde Park or some other high school. She also felt that there was a certain undercurrent among both students and teachers which, every now and then, caused a ripple upon the surface and which might be exaggerated by such a special Negro assembly. I remarked in answer to her first point that Negro children ought to be glad to hear about the exploits of their race and that they ought to feel proud to have these contributions made known to them in the presence of white teachers and students. White students, too, enjoy it as I know from my experience, not only in New York but also in the South. To her second contention, while I admitted that under no circumstances would I knowingly or willingly be party to any action which would fan racial prejudice here, I did not feel that anything I would say could be taken in any different light than the recitation of facts on English or Greek history, which such as a visitor from these countries might bring to the students in a talk.

Mrs. Prescott then replied that the Chicago schools were now facing a crisis as to whether there should be separate schools because of the voluntary segregation practiced by Negroes in herding together in residential districts. (Wendell Phillips is surrounded by the black belt of the South Side). She feared, therefore, to bring in anything in the nature of a segregated talk which might foster a dual school system.

She informed me that there was a history club at the school, consisting of some 90 members. Suggested that I return later in the fall and speak to them.

I took my leave, but could not help feeling that both Mr. Williard and Mrs. Prescott were insincere. The former had passed the "buck" to Mrs. Prescott in order that it might not be said that a white principal had refused to grant a Negro an opportunity to bring a message to a high school student body, more than 90 percent of which was colored. For Mrs. Prescott, if she was sincere, she was wanting in vision. If not, then she lacked the courage to allow me to bring to those Negro children the thing for which their very souls are starving.

Thursday, October 9, 1930. . . . . I was sorely tempted to put my "frat" pin in pawn, for a couple of dollars in order to get the wherewithal to eat. Overcame it, however. Finally caught Rev. Williams in. A very intelligent and refined man. Also widely traveled. Interested in the books, interested to a high degree in my travels and observations. Asked about treatment in the South at the hands of whites, the labor situation of the Negroes there, and many other such kindred queries. Faint and sick as I was, I answered them. Could not purchase the books, however. His savings, like so many others, were tied up in the Binga State Bank debacle. Told me to take care of myself. I was too valuable to the race to die.

I was about at the end of my physical resource when I called upon Dr. Turner. He encouraged me, however, by subscribing, although I was forced to make several substitutions. I received his check for $4.00, which I immediately rushed downstairs to the *Whip* office, where Mr. MacNeal cashed it for me. I went immediately to the Y.M.C.A.—weak, sick, and hungry, as I was—and ordered dinner. The dinner was well-cooked and appetizing, but I was too unwell to eat it.

Walked home and went to bed. Wilkey and his brother came in about an hour later. I was burning with fever and aching terribly. Wilkey was exceedingly kind to me. . . . Told me to remain in bed. He brought me aspirin and some quinine, which I took. Then about 10:00

he came in with the castor oil, which he had had mixed for me at the drug store. It was a terrible dose, but I "downed" it, sucking a lemon afterwards. About twelve o'clock I must confess I felt a little better.

Then something astounding happened. Wilkey's brother came to the room, sat on the bed, and asked me how I felt. I answered a little better. Then he told me of the manner in which the landlady made her money—namely, by selling booze and renting rooms to couples. I had surmised this, now he had confirmed it. Then he told me that there was a couple who wanted to go to bed and, since he had not paid his rent and the landlady had an opportunity to make $2.00, she wanted to give them this room, because it was bigger. I could go out to a smaller room, which was used by Mrs. Clark and her husband. (God forgive me for as slovenly and loose as she appears I certainly did not relish lying in her bed.) I was amazed. He asked me whether it was all right with me. And in my helpless condition what could I say? Even then Mrs. Collins, the landlady, was waiting outside the room door with linen and the couple, like two animals, were also not only waiting, but clamoring to get in. I was sick, mortified, angry, for Wilkey and I would have paid for our lodging irrespective of his brother's delinquency.

Well, I got up, but found I was so weak I could scarcely stand. When I started out to the other room I found that it was not yet ready for me and while it was being prepared, I nearly fainted. Only seating myself saved me. Then Wilkey, who was lying on a couch in the dining room, and who all along had been ignorant of the proceedings, asked me whether I felt so good that I had got up. His brother then told him that the landlady had taken the room and was changing me to another one. Then Wilkey performed. I did not know he was that loyal to me. He excoriated his brother for abetting such a thing. . . . And while they argued again I nearly fainted. I tried to get to the bathroom because of the violent action of the castor oil. Some one was there.

When I finally got in Mrs. Clark nearly knocked the door down trying to seek entry, although she knew I was in there. Truly nothing had ever disgusted me or embarrassed me so much in all my life.

After going to bed in her former room, I was not even permitted to stay there. Wilkey's brother came in to ask me whether I desired to sleep in the dining room where there was a day bed and consequently more air, because of two windows. It did not require the brain of a seer to perceive what was meant. Therefore, I was moved again.

During the night the castor oil must have exerted an unprecedented action on me, for the first time in my life an accident happened. All signs were well removed, however, when the other people rose. But as

---

long as I live, I shall never forget this night. It was hideous, yet not necessary; for I could easily have secured some money.

Friday, October 10, 1930. Wilkey and I packed our things to leave. His brother—whom God knows I wish I had never met—asked us in a frightening tone, whether we meant to leave him there. I asked him where he was going. With me? Good heaven, no!

Went to the *Chicago Defender* to get a copy of my article. A young fellow, [Barfoot] Gordon, had not begun to type it. Promised to give it to me at 1:00 p.m. tomorrow. I returned to the Associated Negro Press. Met, Mr. [Claude] Barnett. I talked with him about conditions in the South. He asked me to give him a story of about 500 words covering travels. He knows Woodson personally. Feels it would help the cause. Promised to do so and see him tomorrow. He had to hurry to catch a train.

One of the most hopeful tendencies of the present unemployment situation is the comparative rapidity with which Negroes are turning to small independent ventures, like popcorn, fruit, vegetables, hot dogs, tamales, and other such commodities. In most instances, they are pushing carts laden with vegetables. Others vend one commodity only such as grapes. When one contemplates the rising new labor psychology of the Negro when he is faced by actual destitution, one almost rejoices that he is being forced out of his lowly employment. This may be the means, perhaps, of bringing forth a small independent class of entrepreneur. . . . The ultimate result of all this labor upheaval may react to make our group less menial-minded, to feel that something better awaits them in the matter of employment than "waiting," "portering," and the like.

Wilkey met me at the Y.M.C.A. at 5:00 p.m. Had dinner there. Would have secured some rooms there, but the price was prohibitive.

Finally we came to Mrs. Wilkey's to wash up before going to speak at Dr. Mansefield's. He had invited me since Tuesday to speak to some of his friends and club members at his office.

Wilkey told me that while getting out of the car today, he was suddenly told to "stick 'em up." He turned about to see himself gazing into the muzzle of three pistols, held by policemen. The police believed he might have stolen the car. After quizzing him, however, they allowed him to depart.

Sunday, October 12, 1930. I was awakened at 10:30 by Wilkey coming in. Claimed he had met a friend who took him to a party and afterwards he had spent the night at his home. I was skeptical, but reprimanded him because of possible injury to his health.

Went out to his aunt's in Maywood to breakfast. At the intersection of Michigan Avenue and 33rd Street, Wilkey failed to stop at the boulevard sign. Neither did the other drivers. Yet, a cop hailed us. We stopped. He told us he was going to take us in. Wilkey pleaded he did not see the sign. Of course, that was no excuse. . . . They were looking for graft and only decided to let us go when we told him that we were trying to sell books. . . . Another cop had come up by this time. Between them they evidently realized we had nothing, therefore, allowed us to depart. It was purely an attempt to fleece "scared" niggers, nothing more. I would have allowed them to arrest me first.

Thursday, October 16, 1930. . . . Left Cincinnati at 5:10. Outside of Ripley—that is, before coming into the town—I saw several Negro farmers. This is a unique sight in the North. Their farms were very small, but well kept. Most of them showed the industry of these people who had cleared the mountainside and planted crops there. Ripley is in Brown County, just across the Ohio from Kentucky. This county contained a goodly number of Negro farmers as far back as 1828. Many ran away from their master; others were liberated, and settled here; still others were given land by benevolent whites. The Ohio Antislavery Society Bulletin for 1838 speaks of them. Many, no doubt, are their descendants. There are also a number of colored mechanics here, a Negro painter told us. In Ripley, unlike Cincinnati, both races attend the same school and I beheld a sight that reminded me of my school days, and one I had not seen since I left New York—namely, white and colored girls going to school together.

We picked up a white man outside of Huntington and gave him a lift to West Virginia State College at Institute, West Virginia.[20] Told him we would meet him at seven o'clock the next morning at the state capitol in Charleston, and we would take him to Lynchburg. He is from Binghamton, New York, and seemed to be a pretty decent chap. His name is Bentley. He told us he is trying to locate a friend.

I met John W. Davis, president of West Virginia State College, whom I had met on several occasions before. Dr. Woodson was instrumental in getting him his position here. Davis is a good friend of the latter. He

---

[20] The state legislature of West Virginia established West Virginia Colored Institute in 1890 as the land-grant institution for African Americans. The school formally opened in 1892, and in 1915 the name was changed to the West Virginia Collegiate Institute, now West Virginia State College. Carter G. Woodson was offered the presidency of the school in 1919, but he declined and recommended his friend John W. Davis. When Woodson was fired from his position at Howard University, after a disagreement with the president, Davis employed Woodson as Dean of the College Department at West Virginia State. Woodson remained there from 1920 to 1922.

was glad to see us and put me up in a guest room with fine accommodations.

A few hours later I was introduced to a Mr. McKenzie, a teacher of History. He promised to call on me at 8:00 p.m.

After dinner I wrote in my diary for a while. Two teachers, McKenzie and [D. P.] Lincoln, came to see me. . . . Lincoln is going to our annual meeting of the Association for the Study of Negro Life and History. I told him I might come by for him. I promised to write him. Was very much impressed by both men. They were amazed at the information I had concerning the Southern Negro and his economic problems.

Saturday, October 25, 1930. Went to the office at 10:20 a.m. Woodson seemed sarcastic in his greeting. He wanted to know whether I had become "Doctor," "Professor," or what, in Lynchburg. Equally sarcastic, I told him I had. Said he wondered what had become of me. I told him there was no need to write when there was nothing to report.

Felt the campaign would go, but stated that return packages were eating up the profit. He said that the office was receiving two sets of books back each day. One came while I was there. It is his own fault. Told him in the beginning he ought to include postage. Persons will not bargain for one thing and then pay another, even if the difference is twenty-five cents.

He wants someone to go to Cleveland to the meeting. I told him I would go. He asked if I would take Wilkey. Told him yes, but in reality, he is just for company only. He does not fit.

He told me that [S. W.] Rutherford wants someone to make a survey of Negro unemployment in Washington. He had asked Rutherford to give it to me. I may accept it, may not. I would rather write a pamphlet on Negro unemployment in the South, its causes, and remedies, and sell it.

THE GREEN SUIT/*Dwight Allen*

ONCE UPON A TIME—September of 1976, to be exact—I went to New York. I was twenty-three. I had a diploma from a college in the hills of eastern Tennessee, a school that until my junior year had not admitted women. As I drove to New York from Kentucky, where my parents lived, I sometimes looked at myself in the rear-view mirror. I had longish hair and dismayingly round, soft cheeks that required little shaving. My small, turned-down mouth showed the effect of my wanting to be taken seriously. In my eyes I thought I saw something flashing, some twitchy eagerness I'd failed to suppress in my desire to be a person whom life wouldn't burn. When I stopped at the George Washington Bridge tollbooth and looked at myself a final time before entering Manhattan, I saw someone who had drunk seven or eight cups of coffee and smoked a pack of cigarettes between the Ohio River and the Hudson. The thrumming I felt at my temples was almost visible.

I'd made arrangements to stay at my Aunt Vi's apartment on the upper West Side. Aunt Vi was my mother's older sister, a painter, twice-divorced. She had a house out in Westchester, her primary residence, which she shared with two Airedales. I was supposed to get the keys to her apartment from a man named Elvin.

It was after eleven when I found my aunt's building, a brownstone between Central Park West and Columbus Avenue. A man was sitting out on the stoop, taking the mild September air. He wore a lizardy green suit. The trousers were flared and the jacket lapels were as big as wings. The suit brought words to mind—predatory, naive, hopeful— but none of them seemed quite right. The suit shined in the sulphurous glow of the street lights, but it would have shined in pitch dark, too.

The man, who wore a white T-shirt beneath the jacket, didn't look at me as I came up the stoop with my luggage. He was smoking a cigarette. He had thick, dark, wetted-back hair, like an otter, and a pale, bony face that was not unhandsome despite the crooked nose. Under his right eye was a purplish smudge—the remnant of a shiner, perhaps. I thought he might have been in his late twenties, older than me by several years, anyway.

Across the street two men were shouting at each other in Spanish. Their curses flew back and forth, blurring the air.

"I'm looking for somebody named Elvin," I said to the man on the stoop. I remembered that my aunt had said that Elvin was from down

South—Mississippi, maybe. "He's a hick just like you, honey," she'd said, "except he's got a lot of mustard on him."

The man picked a piece of tobacco off the tip of his tongue and flicked it away. "You're looking at him, bro," he said.

"You're the building superintendent, right?"

"I guess I am," Elvin said. "I'd rather be the Sultan of Swing, but you got to deal with the cards that get dealt to you, don't you?" He was watching the two men across the street; one stalked away from the other and then turned back quickly to deliver an elaborate, gaudy curse. New York was like opera, I'd read somewhere. People in costumes discussing things at the top of their lungs.

Elvin said, "So you must be Violet's nephew. Come to get down in the big city." He smiled and brushed something visible only to himself off the sleeve of his jacket. Where, I wondered, did Elvin go in his suit and his ankle-high black boots that zipped up the side?

"Peter Smith," I said, holding out my hand.

"Pleased to meet you," he said. He clasped my hand soul-brother style. "What you got in that box there?" He pointed to the case that held my new Olivetti, a graduation gift.

"A typewriter," I said.

"Ah," he said. "Tap, tap, tap into the night, right?" He dragged on his cigarette and then launched it toward the sidewalk. "I used to know this writer who lived in New Orleans. He died of a brain tumor or something." Elvin rose from the stoop and looked skyward. He'd been sitting on a magazine to keep his trousers clean.

"Looks like we got a big, old, hairy moon on our hands," he said.

I'd seen the moon earlier, driving across New Jersey toward New York. It was a harvest moon, the dying grass moon. Seeing it had made me shiver a little. Then it had slid behind clouds. Now, when I saw it again, hanging above apartment buildings topped with water tanks, it seemed no more than an ordinary celestial body on its appointed rounds. A big, old, cratered thing shedding a little extra light on over-lit New York.

"My old man used to say 'Katy, bar the door' when the moon got full," Elvin said. "I used not to believe any of that ass-trology stuff, but I might have to change my mind. I'm feeling a tad werewolfish tonight." He undid the middle button of his jacket.

"You're going out now?" I asked. "It's a little late, isn't it?"

"Never too late for love, bro," Elvin said. "Never too late for some of that."

A few days later, I took a typing test at a temporary employment agency. It was decided that I was a "pretty good" typist, even though I made a slew of errors while typing at a rate of thirty-five words per minute. I was thought to be presentable—a smooth-cheeked college graduate who didn't have straw in his hair or cowshit on his Desert Boots—and the agency sent me off to midtown companies in need of secretarial help. I worked for a direct-marketing firm, a bank, a company that sold gag items such as hand buzzers, an oil company, a cosmetics firm. I wore my tweed coat with the elbow patches and read Faulkner on my lunch breaks. I doused my typing mistakes with correction fluid, hoping I wouldn't be exposed as a charlatan. Late that winter the agency sent me to a publishing house on Fifth Avenue. I was put in the office of a vacationing editor and given a piece of a manuscript to retype. "Be careful you don't spill anything on the original," an editor, a woman in a black pants suit, said, tapping the top of a Thermos of coffee I'd brought with me. The manuscript pages were faded yellow second sheets; they looked as delicate as dried flower petals. After the editor went back to her desk, I held a page to my nose and sniffed it.

The section of the manuscript I typed was about an American couple travelling in the south of France. She had cut her hair short to make herself look like a boy. He wrote stories in cheap notebooks with sharp pencils. They swam naked in the cold blue sea and drank absinthe in cafes and made love. I had read most of the prescribed Hemingway in school, and I thought that what I was typing now, on an old manual Olympia, must be more of him or at least a very good imitation. I was excited. I was enthroned in an office five flights above Fifth Avenue and black New York coffee was running through my veins and sunlight was flowing in the windows—late-winter sunlight that seemed to illuminate the pleasure I felt in being where I was (however fleeting my tenancy was likely to be) and to promise more: spring, love, a life in literature. Now and then the editor put her head in the door to check on me. Once, when she came all the way into the room, I felt an urge to tell her how much I liked her black pants suit, which was Asian in style and rustled slightly when she moved. But I lost my nerve.

A few weeks later I got a permanent job at a publishing house called Church & Purviance, a sleepy, old-line company. (It was thought by some people in the publishing industry to be in a coma from which it was not likely to recover.) I worked for an elderly editor named Mr. Stawicki, who had a corner of the C & P building all to himself. He was responsible for the house's military history books. He had white hair that streamed away from his pale, speckled forehead—one could imagine him on the deck of a frigate, spyglass in hand, studying the horizon for enemy cutters—and in close quarters he gave off a sweetish scent that was a mix of talcum powder, butterscotch candy, and decrepitude. Mr. Stawicki had trouble getting my name right, for some reason that seemed only partly related to his age. He called me Son or Champ or, once, William, which was the name of a nephew of his who sold bonds on Wall Street. "Well, William," he said, " I think it's time for Mr. Powell's morning constitutional." Mr. Powell was Mr. Stawicki's thirteen-year-old Sealyham, whom I was required to walk two or three times a day.

One reason that Mr. Stawicki may have been unable to utter my name was that my predecessor's name, Petra, was close to my own. Mr. Stawicki carried a torch for Petra, who had left him to work for an editor named Marshall Hogue. On the one occasion when Mr. Stawicki and I went to lunch together, at a dark Lexington Avenue bar where both he and his dog were known, he said, following his second Rob Roy, "You know, son, you're a nice boy, but I can't forgive that man Hogue for stealing Petra from me." He pronounced her name with a soft "e" and a trilled "r." And then he alluded to the dust bin of history—he called it the "dust bed" of history—and predicted that he would soon be lying in it.

I'd gotten my job at C & P through Mr. Hogue, whom I'd met at a party at my aunt's house in Westchester. He grew up in Louisville with Aunt Vi and my mother, who sat next to him in fifth grade. He went away to boarding school, and then to college and into the service, and he returned to Louisville only for the occasional holiday. But he had acquired a certain allure while away, and when he did come back he became an object of interest to the girls of my mother's set. My mother went to dances with him. But he was just passing through. He wasn't going to stay put. Like Vi, who'd gone to New York to study painting, he was bound for other places.

At my aunt's party, Mr. Hogue and I drank wassail and ate salty country ham on beaten biscuits and talked about the town where we no longer lived. His voice had been whisked clean of all but a trace of an accent. He had a tidy grayish beard and close-cropped hair and he wore wire-rimmed glasses. He was tall and thin, like a swizzle stick. He told me that I looked like my mother, a comment I'd heard before. It flustered me nonetheless, for it confirmed my fear that the softness of feature my mother had bestowed on me suggested a certain lack of personality. I swallowed some wassail, the scent of cinnamon riding up my nose, and stammered something. Then Mr. Hogue told me that I should come see him whenever I decided to give up the temporary employment racket. Spaces opened up at C & P now and then, he said. Of course, the pay was dreadful and much of the work was humdrum, but literature must be served, mustn't it? He laughed a small, refined laugh.

In the evening, after I had finished my work for Mr. Stawicki, I went home to my aunt's apartment. The building was near the Columbus Avenue end of the block, the less genteel end, across the street from an empty, paved-over lot where kids played stickball and a man once stood with a goat in the rain and read from the Book of Isaiah. Aunt Vi had moved into the building in 1959, after bouncing around the Village for more than a decade. For a number of years she used a second apartment in the brownstone as a studio. Then, around 1970, she decided to move her easels to the countryside. The apartment she left behind, the one I sublet, didn't receive much light, but the ceilings were high and the claw-footed bathtub was large and the bedroom looked down upon a kind of courtyard that the two Irish sisters who lived below me had planted with vinca and lamium. Sometimes I would see Grace and Betty down there on warm evenings, sitting in matching aluminum-tube lawn chairs, sipping Dubonnet.

Aunt Vi's apartment was sparsely furnished. There was a card table, folding chairs, a metal cot, a worn red velvet sofa that might have passed for cathouse furniture, kitchenware (including several Kentucky Derby souvenir glasses), a small pine desk, and a couple of Aunt Vi's paintings. One was a nature morte—a sea bass on a platter, its mouth agape and eye bulging. In the other, Aunt Vi stared at the viewer through big, black-framed glasses. She had a cigarette in the corner of her mouth. Her chin was uptilted, as if she were waiting for an answer to a question. Her skin she'd painted a hazy rose color, the color of smoke mixed with the tomatoey hue that years of drinking produces in some people. The painting hung above the desk where I sat most evenings, trying to write a story called "The Green Suit." After several months of looking at my aunt looking at me and failing to make much progress with "The Green Suit" or its spinoffs (I rarely got beyond an opening page, which I obsessively re-wrote, with a Bic, in a narrow-lined, spiral notebook), I decided to cover the painting with a dishtowel whenever I sat down at the desk. Covering the portrait seemed less radical than taking it down or moving the desk to the opposite wall, where the dead fish was hung. I imagined that if I removed that picture of my aunt scrutinizing me, I'd be upsetting a certain balance of forces in the apartment.

One reason I had trouble writing was that I had a crush on Mr. Stawicki's former assistant, Petra Saunders. I sometimes found myself thinking about Petra in the midst of trying to imagine what Elvin did when he stepped out in his green suit. (I'd learned that he sometimes went to New Jersey—"the land of opportunity," he called it—and so I thought of his suit as his going-over-to-Jersey outfit.) Or I would find myself thinking about Petra while trying to light upon the word to describe the complexions of Grace and Betty, who were both tellers at a bank in Chelsea, who both wore white gloves to work. Grace and Betty were going to be in "The Green Suit," a story in which the narrator, a boy from the provinces not unlike myself, is drawn into the peculiar New York life of a man not unlike Elvin. I foresaw the story turning violent at some point—Grace and Betty mugged? Elvin wild with anger?—though I was a long way from reaching that point. The distance between where I was and where I wanted to be seemed immense, and I often found it easier to retire to Aunt Vi's dilapidated sofa, where I could give myself up to thoughts of Petra.

Not too long after I'd been hired at Church & Purviance, Mr. Hogue took me out to lunch. Petra came along. "You don't mind, do you?" he asked. We went to an expensive Chinese restaurant. I drank two gin-and-tonics and struggled with my chopsticks and confessed to liking Faulkner and Hemingway. "Faulkner more," I added.

"The big boys," Mr. Hogue said, pinching a snow pea with his chopsticks.

Petra didn't comment on my literary tastes, though I guessed, from the way she sipped her ice water and averted her eyes, that she didn't approve. She was quiet—even, I thought at first, evasive. Some part of her face always seemed to be in shadow, eclipsed by her long, dark, wayward hair or by a hand pushing the hair back. When I asked her where she'd grown up, she said, "Oh, you know, all around. My father was in the Foreign Service." She said this as if it were common for American children to grow up in Rome, Addis Ababa, and Bethesda. When I went back to the office that afternoon, my head full of gin and tea and fish sauce, I got my diary out of my desk and wrote, *Is she supercilious or am I blind? Perhaps the latter? She doesn't drink—at least not at lunch. She's reading an obscure Japanese novelist—obscure to me, anyway—which Marshall, as she calls Mr. Hogue, recommended. She looks at Mr. Hogue fondly. When she says the words Addis Ababa, I think of all those soft "a"s tumbling around in her mouth. She has a large mole between her collarbone and left breast. She wore a scoop-necked summer dress—blue, beltless.*

One afternoon a couple of weeks later, after I'd walked Mr. Powell and returned him to his cedar-scented bed in Mr. Stawicki's office, I went downstairs to the C & P library. Mr. Stawicki had asked me to look up something about a diplomat who had attended a naval conference in London in 1930. By the time I reached the library, I'd forgotten the diplomat's name. The library, which was small and windowless, smelled of orange. Petra was sitting at the table, a handsome old oak piece on which the first Mr. Purviance (so the story went) had once been pinned by an author armed with a penknife. Petra didn't look up when I entered the library. She was reading, one hand lost in her dark hair. Then I saw that hand reach for a slice of orange—it was laid out in sections on a napkin—and convey it to her mouth. The name of the naval conference participant suddenly came to me, or almost came to me, but when Petra looked up, her mouth full of orange, the name squirted away, leaving a sort of bubbly, phosphorescent trail in my brain.

"I'm doing research for the Colonel," I said, referring to Mr. Stawicki by his nickname. "For his encyclopedia of warships. The two-volume thing. I can't remember what I was supposed to look up."

"That's a problem," Petra said. She was wearing a plain white blouse and a dark skirt. The mole below her collarbone wasn't visible. With her book and her lunchbox, she looked like a proper schoolgirl. Except that her lunchbox had a picture of Mickey and Minnie on it. I took this to mean that she might have a sense of humor.

"Are you still reading that Japanese guy?" I asked. I waited for his name to surface. "Tanizaki?"

"I finished him," she said. She put another section of orange in her mouth. "Marshall asked me to read this Yugoslav writer to see if we should commission a translation." She held the book out toward me. I came closer. Her fingers and wrists were bare, no jewelry. On the cover of the book, crows or bats were swirling around a man wearing a derby and a clownish cravat. "It's sort of a surrealist satire of life under Tito. This is the Italian translation."

"Are you going to be reading that book tonight, after work, I mean?" I put my hands in the pockets of my khakis.

"What?" she asked.

"Does Mr. Hogue—Marshall—send you home with work at night?" Though I was up to my neck in desire and self-pity—I could count on one finger the number of times I'd kissed anybody during the nine months I'd lived in New York—it seemed prudent to backpedal. Backpedaling was something I could almost do with my eyes shut. "Is Mr. Hogue fun to work for?"

"He does interesting books," she said. She put the orange peels and napkin in her lunchbox, which, I saw, also contained a Milky Way candy bar. I found it comforting that she had a vice.

"And you don't have to walk a dog," I said.

"No," she said, latching her lunchbox and getting up from the table. "But I didn't mind walking Mr. Powell. I went all over town with him. I could be gone for two hours and Mr. Stawicki wouldn't say anything."

"He's sweet on you," I said.

"He's kind of lonely, don't you think?" Petra said. "Well, good luck with your research."

After work that day I walked over to Korvettes to buy a window fan. The weather had turned hot, summer having laid its heavy hand on the city before May was out. The day's heat was in the sidewalks, in the buildings I walked past, in the sweaty, pockmarked face of the blind man who stood with his tin cup and his guide dog at the corner of Fifth and Forty-eighth, rocking back and forth like a man taken over by spirits.

When I came out of Korvettes with my fan and began to walk up Fifth Avenue, I saw, a half-block ahead, Mr. Hogue and Petra. They seemed to not be walking so much as gliding—as far as that was possible on a crowded sidewalk. At several points, Mr. Hogue, who was wearing an olive-green suit (cuffed trousers, narrow lapels), touched Petra on the arm and guided her around a clot of slow-moving tourists or out of the way of some speeding local. I remembered that my mother had said of Mr. Hogue in a recent phone conversation, "He was quite a dancer in his heyday. All the girls wanted to be led by him. Little did they know!"

"Little did they know what?" I'd asked.

"That he preferred men to women," she'd said. "Haven't you figured that out yet?" She sounded perturbed.

Instead of turning left, toward Sixth Avenue, where I could catch an uptown train, I followed Petra and Mr. Hogue up Fifth Avenue. Where were they going—Petra with her lunchbox and musette bag, Mr. Hogue with his Moroccan leather satchel? Neither lived in the direction they were walking. (Petra lived way over in the east eighties; once, after going to a movie in her neighborhood, I'd walked by her building, a drab, yellow-brick sliver squeezed between brownstones.) Perhaps they were going to meet an agent or an author for a drink. Perhaps they were going to an early movie and then to supper at some Turkish or Balinese place Mr. Hogue would know about and then—my mother's assertion about Mr. Hogue's sexual preferences notwithstanding—to a mutual bed. Wasn't it possible that they were lovers, even if (to coin a phrase) Mr. Hogue was old enough to be Petra's father? There was that moment, for instance, outside the tobacconist's at Fifty-fifth, where Mr. Hogue held Petra's lunchbox while she fished around in her musette bag for money to give to a legless man who rolled himself along the sidewalk on a little furniture dolly. And then, after Mr. Hogue returned the lunchbox to Petra, there was the way, too delicate to be fatherly, he touched the small of her back, nudging her toward wherever they were going.

I followed a half-block behind, humping my three-speed fan and my briefcase, sweating through my seersucker jacket. At Grand Army Plaza, where I stopped to light a cigarette, I got caught in an auto-pedestrian crosswalk snarl and fell a block behind. I lost sight of my quarry for a minute, and then I spotted them disappearing under the canopy at the Hotel Pierre.

I walked across the Park, toward the West Side, secure in the knowledge that the life I wanted to possess was going to elude me. I saw a man drinking a carton of orange juice while riding a unicycle. I saw some Hare Krishnas crossing the Sheep Meadow in their saffron robes. Then, on a path near the Lake, a man wearing a floppy red-velvet beret-like hat on top of his Afro stopped me and asked for my wallet. He showed me an X-Acto knife, no more than an inch of blade sticking out of its gray metal housing. I gave him my wallet and stared at the carotid artery in his neck, which seemed to be throbbing. He went through my wallet without saying a word. I felt I should say something, and so I asked him if he wanted my fan, too.

"No, I don't want your dumb-ass fan, you dumb-ass bitch," he said. He dropped the wallet on the ground and walked off. He'd taken the cash and a ticket I'd bought for *La Bohème.*

I walked out of the Park and up Central Park West. By the time I'd reached the Museum of Natural History, I'd stopped shaking. By the time I reached my street I felt oddly at ease, as if I could float the final half-block past the spindly young trees whose trunks were wrapped with tape, right on up the stoop, on which Grace and Betty had set a pot of geraniums. I picked a cigarette butt out of the geranium pot, flicked it away, and went up to my apartment. The door was ajar. I heard Aunt Vi's voice, and then I saw Elvin sitting on the couch, smoking.

"Hey, bro," Elvin said. "You're just in time for cocktails." Elvin was wearing a black sleeveless T-shirt and blue jeans. No shoes. The shirt was made of a shimmery material, like his green suit. He was all muscle and bone, and he gave you the impression that he'd done nothing to achieve it, except perhaps smoke to curb his appetite. At one time, he'd told me, he'd worked as a mud logger on an oil rig in the Gulf of Mexico and commuted with wads of cash between New Orleans and New York. Before that, he'd been in the Army, but had somehow avoided a tour in Vietnam. More recently he'd worked as a car jockey in a parking garage in Midtown. Now he did odd jobs for the landlord to pay off his rent. And occasionally earned beer money by modeling for Aunt Vi.

Aunt Vi came out of the kitchen with a drink in each hand. "I let myself in, Petey," she said. "I hope you don't mind." She gave Elvin his drink and surveyed me through her big black glasses. The glasses made her seem both distant and overbearing, like a bird of prey.

"No, I don't mind," I said, setting down the fan but leaving my jacket on for the moment. I didn't consider the apartment to be mine, any more than I considered myself to be a resident of New York.

"I had to come into town to see Dr. Bickel, so he can pay for the addition on his summer house in Quogue," Aunt Vi said, laughing her heavy, tobacco-crackled laugh. "The old buzzard would cap every one of my teeth if he could."

I looked around the room, as if some clue to my existence were to be found there. On the mantel above the non-working fireplace, I saw the wine bottle that I'd not quite emptied the night before while sitting at my desk, waiting for inspiration to blow through me and prickle the hairs on the back of my hand. Beside the sofa, not far from Elvin's bare feet, the pale, bony dogs which had carried him far from Mississippi, were one blue sock and a packet of newspaper clippings my mother had sent me from Kentucky. On the wall was Aunt Vi's painting of her ripe, florid self; I'd had the foresight to remove the dishtowel.

"You look like you could use a drink," Aunt Vi said.

"You've been working too hard, bro," Elvin said, hoisting his glass, grinning. "Take a load off."

"I wouldn't mind having a drink," I said to Aunt Vi. I thought I probably wouldn't tell her and Elvin about my run-in in the Park.

My aunt went back into the kitchen. Elvin said, "I'm thinking of going over to Jersey on Saturday. You want to come?"

"What do you do there?" I asked.

"Study the landscape, do a little recon," Elvin said, blowing a stream of unfiltered smoke toward the ceiling. "Go bowling sometimes. See this girl I know."

I wondered if Elvin went bowling in his green suit, or if he took a change of clothes.

"Sounds nice," I said, not wishing to offend Elvin, who was, after all, the building's super and could requisition me an extra door lock, if I should ever need one. "I'll check my social calendar."

Aunt Vi returned with my drink, a gin-and-tonic, heavy on the gin, in a Kentucky Derby glass. The gin went straight to that part of me that wished to lie down, and so I excused myself, saying I was going to change out of my work clothes.

"Sound your funky horn, man," Elvin said, snorting.

"What's that supposed to mean, Elvin?" Aunt Vi asked.

"It's just a song I used to sort of like," Elvin said, dreamily.

I went into the bedroom, undressed, polished off the gin, and lay down on the cot. I looked at the Monet poster I'd stuck on the wall—a sun-drenched beach scene, flags rippling in the breeze.

"The boy needs to get laid," I heard Elvin say. He made two syllables out of "laid."

"I'm sure he'd be touched by your concern," Aunt Vi said. "When are you going to sit for me again?" Elvin was one of my aunt's favorite subjects. She'd painted him clothed and unclothed—once in repose on a couch, in the manner of Manet's "Olympia," with a Mets cap covering his genitals. His eyes were near to being closed. "Drowsy Elvin," my aunt called the painting.

They talked about dates and fees. I started to drift off, my body tingling as I went. At one point, I heard Aunt Vi ask me if I wanted to go out for supper. No, I thought. I'll just lie here forever.

Three weeks later, a warm mid-June evening, I lay upon the same bed, absorbing the breeze generated by my fan. I was wearing basketball shorts and a University of the South T-shirt. Now and then I heard firecrackers explode. The Fourth was approaching, and every kid in the neighborhood was armed to the teeth. Below my window, in the dim courtyard, Grace and Betty sipped cocktails and discussed the events of the day: the rudeness of a young officer at the bank, the elderly Negro man whom they no longer saw on the Number 11 downtown bus, Elvin's failure to fix a dripping faucet, whether the church they went to could afford to install air-conditioning.

I'd been home since about three in the afternoon, having fled the office in the wake of Mr. Powell's death. I'd taken Mr. Powell for a lunchtime walk over in Turtle Bay, where trees provided shade and there was the occasional poodle or Boston terrier for my charge to sniff. On Second Avenue I slipped Mr. Powell's leash around the top of a fire hydrant and went into a deli to buy a sandwich. Mr. Powell, being old, wasn't frisky, and I expected him to do no more than wait patiently on the curb while I got my turkey on rye. But he stretched his leash and wandered off the curb into the gutter, where there was garbage to be inspected. I didn't witness the accident, but I was told by a pedestrian, a well-dressed man walking a Chow, that a cab turning left and cutting the corner close had struck Mr. Powell, that the driver had hit his brakes, but then had gone on, perhaps at the urging of his fare.

Mr. Powell had been killed instantly, but as I carried him back to the office, in a black garbage bag that the deli manager had given me, I kept thinking, absurdly, Maybe he's just sleeping. When I'd picked him up out of the gutter there hadn't been any blood on his thick white coat and the only certain sign of death that I could see was in his eyes, which were open but of no apparent use. However, he didn't stir as I bore him toward his master, and toward, I felt increasingly sure, my own termination. Mr. Powell grew heavier as I rode in the elevator to my floor, accompanied by silent Jimmy, the uniformed elevator operator, who was the most phlegmatic man in New York.

When Mr. Stawicki saw me with the garbage bag, he said, "Please don't tell me that's my dog." I said it was and that I was very sorry and that it had happened suddenly and that Mr. Powell hadn't seemed to suffer much, if at all.

Mr. Stawicki looked stricken. He waved me out of his office.

I sat down at my desk and wrote him a note of apology, restating my remorse at his loss, saying that I planned to look for work elsewhere but would stay on until he found a replacement. I put the note in the In box outside his door. Then I went downstairs to the main editorial floor to see Mr. Hogue and tell him about Mr. Powell and my decision to leave Church & Purviance.

But Mr. Hogue was not in his office. Nor was Petra in her adjoining nook, though the coffee in her mug was warm. So I went back upstairs, got my briefcase, and walked home, via the Park, where I encountered no muggers, only a violinist dressed up in a bear suit. At the apartment, I drank plain lemonade and listened to Mississippi John Hurt sing "Candy Man" in his gentle, rocking-chair voice. Then I lay down on the bed and napped, dreaming that I was a child sick in bed and that Grace and Betty were ministering to me, bringing me broth (in a church collection plate) and magazines and stuffed animals.

Later, awake, listening to the drone of the fan and the voices of Grace and Betty, I considered the idea of returning home to Louisville and hooking on with my grandfather's brokerage firm and eating high-cholesterol lunches with my father at the downtown club where he played penny-a-point bridge and marrying any one of several young women I knew whose interest in literature was about the same as their interest in ethnography or limnology. This notion occupied me for several minutes—deeply enough that the sound of my door buzzer didn't immediately rouse me. When I did finally leave my cot and go downstairs, I at first saw only Elvin, shirtless, standing in the vestibule, where the mailboxes were. Then, beyond the outer door, on the stoop, I saw Petra, her musette bag over her shoulder. She was leaving. I opened the door and called her name.

Elvin, scratching his flat, naked belly, said, sotto voce, "Hey, man, if she's the reason you bugged out on me, I forgive you."

I hadn't gone bowling with Elvin in New Jersey. I'd pleaded a tight schedule.

"Thanks," I said. I was happy to be on Elvin's good side. I stepped out the door onto the stoop. Elvin remained in the vestibule.

"I was sorry to hear about Mr. Powell," Petra said. She was wearing a white, open-necked blouse and a blue jean skirt.

"Thanks," I said. The stoop felt warm on my bare feet.

"I'm coming from my dentist," she said, "down on Eighty-first. Dr. Fingerhut. He's this old guy whose only flaw is that he believes in minimal anesthesia. He plays Schubert or Mozart while he's scraping tartar off your teeth. 'Ah, my dear, you haf vut looks like a very sweet tooth. Ve must repair before it becomes a very tot tooth.' Marshall told me about him. He's cute, except for his ideas about anesthesia." She paused, as if to consider her presence on my stoop.

I didn't know what was more improbable: a suddenly chatty Petra or the fact that she was standing near me on a warm summer evening. The air—the grimy, hazy, fume-laden air of Manhattan—seemed almost fresh. There was nearly enough oxygen in it to make your head spin.

"Dr. Fingerhut told me about this Cuban-Chinese restaurant on Amsterdam somewhere," Petra said. "I thought you might be able to help me find it."

"I'll get my shoes," I said.

We found the Cuban-Chinese place, up Amsterdam, in the shadow of a new housing project, but it didn't serve liquor, which, it turned out, Petra avoided only during work hours. We walked back to a bar called the Yukon, down the block from the laundromat that I and Elvin and Grace and Betty frequented. I'd watched some baseball in the Yukon, and had even, once, tried writing there. Except for the refrigerated air, there wasn't anything in the Yukon that suggested the remote Canadian Northwest. No pictures of Jack London or sled dogs, anyway.

We sat toward the back, in a booth that had a view of the dartboard. A fat, bearded man and his petite female companion were playing.

"Tell me again how Mr. Powell got killed," Petra said. She'd been out of the office for part of the afternoon, and had heard about the incident fourthhand, from Mrs. Berlin, the receptionist.

I told Petra the story of Mr. Powell's death, and then I said that I was going to look for work elsewhere and was even thinking of moving back to Kentucky, where I could whittle sticks with my friends. I was hoping, of course, that she would try to dissuade me from the latter idea and give me room to imagine that I could displace Mr. Hogue as her lover. The notion that she was Mr. Hogue's lover had taken root and flourished in the little hothouse of my mind.

"I've never been to Kentucky," Petra said, turning the frosted glass that contained her vodka-and-tonic. "Marshall talks about spring down there, how pretty it is."

"Um," I said. I let pass the chance to ask about her relationship with Mr. Hogue. A couple more beers and I might have managed it. "What was spring in Addis Ababa like?"

"It was nice, mild. Addis Ababa is eight thousand feet above sea level, you know," Petra said. She was looking past me. She laid her hand on my free hand, the one that wasn't gripping the bottle of Rheingold, and nodded in the direction of the dart players.

"Look," she whispered. "On the floor. The bag."

I turned and leaned out of the booth and saw a gym bag under the table that held the dart players' drinks. Then I saw the man, who was wearing a billowy shirt that had a tropical theme, flick a dart toward the target. The motion his hand made was dainty and precise; it was if he were dotting an i.

"What?" I asked Petra. She'd removed her hand from mine almost as quickly as she'd put it there. If she touched me again, I thought, that would mean something. I was a boy who required reassurance, an appalling trait to have in a place like New York.

"The bag," Petra said. "It's moving. There's something in it."

I rubbernecked again, and saw that there was indeed something moving inside the bag, flexing it this way and that.

"'Maybe it's a ferret." I looked at the mole below her collarbone; I wanted to put my thumb on it.

"No," Petra said, firmly. "It's a snake. Those people look like snake owners."

I turned around once more. The woman was studying us. She did somewhat resemble a person you might see at a roadside reptile farm—the proprietor's thin-lipped wife, who keeps the books and dreams about running off with the guy who stocks the farm's Coke machine. She had a hard face that was once pretty.

"You don't like snakes?" I asked Petra.

"I don't expect to see one in a bar," she said. "It kind of takes the wind out of your sails."

"I know what you mean." As she finished her drink, I thought I could see her considering whether to take a cross-town bus home or to spring for a cab. If she was going home, that is. In any event, it seemed clear that she didn't wish to spend any more time in the Yukon.

I paid for the drinks and waited by the jukebox while Petra used the Ladies'. When she came out, she stopped to talk with the dart players. Then she came on toward me, the news that she'd been right about the contents of the bag written on her face. She was a person who took some satisfaction in being right.

"It's a python," she said. "A baby python. They have a bunch."

We walked out into the warm, jarring air. The sky was still an hour short of turning the smudgy color that was the local version of night-time. Yellow cabs were streaking down Columbus. A man wearing beltless, crimson slacks and a shirt of several hideous colors came up the avenue, cutting a wide swath, singing, muttering, nodding violently to himself.

"I guess I'll go now," Petra said. She stepped off the curb and waved for a cab.

"O.K.," I said.

A cab cut across two lanes and came to a halt a yard or so from Petra's sandaled foot. She didn't flinch. "Don't feel too bad about Mr. Powell," she said. "And don't go home to Kentucky with your tail between your legs. Be brave." She gave me a quick kiss on the cheek. Its delicate placement reminded me of the way the fat man had thrown the dart.

"What are you reading nowadays?" I asked, as she got into the cab, a part of her leg that I'd not seen before becoming briefly visible.

The thought that I was homosexual had of course occurred to me now and again—for instance, on those occasions when I'd lain on my narrow, squeaky cot, solemnly holding myself. But if this were true, why did the sight of Petra's thigh, not to mention the touch of her mouth, move me so?

"Proust," she said, pulling the door to. "He's great. You should try him. He'll make you want to . . ." The cab shot away, like a cork flying out of a bottle, leaving me to imagine what she thought Proust would make me want to do. Learn French? Run naked down Broadway shouting "Hallelujah"? Sleep with men? Proust, I knew, had been homosexual. That was about all I knew about him. He hadn't been on the syllabus at my college in east Tennessee.

I headed back up Columbus. Standing in the doorway of the laundromat, smoking, watching the world rush by, was Elvin. He signaled to me. Over his jeans, he was wearing what looked like a pajama shirt, v-necked, with red piping. His muscle shirts must have been in the wash.

"Hey, bro," he said, "maybe we can double sometime."

"Double?" I asked, thinking this was street slang I'd failed to absorb.

"Double date," he said. "You and your chick, me and mine."

"Yeah," I said. "Maybe we could do something like that."

Elvin drove up the Henry Hudson Parkway, slaloming in and out of the thick Saturday afternoon traffic like a stunt driver—a style that made it difficult for me to concentrate on the long sentences describing the amatory practices of M. Swann. So I put my book down. But watching Elvin drive—one-handed, mostly, while he sucked on a joint—was too frightening. And looking out the window at the river, sparkling though it was in the July sun, was insufficiently distracting. So I fixed upon Connie's dark, shag-cut head. Connie, who was Elvin's girlfriend. Who was—as far as I could deduce—not much older than sixteen. She had an operator's license, anyway; she'd driven the car, her father's, over from Jersey before giving the wheel to Elvin. Connie, who had said to Elvin as he laid down rubber at the last stop we'd see until we hit the Spuyten Duyvil bridge, "My father's going to fucking kill me if you wreck it." To which Elvin had said, "Be cool."

We were going to my aunt's house in the green hills of northern Westchester. It was her fifty-fifth birthday, and she was giving herself a party. She'd invited a great flock of people—painter friends, Village friends, Grace and Betty, my parents, Mr. Hogue, other Kentuckians, her dentist. Grace and Betty declined (they were going to Mystic with a church group), and so did my parents, who, according to my mother, had a long list of conflicts. But Mr. Hogue was coming, and so was the dentist. Petra was supposed to be there, too. In any event, I'd asked her, and she'd said yes, though the yes was provisional, dependent upon whether she could resolve something in her social schedule.

I'd asked Petra to Aunt Vi's party about a week before I was to leave Church & Purviance. One effect of being nearly unemployed was that I didn't feel my usual diffident self around Petra. Anyhow, the sight of her standing next to the copy machine, a cranky, unreliable thing that wheezed and heaved before disgorging paper, had emboldened me. She'd gotten her hair cut quite short; her exposed neck was as pale as a photographic negative. And so I'd asked her for a date, and after she'd startled me with her yes (provisional though it was), I'd also asked if she were no longer seeing Mr. Hogue.

Petra looked at me with her small, bright, critical eyes for as long as it took the copy machine to cough up three pages of somebody's five-hundred-page Bildungsroman.

"I like Marshall and he likes me, but we don't 'see' each other," Petra said, smiling at my foolishness, revealing her teeth, which were imperfect. She had a snaggly upper right canine. "He has other interests."

"Ah," I said, which was the sound of my mind opening slightly to receive important information. Air entering the hothouse.

"Ah," I said again, two weeks later, as I, fully unemployed, rocketed up the Saw Mill with stoned Elvin and his barely legal girlfriend, and without Petra, who would get to Aunt Vi's on her own, if a lunch date she had with Ethiopian friends of her father didn't take forever. The "Ah" this time was the sound of air being nervously expelled. I thought there was a good chance that Elvin would fail to negotiate one of the many curves on the narrow Saw Mill, or, if we got that far, one of the many curves on the even narrower Taconic. I thought, too, that there was a good chance that I wouldn't see Petra, even if Elvin didn't wipe us out. She'd made no promises.

Connie passed me a bottle of beer and smiled. She was wearing a retainer, which made her look even younger than she was. She had a pretty mouth with a fleshy underlip, and brown eyes clouded by worry. How had Elvin acquired her, I wondered. Had he been wearing his green suit when he seduced her? I drank my beer rapidly and asked Connie, who was keeping pace, for another. We made more eye contact. Elvin, singing along with a Peter Frampton song, miraculously steered us off the Taconic and down a snaky, wooded road to my aunt's house.

It felt wonderful to have the ground under my feet, and after I'd kissed my aunt (who was wearing a huge, brocaded sombrero), and after I'd gotten a plate of food and another bottle of beer, I sat down on the grass under a large sugar maple, next to Beau Jack, one of Aunt Vi's two Airedales. Elvin took Connie to see Aunt Vi's studio, an old implements shed that she'd fixed up. Beau Jack panted and watched me eat barbecued chicken. It was a hot, breezeless afternoon. The whirligig on top of the implements shed didn't twitch. Insects crackled. A group of guests sat on the screened-in front porch, under a ceiling fan. I gave Beau Jack a chunk of chicken, and then I saw Mr. Hogue walking across the lawn toward me. He wore long, white pants (cuffed) and a blue polo shirt. The heavy July air seemed to part for him. Sweat didn't sit upon his forehead and it didn't mark his shirt. His wirerimmed glasses caught the light and scattered it.

He settled himself in the grass with his drink, something with a wedge of lime floating in it. "How do you like being retired?" he asked. There was amusement in his eyes, though the amusement was polite. He had offered to help me find a job at another publishing house, but I'd declined, saying I hadn't decided what I was going to do next.

Now I said, "Retirement is O.K. so far. I sleep in and I read Proust. Slowly. All those long sentences, you know, that drag themselves across the page like bloated serpents after a meal." I took a gulp of beer. I was high and was hoping to get higher. I hoped to see Petra soon, before I peaked.

"Petra is reading Proust, I think."

An old wood-panelled Country Squire station wagon rolled up the driveway, crunching gravel. Four men in white shirts got out. Musicians.

"I'm in love with Petra," I said, in a voice that one might use when taking an oath of office.

"I gather you're trying to say you're not queer," Mr. Hogue said evenly.

"No," I said. "I mean, yes, I'm not." I drained my beer and looked toward my aunt's studio. Elvin stood outside the shed, pouring beer down his throat. In the flat mid-afternoon light, he seemed somehow two-dimensional, tinny: Man with a Big Thirst. I didn't see Connie.

"How would you know that you aren't queer?" Mr. Hogue gazed at me in a kindly, schoolmasterly sort of way.

Was there a correct answer? "I can just feel it," I said.

Mr. Hogue rose from the grass and laid his hand on the ridged trunk of the sugar maple. There were tap holes at the tree's waist. "A young friend of mine told me about a drug he once took—MDA, I think he called it—that made him want to fuck trees. Even skinny saplings excited him. He was out in the woods, you see, trying to get in touch with his soul. And he spent hours, under the influence of this drug, dry-humping anything with a trunk. And he was perfectly happy. Don't you think it's odd that a little chemical adjustment, a jot of this or that, is enough to make you surrender to a tree?"

"You have to watch what you put in your mouth," I said smartly.

"But then a tree is always there for you, isn't it?" Mr. Hogue said. "Well, let me know if you change your mind and want to get back into the publishing business. I won't tell anybody that you killed Stawicki's dog." He smiled pleasantly and walked away.

I drank more beer and kept an eye out for Petra while playing croquet with Elvin, my aunt, and her dentist, Dr. Bickel. With a cigarette
clamped between her lips and her sombrero set securely on her head,
Aunt Vi drove Dr. Bickel's ball thirty yards off the course, into the
weeds beyond the edge of the lawn. "Oh, doctor," she shouted joyfully,
"when you fetch that ball, beware the stinging nettle and the wily cop-
perhead!"

The band, which was set up on the other side of the house, played
"Blueberry Hill." Elvin sang along and drove my ball into the nettles
and fleabane. "Take a hike, bro," Elvin said, and then cruised around
the course in a single turn. "It's scary how good I am," he said. "And
I'm stoned out of my mind."

The band played a slow blues number and I went for a hike. I
walked past Aunt Vi's studio—through the window I saw a large canvas of Elvin sitting in a high-backed rattan chair in his green suit; he
looked like a small-time criminal dressed for dinner—and then I
walked through a field toward a spring-fed pond that was at the back
of the property. I'd had five beers, but I could still walk a fairly straight
line and identify some of the plants that grew in the field: goldenrod,
wild carrot, fleabane. Down in a swale, fifty yards from the pond, was
a clump of purple loosestrife. The sun shone brightly and the high
grass brushed against my shins, making them itch. I felt some throbbing in the neighborhood of my left eye: pain gathering for a frontal
assault. I'd just about given up on Petra's coming. I was looking forward to sticking my head in the water.

There was a swimmer in the pond—three, actually, if you counted
Beau Jack and his mother, Cornelia, who were wading in the reedy
shallows. The human swimmer was Connie. She was naked as a
baby, her white bottom pointed at the pale blue sky. Her head was
turned away from me. Then she dove under and when she re-
surfaced, her black hair sleek and shiny, she saw me. I was standing
on the grassy bank, unbuttoning my shirt. She seemed unalarmed by
my presence. She'd given me that lingering look in the car, after all,
which I'd interpreted to mean: I wouldn't mind it if you saved me
from Elvin. Though this reading of things was perhaps nothing more
than vanity on my part. I had a habit of seeing sparks where there
were none.

"How's the water?" I asked. I put my shirt on the ground, next to
Connie's pile of clothes. The dogs came over to sniff me.

"O.K.," she said. "Cool."

She looked away as I got out of my shorts and underwear. Had she
seen me trembling, my heart whanging away under my bare chest?

Proust: "We do not tremble except for ourselves, or for those whom we love." I didn't love Connie, needless to say.

I waded into the pond, soft, oozy mud sucking at my feet, and then I dove out toward the middle, beneath the sunstruck surface. The cool water gripped me, held me under. I could see nothing. If I kept swimming, I thought, I could end up on the other side of the world, far from harm. But the other side of the world wasn't really where I wanted to be now.

I came up behind Connie, my mouth inches from her shoulder blade and knobby vertebrae. She turned and pushed away from me a bit. Her arms were folded across her breasts. She was wearing a cross around her neck.

"Where'd you meet Elvin?" I asked.

"The Moon Bowl," she said. "In Moonachie. Where I go bowling."

"Do you like him?" I heard the band—the boom-da-boom of the bass, an undulant melody from the saxophone. Cornelia caught the scent of something and ran into the field. Beau Jack continued to work the pond shallows.

"Yeah, sure," Connie said. "Except he's kind of crazy, you know." She smiled and I saw the retainer wire across her teeth. "He has this, like, Saturday Night Special that he bought from this guy at the bowling alley. He got it so he could protect himself from nuts and stuff."

"Would he shoot me," I asked, "if he saw us getting it on?" I moved toward Connie. The pain above my eye had increased.

"Don't," she said, backing toward the shore, her hands still covering her chest. I saw the fear on her face, the way her wet, dark hair framed her tightening features. But I said nothing. I half-closed my eyes and lunged at her. Bone knocked against bone as she fell back. Her head went under for a second. I pulled her up toward me. She'd swallowed water and was coughing. I pressed my mouth against hers and tried to insert my tongue between her teeth. She shook her head free.

I let go. "I'm sorry," I said.

"Go die," she said. She coughed and wiped her mouth against her forearm. She was sitting where the water was perhaps a foot deep. Her breasts were small and waifish.

I turned away and drifted toward the middle of the pond, where the water came up to my chest. I squatted there, in the brilliant sunshine. I heard Connie get out of the water, but I didn't move. I heard Beau Jack's collar tags jangling. I stayed in the water for a long time, watching the skin on my fingers pucker, waiting to hear Elvin's voice. Would he ask me to turn around before he shot me with his Saturday Night

Special? If, for some reason, he didn't shoot me, I thought I might try to resuscitate the story I'd been writing about him.

The sun slipped down the sky and swallows made passes over the pond. I wanted a cigarette and got out of the water. My clothes weren't where I thought I'd left them, however, nor were they anywhere nearby. Connie had removed them, apparently. I walked out into the field and there, among the loosestrife, found one of my sneakers. With the sneaker in my hand, I walked back and forth across the field, stepping lightly among the milkweed and fleabane and hairy-stemmed ragweed, looking for the rest of my clothes. After a while, I sat down, using my shoe as a cushion. I was a hundred yards from my aunt's house. I could see people playing croquet, my aunt among them, with her absurd flying saucer of a hat. I could walk naked to my aunt's house now or later. Or I could simply sit here and wait for the turkey vulture, making black circles in the sky to the south, to descend upon me.

Then I saw two figures crossing the field. One was Elvin, his shimmery blue muscle shirt hanging out of his jeans. The other was a young woman wearing a dark skirt and white shirt. Petra. She trotted to keep up with Elvin, who was making tracks, despite being unable to walk straight. They were talking. I heard Elvin say, "I don't know what exactly he did. All I know is what my girl told me."

Petra stopped and held her hand up against the declining sun. Elvin came on. I rose to my feet. I held the sneaker in front of my crotch.

"You look like fucking Mr. Pitiful, bro," Elvin said, squinting, angling his head so that the sun wouldn't strike it so directly. I did not think it was to my advantage that he was wobbly drunk. "But I'm going to hit you anyway. You know why."

I didn't say anything smart or brave. I didn't say anything at all. I just stood there, hiding my privates behind my shoe, looking past Elvin at Petra, wondering where she and her Ethiopian friends had gone for lunch. Wasn't there an Ethiopian dish called *wat*? A hot, peppery dish that made your lips burn? Perhaps she'd had some of that for lunch, perhaps the taste of it was still there on her tongue.

Dwight Allen's stories have appeared in *American Short Fiction* and *Gulf Coast*.

Reviews

Undaunted Courage: Meriwether Lewis, Thomas Jefferson, and the Opening of the American West
by Stephen C. Ambrose
Simon & Schuster, 1996, 511 pp.,
$27.50

Long before the Louisiana Purchase, Thomas Jefferson had supported plans for exploring the American West. As the leading American thinker of the Enlightenment, and an amateur scientist, he nourished an active interest in the Louisiana country and was fascinated by the native Americans, the geography, and the flora and fauna of the Western wilderness. When, in October 1803, through an unusual series of events, the Louisiana territory fell into American hands, Jefferson's plan for a full-scale expedition to explore what he had just bought was ready to be launched; earlier that year he had persuaded Congress to secretly appropriate money for such a venture. In December, President Jefferson dispatched his private secretary and fellow Virginian, Captain Meriwether Lewis, along with William Clark, co-commander and younger brother of the noted Indian fighter George Rogers Clark, on what was perhaps the most famous trek in American history.

In the spring of 1804 Lewis and Clark and a party of nearly forty men set out from the frontier town of St. Louis and followed the Missouri River northward. Guided by Sacagawea, fifteen-year-old pregnant wife of a French fur trader, they crossed the Rockies into then-uncharted territory and descended along the Columbia and Snake Rivers to the Pacific coast. They were instructed by Jefferson to keep careful journals about all the plants, animals, minerals and metals that they encountered, and to note all information about native inhabitants, prospects for trade, and viable routes for overland migration. Lewis had been groomed for the job, having undergone crash tutorials in everything from botany to zoology in preparation for the collection of such diverse data. His journals would stand as perhaps the most undervalued legacy of the expedition (much of their contents would not be published for nearly a century).

Although Lewis was hailed as a national hero upon his return to St. Louis in the autumn of 1806, and despite his subsequent appointment as governor of the territory he had charted, failures in his personal life led him to alcoholism and severe depression. He committed suicide three years after his return.

In *Undaunted Courage*, distinguished historian Stephen E. Ambrose paints an original and readable portrait of Meriwether Lewis, and traces in vivid detail the hazardous odyssey that left an indelible mark on the American imagination. Drawing on new scholarship, Ambrose focuses on Jefferson's initial motivations for Western exploration. He documents the Lewis and Clark expedition, from its clandestine funding by Congress and the initial preparations—even before the vast territory was purchased—through the perilous journey to the soon-to-be "Oregon Country." Aside from the inherent drama of the trip itself, what makes this book so fascinating is Ambrose's ability to convey the sense of wonder experienced by the explorers as they encountered people and places never before seen by Euro-Americans. Ambrose also includes a portrait of Sacagawea, the remarkable young Shoshone woman who played a key role as guide and go-between during a critical leg of the journey.

Following recent trends in Jeffersonian scholarship, *Undaunted Courage* not only aids in re-establishing Jefferson's importance in American history but stands as an exhaustive and definitive study of Meriwether Lewis and the expedition that whetted American curiosity about the West.

Emerson Among the Eccentrics: A Group Portrait
by Carlos Baker
Viking, 1996, 608 pp., $34.95

If Carlos Baker is even half right, America's first philosopher of spiritual self-development and self-reliance was one of the nicest guys in the history of American literature: supportive, kind, gracious, a great listener, generous—at times self-sacrificial in saving some of his more improvident friends from financial dilemmas—a hard worker on the public-speaking circuit (his principal source of income), long suffering toward his semi-invalid wife, kind and loving toward his children, possessed of a sense of humor even regarding his own mental decline in old age ("I am an imbecile most of the time," he wrote). One almost yearns for a thorn in this rose bush.

His only flaw might be a tendency toward coolness, an inability to truly or passionately love —unlike his friend Hawthorne, who for all his inwardness was warmly devoted to his wife Sophia. Thoreau, on the other hand, was embarrassed, shy, and awkward around women to the point that it sometimes made him blush to walk through a room where they were present. The beak-nosed, irritable author of *Walden* —the most elegant single document of Transcendentalism—did, however, have a natural affection and easy relationship with Lidian Emerson, Waldo's wife. Indeed, Baker suggests that at times Thoreau, working in Emerson's household or living nearby, was more of a soulmate to Lidian than her frequently absent husband.

Baker's book fleshes out the idea, set forth in the now classic *American Renaissance: Art and Expression in the Age of Emerson and Whitman* by F.O. Matthiessen (1941), that the age of Emerson, roughly the 1830s through the '60s, was a particularly vital and coherent era in American literature. Baker generally convinces us that the Transcendentalists and their fellow travelers were important to each other: Bronson Alcott, schoolteacher and idealist; Thoreau, naturalist and ornery philosopher of simplicity; Margaret Fuller, feminist and revolutionary (and in some ways the most romantic personality among them); Nathaniel Hawthorne, handsome, dour novelist; poets Jones Very and, at a distance, Walt Whitman; the Henry James, Sr., family, including sons William and Henry, Jr. Often living near each other (Thoreau's Walden Pond shack was on Emerson's land), having extended visits with each other, writing long and articulate letters to each other, at times reading and criticizing each others' works, the Concord/Boston group formed a coherent intellectual community.

Not that they all agreed with or liked each other. Hawthorne and historian Charles Eliot Norton, were frustrated and perplexed by Emerson's tendency to float off into Neoplatonic clouds in the face of hard questions. In Norton's words, he "refused to entertain instances of misery or crime." However, in a time when publicly turning one's back on organized religion could be thought "dangerous," Emerson's persistent optimism was surely useful. Summarizing his effect on American thought and culture, Oliver Wendell Holmes, who was even more of a free thinker than Emerson, called him "an iconoclast without a hammer, who took down our idols from their pedestals so gently that it seemed like an act of worship."

Ship Fever and Other Stories
by **Andrea Barrett**
Norton, 1996, 254 pp., $21

The widespread phobia about science among literary types has often led to its depiction in fiction as a ruinous force. In this striking story collection, Andrea Barrett investigates science's place in our lives, but she does so with a respect—almost reverence—for the field that many of her predecessors have lacked. Her goal is "to write about the love of science and the science of love." She achieves it by sucessfully coupling these seemingly disparate subjects—love and science.

"The Littoral Zone" tells of two marine biologists who have an affair at a research station on an island off the coast of New Hampshire. As they look back on their relationship, they wonder if their love is worth the pain they have caused their families. In "The Behavior of the Hawkweeds" the wife of a mediocre genetecist who reveres Mendel contemplates what it means to live a life of disappointment. Mendel's work takes on significance to her as well; his theories of heredity were apparently disproven when he encountered hawkweeds, plants that do not pass "their traits serenely through generations." The young Canadian doctor in "Ship Fever" uses his medical training to care for sick Irish immigrants fleeing the Potato Famine. Though the scientific knowledge of the day proves useless in the face of one of the world's worst typhoid epidemics, the doctor learns that love and kindness can be more effective remedies.

Barrett is the author of four novels, and her stories often seem novelistic in scope and technique. Several of them employ historical settings and multiple points of view, and combine real historical figures with imagined characters—practices more common in the novel. These techniques give heft to Barrett's stories and set her apart from the scores of authors still under the influence of minimalism. The result is a memorable collection that glorifies scientific knowledge rather than indicting it.

Equation for Evil
by Philip Caputo
HarperCollins, 1996, 488 pp., $25

In his latest book Caputo, author of the Pulitzer Prize-winning *A Rumor of War*, as well the acclaimed *Horn of Africa* and *Indian Country* tries to transcend the detective novel genre. Unfortunately, the novel is more ambitious than it is successful. Though the ostensible theme of *Equation for Evil* is a metaphysical inquiry into the nature of human evil, most of the book is dedicated instead to endless, nail-biting detective work.

The story begins with the mass murder of a school bus full of Asian-American kids. The killer, neo-Nazi Duane Boggs, blurts out one last unintelligible screed and blows his brains out. As a response to the public outcry over the apparently racist-motivated mass murder, Gabriel Chin, Chinese-American Special Agent for the California Department of Justice, and Leander Heartwood, W.A.S.P. forensic psychiatrist, are appointed to investigate Boggs' crime. Together they muddle through the racism and paranoia of post-L.A. riot California, unravelling the mystery of his complex motives from end to beginning and speculating on the origins of evil.

After a promising start, the story culminates in a Stallone-like, junkyard shootout complete with insipid one-liners. We never learn what the nature of evil really is, either through Chin's shallow existentialist theory or Heartwood's Freudianisms.Chin's contemplation of an extramarital affair is just one example of the unresolved subplots that appear and disappear throughout. Despite its good pacing, *Equation* falls flat on its face. More literary readers will be unimpressed by the pedestrian prose, and mystery lovers will be annoyed by the time-consuming speculation.

Ex Utero
by Laurie Foos
Coffee House, 1995, 199 pp., $16.95

One night, after a hard day of shopping, Rita sits up in bed and realizes that her uterus is missing. When she retraces her steps and discovers that she's misplaced it at the mall, she becomes a poster child for a society obsessed with media exposure and women's reproductive capabilities.

Rita's husband, George, becomes impotent, and spends his days drawing sad pictures of his wilted organ. Rita takes to wearing red high-heeled pumps. Since mall security isn't making much progress on her case, she agrees to appear on the Rod Nodderman program—a syndicated talk show hosted by a Donahue-like Lothario—to solicit the aid of the American public. Her appearance sparks a wave of hysteria among women and men alike. The Society for Fruitless Wombs holds demonstrations at the mall and the TV station. Security guards drool over artist's sketches of Rita's womb on cable. Adele, the ultimate Nodderman fan, feels her vagina seal up in respose to Rita's story while she's making love in front of the TV. Lucy, another Nodderman viewer, experiences even more bizarre, sympathetic effects. And the malls can't keep up with the demand for the size-seven red high heels that have become Rita's trademark.

Rita eventually tires of the publicity and goes on the lam with Adele. The two hole up in a hotel room, eating bonbons and telling each other horror stories about childbirth—though neither of them has experienced it. However, when a young hemophiliac man, inspired by Rita's story, commits suicide with a plastic womb tied around his neck, Rita takes full responsibility and turns herself in. She is then rewarded by the return of her womb, only slightly the worse for wear, which she decides to keep—though not to use for its traditional purpose.

Foos' first novel is a delight of wit and invention. Although it invokes the tradition of the absurd, her satire is almost allegorical in its pointedness and consistency. Some readers may find the narrative explosion of a single joke to be tiresome. However Foos takes the notion of synecdoche —a part standing for the whole—seriously. "Never get the whole story," Nodderman tells his staffers. In this hilarious sendup of media, maternity and misogyny, Foos exploits Nodderman's technique for all it's worth.

The Unconsoled
by Kazuo Ishiguro
Knopf, 1995, 535 pp., $25

Ryder, a world-renowned pianist, arrives in an unnamed Continental city to give a concert. The city is at a crossroads in its history, at a point when it will either experience a renaissance or slide irretrievably into decay. As Ryder finds out, a group of community leaders has arranged his concert as part of a last-ditch effort to shore up the fortunes of the city. For these people, Ryder is nothing less than a savior.

Oddly unconcerned about the huge expectations laid upon him, Ryder wanders dream-like through his days in the city, meeting familiar people he can't quite place. In each case, he realizes after some time that he does indeed know these people— his wife, his child, an old school friend, a childhood playmate. His inability to immediately recognize them doesn't concern him, and there are no teary reunions when he realizes who they are. He continues to keep them at a safe distance.

Because Ryder's behavior and personality are so baffling, we never know for certain if he is delusional or if he is simply visiting a really odd town. The answer, probably, is both. As he did in *The Remains of the Day*, Ishiguro effortlessly inhabits his character, mimicking the stiff-upper-lip detachment and rational- ization of the British upper-middle class. But he's gone one step further here by placing Ryder in a world that is awry at a more basic level than that of *The Remains of the Day*, a world where space, time and perception don't work as we expect them to.

This is an extremely frustrating world, and at 535 pages, *The Unconsoled* gets long. In this self-consciously Great Book, Ishiguro spends a lot of time showing off: even minor characters go on at length about their lives, their motivations, their wounds. In fact, the only character whose life we don't learn about in great detail is Ryder's—we find out only vague facts as he stumbles across them.

Still, *The Unconsoled* offers a story like no other in recent memory, and provides no easy answers—this is not a *Bourne Identity* for the literary set. Ishiguro doesn't lead us to a climactic epiphany, when all the mystery and obfuscation are tidily resolved. In the end, none of the expectations laid upon Ryder when he came to town—that he would be a father and husband, that he would perform a concert, that he would redirect the destiny of a dying city—are fulfilled. Without remorse, Ryder leaves disappointment in his wake and goes in search of breakfast.

Is *The Unconsoled* an impressive achievement? Without a doubt. Is it so impressive that reading it is worth the effort? Possibly not.

The Hudson Letter
by Derek Mahon
Wake Forest, 1996, 63 pp., $8.95

The Hudson Letter is composed of the long sequence from which the collection takes its name, along with four other poems (an adaptation of Ovid's *Metamorphoses,* two poems by Mahon, and a translation of the Irish poet Nuala Ni Dhonhnaill) which have nothing in common with it. "The Hudson Letter" itself shines so brightly, however, that one is tempted to overlook the disunity of the collection.

Composed in eighteen sections, "The Hudson Letter" is an eloquent

blend of high diction and slang, reminiscent of Hart Crane. Mahon works the expatriate Irish theme perfectly, his outsider's perspective capturing New York's cacophony and industry, as well as the violence at the core of its language. Isolation and solitude are the immigrant's predicament— and Mahon's most compelling subject. Mahon speaks in a wide variety of outsiders' voices—from Sappho's to Auden's, to an Irish immigrant girl's. His stark vision seems justified by his observation, "fine worlds are seldom humane."

The Spaces Between Birds: Mother/Daughter Poems, 1967–1995
by Sandra McPherson (with Phoebe McPherson)
Wesleyan, University Press of New England, 1996, 63 pp., $25.00 (cloth), $11.95 (paper)

Sandra McPherson's latest collection contains new and reprinted poems interspersed with previously unpublished poems by her daughter Phoebe. A preface details the horoscope cast at Phoebe's birth, and chronologically, the selections move from evocations of Phoebe's childhood to poems that describe Sandra's final acceptance of her daughter's difference: Asperger's syndrome autism.

In "Precious Metal" Sandra writes of her daughter's uncanny affinity for broken pieces of machines, which Phoebe collects and transforms into new machines, much as Sandra collects words and images and transforms them into poetry: "With each gadget/she translates into being,/ my floral wisdom loses a petal./ Then with new and mystic/trust in welding, gains it back."

Phoebe's own poems, whimsical, beautiful and terrible, provide a naive counterpoint to her mother's: "I was trying to make this house shiny with laughter on the leaf," one of her shortest untitled poems reads; "This place is full of dogs and dumb meanings," says another.

McPherson admires her daughter's creativity, and her inclusion of the pieces with her own work isn't merely out of a compulsion to go public with private hardship. Phoebe's poems are better than curiosities, calm and wondering, in sharp contrast to those of her mother, which voice McPherson's frustrations in dealing with her more- and less-than-normal daughter.

Conceptually, the book is grounded in the idea of negative space, a way of viewing the world not by the boundaries of things, but by the spaces between them—the "spaces between birds." This is Phoebe's vision, backwards and arresting. As McPherson writes in the title poem, "I believe/if we all agreed/to follow each other/in a migratory V.../we would learn to hear the blank-ness/that forms the essence of our going on,/some puff we didn't/ mean to say but which/means *us*."

Accordion Crimes
by E. Annie Proulx
Scribner, 1996, 381pp., $25

Annie Proulx's new novel is a great book to disagree about. Some readers will love it, and for arguably good reasons. Like her previous much-feted *The Shipping News*, it is beautifully written sentence by sentence, as it describes the long life of one accordion, which is built by a craftsman in Italy, brought to America in the 1890s, and which then passes through the hands of many immigrants of various origins—German, Tex-Mex, Cajun, black, Polish, Norwegian, and others.

The immigrants' lives are described in ruthlessly tragi-comic terms, with even their momentary triumphs so woven into a fabric of high-velocity narrative that they move in the course of one sentence from success to despair or death. Proulx dispatches her characters with merciless regularity and speed, even at times resorting to parentheses to remind us in advance of the pitiful end of her poor immigrants.

There is thematic purpose to it all: Proulx is showing in loosely connected segments the lives of filth and poverty that American immigrants led and continue to lead. Whatever our illusions, she is saying, the facts are harsh. Yet the author's virtuosity somehow overwhelms her subject. The book is so jammed with historic references, images, and little details that the reader eventually feels that he is watching a kind of fireworks display, designed almost entirely for spectacular effect. While the novel may be packed with the best research, the most dense verisimilitude, that the author's nerves and money could buy, Proulx seems to forget the people who are supposed to be its subject. There is little apparent selectivity, little breathing room in her zooming low-altitude narrative. When she slows down a little and allows a story to develop, as she does at moments in the novel, one sees what kind of superb writer of fiction she can be.

The virtues of this book are numerous; in places it is thrilling; but reading it, to me, is like being manhandled by a thousand-pound literary gorilla.

The Moor's Last Sigh
by Salman Rushdie
Pantheon, 1995, 435 pp., $25

"Ah, the legends of the battling da Gamas of Cochin! I tell them as they have come down to me, polished and fantasticated by many retellings. These are old ghosts, distant shadows, and I tell their tales to be done with them."

So Moraes Zogoiby, the protagonist of Rushdie's latest novel, begins to narrate his family history. At times fascinating, at times cartoonish, *The Moor's Last Sigh* is an absorbing family saga that slowly meanders through a century of Indian history.

Rushdie peoples his story with colorful characters, like the narrator, Moraes Zogoiby (the Moor), estranged son of a Catholic mother and Jewish father. He is an Indian child who, symbolically, arises out of this mix deformed, with a stump-like arm and a life that moves "double-quick": by the age of ten he is larger than his father, and by twenty-four, with white hair, he appears older than his mother. And there is Vasco Miranda, a family friend-turned-madman (he has a needle coursing through his veins, threatening to pierce his heart at any moment) who forces Moraes to narrate the da Gama-Zogoiby family history.

Moraes' life revolves around several charismatic and ruthless women. His mother, dominates his actions, even after her murder, as her spirit calls him to avenge her death. Then there is his love, Uma Sarasvati, whose treachery leads to his banishment from the family.

Rushdie's 430-page novel is crammed with misfortunes, grief, betrayal, history and magic. His observations on the spice trade, art, cricket, architecture, and the underworld all add flavor to the novel, while the hectic pace of Indian politics reanimates the story when it threatens to become too lethargic.

The Best American Short Stories 1995
Edited by Jane Smiley
Katrina Kenison, Series Editor
Houghton Mifflin, 1995, 366 pp., $24.95

With the 1995 *Best American* anthology, Jane Smiley has assembled a vibrant collection of stories—offbeat and refreshingly unpretentious.

One of the best pieces here is Steven Polansky's "Leg," about a father who, in a desperate attempt to communicate with his son, intentionally lets his injured leg become infected and gangrenous. Despite the grotesque plot, the story does not come off as gimmicky. Instead, the father's actions make the reader first question, then reflect on the extremes to which even ordinary people will go, given the right circum- stances.

Andrea Barrett's "The Behavior of the Hawkweeds," is a complex tale of scientific intrigue. In "Hand Jive," a story about growing up, Andrew Cozine turns a potentially ludicrous-seeming compulsion into a cause for readers' sympathy. Edward Falco's "The Artist" has all the elements of a bad "Miami Vice" episode: guns, drugs, and the frozen body of a dead cop. Yet readers will be amazed and delighted when they discover how Falco has shaped all these elements into a fine story about escaping one's past.

The stories in the 1995 anthology are marked by their originality and their riskiness. You may not like all of Smiley's choices, but you won't close the book feeling like you've read it all before.

An Actual Life
by Abigail Thomas
Algonquin Books, 1996, 252 pp., $16.95

Thomas is the author of a previous story collection, *Getting Over Tom*. In that book she described, with fine comic touches, the lives of pregnant daughters and neglectful mothers, middle-aged loneliness and the pain of unrequited love. Her first novel, *An Actual Life*, is the sad yet funny story of Buddy and Virginia, two characters introduced in the earlier book.

Married out of "necessity" in the 1960s, after Virginia's polite expulsion from college due to her pregnancy, Buddy and Virginia are virtually strangers. Virginia comes to this realization slowly and painfully, upon the birth of their daughter Madeline. The young family temporarily moves in with Buddy's Aunt Dot while Buddy finishes school. Unfortunately, their residence in Buddy's hometown of Hadley, New Jersey, brings them into close contact with Irene, Buddy's high school sweetheart. Though Irene is now married to Buddy's best friend, Chick, the emotional bond that still exists between Irene and Buddy is apparent to Virginia, and takes its toll on both couples.

Told from Virginia's point of view, the story anatomizes all the hopes and fears involved in marriage. If Virginia recognizes her mistake in marrying Buddy, her sense of humor in light of her predicament provides us with a deeper understanding of what it means to learn to live with our choices.

The Trial of Jesus
by Alan Watson
University of Georgia 1995, 219 pp., $24.95

Watson, a Roman law historian, undertakes in this book to discover the most plausible tradition describing Jesus' trial and death. Why was Jesus executed, he asks. What parts did the Hebrew high court, the Sanhedrin, and the Roman authorities play in his trial? Why didn't the Sanhedrin execute Jesus? Did Pilate regard him as innocent yet condemn him nevertheless? In order to answer such questions, Watson sketches a fascinating and dispassionate portrait of Jesus.

He begins by declaring his agreement regarding the generally accepted provenance of Mark—Rome, A.D. 60—and its role as the primary source for the other Synoptic Gospels, Matthew and Luke. He feels that because the writer of Mark was a Roman citizen, he might naturally be inclined to shift the blame for Jesus' death as far from Rome as possible. John, he feels, was written in Jesus' home country some sixty years after Mark, which is also a fairly common view among biblical scholars.

As described in Mark, Jesus ran increasingly afoul of the Jewish educated professional class of Pharisees (scribes, lawyers, etc.) by being arrogant toward them, breaking Sabbath law, and assuming the authority of God—blasphemous behavior in their eyes. Moving into a crisis point in his ministry, he continued to perform miracles—an activity, whether real or counterfeit, that was so widely accepted as to seem almost mundane. During his ministry, he struggled against becoming merely a healer and miracle worker. As time went on, he be-came increasingly incomprehensible in his parables, and frustrated with those who didn't accept him. He shared with charismatic leaders of all ages the desire to divide his followers from their families (in Luke going so far as to say that in order to follow him one had to "hate" his family), as well as a long list of other characteristics, including making the prediction that his followers would be persecuted.

When Jesus went to Nazareth, his home town, those who had known him and his family were astounded by the power of his preaching yet offended and confused by him. Jesus was aggressively critical of what to him was Pharisaic nitpicking—their tendency to forget the basic precepts of Jewish faith and to obfuscate the spirit of the law with useless proscriptions. His charismatic influence seriously challenged their authority.

After his triumphant reentry into Jerusalem, Jesus went into the Temple, overturned tables and ran out moneychangers and the sellers of animals for Passover sacrifice. From the perspective of the Jewish authorities, this was an egregious act,

offending not just the scribe class but also the Sadducees, the elite class of priests who controlled the Temple. In John this act occurs at the beginning of Jesus' ministry, one of several pieces of evidence, according to Watson, for the greater plausibility of the chronology in Mark, since anyone doing such a thing would have little chance of escaping with his life.

Watson believes that Jesus, who prophesied his own death at least three times came back into Jerusalem fully intending and expecting to be condemned and stoned to death by the Sanhedrin—their usual method of execution. While the Sanhedrin did find him guilty during an emergency (and illegal) night meeting, the next day, possibly fearing riots, they decided to pass the buck to the Romans. Pilate gave the crowd their choice of one prisoner to be released, and they chose Barabbas. Because Jesus was not interested in secular politics, his death was a genuine tragedy, as he suffered a meaningless execution by crucifixion at the hands of Romans, for whom he cared nothing.

Watson writes plainly and concisely about one of the most important trials in Western history and in doing so produces a fresh portrait of the accused.

The Oxford Companion to American Literature
Sixth Edition
Edited by James D. Hart, revisions and additions by Philip W. Leininger
Oxford University Press, 1995, 779 pp., $49.95

The Oxford Companion to English Literature
Fifth Edition
Edited by Margaret Drabble
Oxford University Press, 1995,
1171 pp., $49.95

The revised editions of these two hefty references include updates of previous entries, as well as new entries (over 180 for the *Companion to American Literature*, 59 for the *Companion to English Literature*) designed to bring them up to the minute and to broaden their scope. Both volumes have considerable bookshelf presence—dignified but vividly hued jackets, with details from the cover art reproduced on the spine. Each includes an appendix, a literary chronology, in which publishing events are arranged side by side with sociopolitical ones, to provide a historical context for the literature. *The Companion to English Literature* also lists, in additional appendices, poets laureate of England and winners of major literary prizes.

The stated purpose of the two books is, as Drabble puts it in her Preface to the English *Companion*, to "quickly, easily and clearly satisfy the immediate curiosity of the common reader, and direct that reader, where appropriate, to further sources of information." Both *Companions* have been fulfilling that purpose admirably for over fifty years. Additions to the *Companion to American Literature* include entries on such relative newcomers to the American literary scene as Tim O'Brien, Louise Erdrich, Rita Dove and Wendy Wasserstein. There are new entries on popular writers, like Louis L'Amour; also on important peripheral figures

—historians (William Manchester), critics (Richard Ellman, Camille Paglia), etc. Not surprisingly, the jacket blurb for the American *Companion* advertises more multicultural entries—something the publicity for the English Companion does not do, by the way. The more conservative revisions to that volume include entries on significant "new" British writers (Martin Amis, Peter Ackroyd, Salman Rushdie), genre writers (P.D. James, Ruth Rendell) and foreign writers (Robertson Davies, Toni Morrison, J. M. Coetzee).

Whether you're just browsing, or seeking specific answers, you'll find both books informative, well edited and carefully cross-referenced. You'll also find them very different. To say that the English *Companion* is very English and the American *Companion* is very American may be too reductive, but in many ways it's true. Sir Paul Harvey's original 1932 *Companion to English Literature* was an encyclopedic endeavor that attempted to encompass the grand tradition of literature—a labor of love which included classical allusions, entries on British and Irish mythology and "allusions commonly met with, or likely to be met with, in English literature." Though Drabble cut many of the more far-flung entries in her 1985 edition, she has retained the spirit of Harvey's reference, "highly conscious," as she writes, "of the responsibility of revising a much-loved volume." In addition to providing information about British authors and their published works, *The Companion to English Literature* continues to offer entries on British and Celtic mythology, classical authors (but not classical mythology), literary magazines and publishers, and major foreign authors, especially—but not limited to—those writing in English. A small proportion of the entries are devoted to non-literary figures who have had a significant impact on English literature.

While the scope of Drabble's *Companion* is admittedly narrower than that of Harvey's, it is nevertheless considerably more comprehensive than that of James Hart's American *Companion*. Hart died in 1990, and the revisions and additions have mostly been made by Philip Leinin-ger, a consulting editor at Oxford University Press and an experienced editor of literary reference books. *The American Companion* demonstrates the extent to which the themes and conflicts in American literature are home-grown—and evidences the strong American pride in that fact. You won't find Aristotle here, but you'll find substantial discussions of many American presidents, and others of such historical events as the Civil War. (Kings don't generally rate in the English Companion unless their names are the titles of literary works, and there are no entries for either of the World Wars in Drabble's volume, despite their profound impact on British literature.) Foreign authors aren't included in Hart's reference, except in very rare instances. Dickens gets a paragraph because he toured the U.S. and wrote about it. Flaubert and Zola, whose influence on American Naturalism was seminal, don't get their own entries, though they are briefly mentioned in the discussion of that literary movement. On the other hand, Hart is somewhat more willing than Drabble to assess the critical reputation of authors.

Each of the two volumes provides a wealth of reliable information about literature in English, and related subjects; however necessity demands that a reference book of this kind omit more information than it includes. At almost fifty dollars apiece, the Oxford *Companions* make expensive bookends. If you're thinking of investing in one, take some time first to browse through it, to make sure it's the reference book you need.

Reviews by:
Brett Rogers, Speer Morgan, Kris Somerville, Reeves Hamilton, Trudy Lewis, Willoughby Johnson, Jeff Thomson, Kirsten Rogers, Abel Klainbaum, Hoa Ngo, Rebecca Fuhrman, Evelyn Somers